PRAISE FOR THE PLAYS PUBLISHED IN THIS VOLUME

The Death of Eurydice

"[A] shining achievement . . . Retellings that bring to light new ideas in ancient stories . . . are some of my favorite things in the world, and Stewart pulls this off beautifully! . . . Not only was the writing solid and interesting, it was accompanied by standout performances by Rachel Baird (who also directed) and Adam Argyle."

— Bianca Dillard, *Utah Theatre Bloggers Association*

"Mahonri Stewart's plays never fail to inspire."

— Hillary Stirling, guest post at *A Motley Vision*

"This was an amazing display of Utah Theater at its finest . . . I left the theatre with great respect for Mahonri Stewart, a playwright who clearly knows how to tell a story that makes you think long after the curtain closes."

— Rebecca Gunyan, *Front Row Reviewers*

The Snow Queen

"*The Snow Queen*—a story that follows young Gerda . . . and Kai . . . in a parable about good versus evil, the power of love, and the lie that is pessimism . . . The plays were well acted, always well staged, and left me with questions and a lot to discuss with my date. I recommend this show as a stimulating experience for all."

— Jocelyn Gibbons, *Utah Theatre Bloggers Association*

Jinn

"It is cathartic to experience a play like Zion Theatre Company's portrayal of Mahonri Stewart's *Jinn and Other Myths*. This performance does not just entertain, but also challenges you to analyze the artistic material and also yourself."

— Jocelyn Gibbons, *Utah Theatre Bloggers Association*

"It's a powerful commentary on us as a society and as individuals. Her challenge is ours and ultimately it becomes a rather ironic question of self-determination. Do we face our past mistakes, grapple with the grief, and become better people for it? Or do we bottle it all up and, in so doing, let those mistakes control our lives while we ourselves remain broken? The question is almost too easy to answer, but the play artfully captures the human elements that make it so hard for Calypso (and symbolically us as a society) to make the healthy choice. Facing one's mistakes is a very punishing process emotionally, and even after Calypso makes her choice, I was none too certain that I would have had her courage."

— Hillary Stirling, guest post at *A Motley Vision*

Evening Eucalyptus

"Mahonri Stewart's script conveys the perfect mood to match [the early 20th century] Australian setting of the play . . . *Evening Eucalyptus* is a play that pushes the boundaries of theatrical convention . . . and the sweet story of a broken man and a strong woman in an enchanted land is one that I won't forget soon."

— Russell Warne, *Utah Theatre Bloggers Association*

"[*Evening Eucalyptus*] does a good job of weaving together several story lines with a sense of magic . . . the last lines of the play linger in the mind long after curtain call . . . an exciting climax and compelling resolution. There is a lot to recommend *Evening Eucalyptus* for a night of thought-provoking entertainment."

— Kristin Perkins, *Front Row Reviewers*

"I was touched by the excellent writing and the introduction to the Aboriginal culture. Mahonri is a masterful writer . . . and it is always a pleasure to grapple intellectually with what his clever mind produces time after time."

— Marilyn Brown, *Dawning of a Brighter Day*

Rings of the Tree

"*Rings of the Tree* has broad appeal. Folks from 8 to 80, especially feminists and young women will enjoy the play . . . The thought provoking plot twists and turns make the play interesting and keep the audience fully engaged. This is a play you can't leave at the theater; you take it home with you. Stewart has a gift for writing dialogue. His conversations are well thought out and go a long way in developing the characters. For an ensemble cast, I found all the characters surprisingly well developed."

— Nan McCulloch, *AML-List*

"The plot was interesting, unconventional, unpredictable, and definitely trending right now . . . it's innovative and bold . . . a truly daring show."

— Paige Guthrie, *Utah Theatre Bloggers Association*

The Opposing Wheel

"*The Opposing Wheel* is something we don't get on stage very often: high fantasy . . . Stewart's script is complex and full of detail . . . [if you] enjoy fantasy stories like the Narnia books, then the show should be irresistible."

— Russell Warne, *Utah Theater Bloggers Association*

"I wish I could have gotten a shot of the nearly full moon peeking out of the clouds behind us as it rose above the mountain top [at the outdoor Castle Theater]. It was magical, just like Mahonri's play. Literally. Magical spells and all. What a thought provoking, crazy mix of characters from Camelot, minions of the devil, a lovely pagan trapped in a tower, and a Mormon . . . But nothing turns out the way you expect. It's pretty difficult to figure out who the real heroes are because everyone has goodness and everyone has flaws. It's a whole new reality that isn't so hard to believe if you allow yourself to consider the possibilities. And even if you don't, it's still an amusing, touching, modern fairy tale. With a nice feminist twist, I might add. Keep your eyes on this Mahonri Stewart, people."

— Margy Layton, *Shove Me in the Shallow Water*

"On the surface it's a quirky romance set against a supernatural background, and it can be enjoyed as simply that. Scratch that surface and you find a fascinating merger of Arthurian and Biblical prophesies about the End Times with the characters teaming up in preparation to fight on the side of the divine. Go a few layers deeper, though, and an underlying yin-yang tension is what truly drives the play: ancient and modern, fantastic and mundane, pagan and Christian, past and future, and even life and death. More critical than any of these is the age-old tension between male and female. At the center of all the witty dialogue and the fun of a good mystery is a surprisingly cerebral story . . . Mahonri is unequivocally the most brilliant feminist I've ever encountered, and that really shines through in *The Opposing Wheel*."

— Hillary Stirling, Audience Response

Emperor Wolf

"I was attracted to the challenges posed by Mahonri's script (realizing the scale of the mythic world with minimal resources; taking the audience on an epic journey in a small blackbox), and to the ultimate triumph of mercy over justice, which, despite the relative absence of organized religion in my own upbringing and background, is something my own morality can support."

— Brian Foley,
Director of Arizona State University's production of *Emperor Wolf*

Evening Eucalyptus

and

Other Enchanted Plays

BY

Mahonri Stewart

For production rights to any of Mahonri Stewart's plays, contact him directly at mahonristewart@gmail.com.

ISBN 978-0-9883233-8-4

Front cover art: Liz Pulido

Published by:
Zarahemla Books
869 East 2680 North
Provo, UT 84604
info@zarahemlabooks.com
ZarahemlaBooks.com

Printed in the U.S.A.

Contents

Introduction:
Magic, Miracle, and Incarnation

The great god of Middle-earth, J. R. R. Tolkien, was a jealous god. He had very specific commandments as to who could ascend the Smoky Mountain of the Fantasy Builder. In speaking of the kind of writers who were qualified to create fantasy and fairy stories, Tolkien wrote:

> In human art Fantasy is a thing best left to words, to true literature. In painting, for instance, the visible presentation of the fantastic image is technically too easy; the hand tends to outrun the mind, even to overthrow it. Silliness or morbidity are frequent results.[1]

Tolkien is already walking on shaky ground for me when he dismisses Fantasy Painting out of hand.[2] The 19th-Century Pre-Raphaelites, whose art included Fantasy paintings of mermaids, sorceresses, and the Lady of Shallot, are among my favorite artists. Their work stirs something in the depths of my imagination that few other things do, creating a vivid desire and creative awakening that sends me off into spiraling revelries. Bad enough that Tolkien disparages this achingly beautiful Fantasy art, but he then sets his sights on my own chosen field, Theatre/Drama, which obviously ruffles my feathers a bit:

> It is a misfortune that Drama, an art that fundamentally distinct from Literature, should so commonly be considered together with it, or a branch of it. Among these misfortunes

---

1. J. R. R. Tolkien, *Tree and Leaf,* "On Fairy Stories," (London: Unwin Books, 1964), 45

2. Doubly ironic, considering Tolkien was known to dabble in fantasy art himself. His illustration of Smaug graces the covers of many editions of *The Hobbit,* including the one I own.

we may reckon the depreciation of Fantasy. For in part at least this depreciation is due to the natural desire of critics to cry up the forms of literature or 'imagination' that they themselves, innately or by training, prefer. And criticism in a country that has produced so great a Drama, and possesses the works of William Shakespeare, tends to be far too dramatic. But Drama is naturally hostile to fantasy. Fantasy, even of the simplest kind, hardly ever succeeds in Drama, when that is presented as it should be, visibly and audibly acted. Fantastic forms are not to be counterfeited. Men dressed up as talking animals may achieve buffoonery or mimicry, but they do not achieve Fantasy.[3]

In putting forward these enchanted plays of fantasy that I have written, I think of Tolkien and other critics, and how they may have received them. However, at least I am in good company, for Tolkien goes on to particularly attack the work of Shakespeare, calling the Three Witches in *Macbeth* "almost intolerable" (better read than to see performed, he condescendingly concedes). Tolkien felt that if Shakespeare had "the skill or patience for the art," the Bard could have made it into a good piece of literature for a book, but since Shakespeare dares to indulge in the "bogus," "substitute magic" of presenting *"the visible and audible presentations of imaginary men in a story.* That is in itself an attempt to counterfeit the Magician's wand" (emphasis Tolkien's),[4] then the work is not slipped into his idea of legitimate fairy canon. So, basically, in Tolkien's mind, we Dramatists, we Playwrights, even the likes of Shakespeare, are second rate "counterfeits" that are working within a sub-rate genre that does not ascend to the height of "true literature," and thus not worth including in the genre of high fantasy literature.

Like his own creation from *The Hobbit,* Smaug the dragon, Tolkien hordes the golden privilege of legitimate Fantasy writing to himself and his race of Faërie Literati. Ironically, Tolkien's commentary

---

3. Ibid, 45–46.
4. Ibid, 46–47.

about the "natural desire of critics to cry up the forms of literature or 'imagination' that they themselves, innately or by training, prefer," could equally be applied to himself in this case. His evident disdain for Theatre and Drama, creates a blindness towards his own "dragon sickness" that is troubling.

Now I want it to be noted that I am a particular fan of Tolkien's work, and I have enjoyed studying about his life. He was a great writer, as well as a very good man. Reading *The Lord of the Rings* was a spiritual experience for me in high school. Frodo, Gollum, Samwise, Eowyn, Gandalf, and Aragon were all very real and moving characters to me. When I read of their adventures, I was enraptured, and they have stayed with me and influenced my life in some surprisingly personal ways. I have fond memories of reading *The Hobbit* when I was a teen, and then reading it to my son at bedtime more recently. Tolkien has truly blessed my life with a ritual of imagination that has been truly efficacious.

However, I find it ironic that the man who created such humble hobbits, could at times be full of such dogmatic disdain himself. He had such contempt for most things that were considered "modern" in his age, from T.S. Eliot to automobiles; for many types of literature and genres (really, most works past the Middle Ages); even for many of his own fans, especially those of the 1960's generation who took to his work with particular, revolutionary fervor, crying "Gandalf for President" and "Frodo Lives!" Tolkien described them as "my deplorable cultus."[5]

Even his friend and fellow Inkling C.S. Lewis came to be on the receiving end of Tolkien's disdain. Tolkien eviscerated the Narnia books, despising the multiple types of myths drawn into the stories; the inclusion of Father Christmas in *The Lion, the Witch, and the Wardrobe*; as well as many other similar complaints.[6] Not even the great C.S. Lewis fit into the particular and personal ideal Tolkien believed Fantasy Literature should achieve.

5. Humphrey Carpenter, *J.R.R. Tolkien: A Biography* (Boston/New York: Houghton Mifflin, 1977), 233.

6. George Sayer, *Jack: A Life of C.S. Lewis* (Wheaton, Illinois: Crossway Books, 1988), 312–313.

C. S. Lewis's marriage to divorcee Joy Davidman; his friendship with fringe supernatural author Charles Williams; and Lewis's adherence to Protestant beliefs rather than Tolkien's beloved Catholicism, despite Tolkien being partially responsible for bringing Lewis back into a belief in God after years of adamant atheism; all contributed to a falling out later in their lives. Tolkien couldn't overcome the disappointment that his once fond friend C. S. "Jack" Lewis didn't quite shape into the statue Tolkien's Pygmalionesque expectations had hoped for. Like Frodo and Samwise Gamgee, together they had walked to Mordor and back again, only to find themselves drawing apart. This kind of personal disdain is the most painful of all for me to note in Tolkien, who otherwise was a most wise and gentle man.

No doubt, Tolkien's particular revulsion to Fantasy Drama would translate to similar feelings about Fantasy Cinema. He most likely would not only have despised what Hollywood did to his beloved *Hobbit* (perhaps he would have felt kinder to the more faithful Rankin/Bass animated version?), but almost certainly would also have had grave misgivings of the much superior *Lord of the Rings* films. I have often played out the odd fantasy in my head of what it would be like show Tolkien and C. S. Lewis the films that were made of their work, and how delightful it would be for them to see their work come to life in such a way. However, that private fantasy is now tempered, realizing that they probably wouldn't have liked the films based on their work very much at all, especially Tolkien. Not because some of the films aren't great, which at least the *Lord of the Rings* films decidedly are (and I, for the most part, have a fond place in my heart for the recent Narnia films), but because Tolkien believed that Fantasy best existed in the mind. In his opinion, Fantasy should never actually take real, visual, tangible flesh and blood, lest it loses its magic.

Tolkien's type of arguments are only one side of the equation. On the other side of the divide are those who agree that Fantasy has little place in Drama, but for the opposite reason: they believe that Theatre is too high minded for childish fairy tales. I once had a theatre professor I really respect ask me why I was suddenly writing so much work that had a Fantasy bent. I could have misinterpreted the intent behind the question, but the implication seemed to be that so many Fantasy plays were beneath me and that I should focus on more "high minded" and realistic work.

I've kept in mind these criticisms about the genre, but my thoughts keep going back to the man Tolkien disparaged, William Shakespeare. I think particularly about what we often call his Romance plays. These plays aren't Romances in the sense that we consider the word today: they are not merely love stories (although sometimes a subplot about lovers is included). The Romances were written in the last years of Shakespeare's life and were plays that dealt with redemption, forgiveness, family, spirituality, as well as magic and the supernatural. They were the Epic Fantasies of their day, Jacobean Faërie stories. Plays like *The Tempest, Pericles, A Winter's Tale,* and *Cymbeline* had wizards, monsters, nymphs, murderous bears, resurrections, evil step mothers, and fire from the sky that killed incestuous villains. These Romances had gods who gave magical books to sleeping soldiers; promptings to wise, virtuous women; and visions to grieved kings.

The Romances were written by a more mature Shakespeare, who had passed out of the giddy-comical love stories, studious histories, and the wracked tragedies of his previous work. His was brilliant work, all, yet in his old age Shakespeare wrote fantasies that had a redemptive edge. To me, the fact that he chose to focus on such fantasy stories with spiritual themes as he drew closer to his own passing over into another world, well, that speaks volumes. Add to those stories *A Midsummer's Night Dream, Hamlet,* and *Macbeth,* and I think we can see that Shakespeare was more than a little enchanted, and that this was no fault in him. Rather, it's part of what lures us back into his spells time and time again.

I played Prospero once at Utah Valley University[7] in an ingenious production by director Christopher Clark, wherein he separated the bodies and the voices of the actors so that it played out like a kind of human puppet show. I played the non-speaking body of Prospero, my

---

7. UVU posted a very good video of the production on You Tube: https://www.youtube.com/watch?v=zk3EvgO78FI&index=32&list=PL5DC905FD1501690F

favorite role that I have had the chance to play. Although, because of the separation of voice and body, I said not a word in the production, I felt transported to that mystical island. I felt true magic when I listened to my fellow actor, my fellow Prospero Benjamin King, intonate the speech where Prospero meditates upon his powers, but then finally decides to give up his supernatural arts. As I physically enacted the spell, I also felt the magic of the words:

> Ye elves of hills, brooks, standing lakes and groves,
> And ye that on the sands with printless foot
> Do chase the ebbing Neptune and do fly him
> When he comes back; you demi-puppets that
> By moonshine do the green sour ringlets make,
> Whereof the ewe not bites, and you whose pastime
> Is to make midnight mushrumps, that rejoice
> To hear the solemn curfew; by whose aid,
> Weak masters though ye be, I have bedimm'd
> The noontide sun, call'd forth the mutinous winds,
> And 'twixt the green sea and the azured vault
> Set roaring war: to the dread rattling thunder
> Have I given fire and rifted Jove's stout oak
> With his own bolt; the strong-based promontory
> Have I made shake and by the spurs pluck'd up
> The pine and cedar: graves at my command
> Have waked their sleepers, oped, and let 'em forth
> By my so potent art. But this rough magic
> I here abjure, and, when I have requir'd
> Some heavenly music, which even now I do,
> To work mine end upon their senses that
> This airy charm is for, I'll break my staff,
> Bury it certain fathoms in the earth,
> And deeper than did ever plummet sound
> I'll drown my book.[8]

---

8. William Shakespeare, *The Tempest*, Act V, Scene I.

At that moment, criticisms like Tolkien's would have been the last thing in my heart. Far from my suspension of disbelief being "hung, drawn, and quartered,"[9] as Tolkien cynically suggests, Fantasy Drama allows me a new, ritualistic way to experience the story, with no less artistry or lyricism. My imagination taking flesh and blood is no less powerful because I can see the visions, than taking Christ's hands into mine would be, rather than reading his words in the Gospels. When the magical is made real, it is no less powerful, but rather transcends into the realm of miracle.

As many fantasy works are written for children (as "The Snow Queen" and *Emperor Wolf* are in this volume), I am also very cognizant the power Theatre can have on the young. My son Hyrum and I often go to plays together, and we recently saw a production of the premiere run of Susan Zeder's *The Milk Dragon*, which I thought was a delightful play. What an enchanting experience it was to see my son respond to the imaginative ways that beautiful Fantasy Play was staged, and how the magic was translated into a living, breathing, theatrical space. His enthusiasm for the play was just as strong as when we have read *The Chronicles of Narnia* together, or *Wizard of Oz*, or *Peter Pan*. There was no less magic than the written word. Perhaps Drama even contains a little more of that miracle of Incarnation than Tolkien's supposedly more "real" Literature does.

Many great plays are formed with fantasy and magic. Mary Zimmerman's *Metamorphoses*, Tony Kushner's *Angels in America*, August Wilson's *The Piano Lesson*, Sarah Ruhl's *Eurydice*, and Nilo Cruz's *Lorca in a Green Dress*, are only a few of the modern plays I can think of off the top of my head that utilize magical, supernatural, or fantastical elements. The Fantasy Play is far from dead, and far from irrelevant. Using the magical in the theatrical art form for me is like what Caliban says in *The Tempest*, I "had waked after long sleep, Will make me sleep again: and then, in dreaming, The clouds methought would open and

---

9. *Tree and Leaf*, 46.

show riches Ready to drop upon me that, when I waked, I cried to dream again."[10]

The fact that when I "waked" the second time, I could then touch my Vision, that didn't drive away the dream, but made it all the sweeter.

So I give you these spells, written in this mystical book, that can then be performed by airy spirits and nymphs. "The Death of Eurydice," "The Snow Queen," and "Jinn" are all short incantations, but no less potent. *Evening Eucalyptus* is a native enchantment I learned while I lived a couple of years in what some call Australia, but what is really the magical land of Oz. *Rings of the Tree* is one of my early plays, but one that still holds its spell on me and many others. *The Opposing Wheel* takes a page from Merlin's book, as well as Tennyson's. *Emperor Wolf*, finally, is my work that I leave as a legacy to my sorcerer's apprentices, my children. Like C. S. "Jack" Lewis, I find that a child's inclusion in our magic circle creates no depreciation of its potency.

Call them Fantasy Plays, Romances, Fantasias, what you will. Their purpose is Enchantment of the most serious sort, and Manifestations of the most whimsical.

---

10. Act III, Scene II.

The Death of Eurydice

A One Act Play

Production History

"The Death of Eurydice" was originally written as part of the full length play about world mythology, *Manifest,* which has yet to be performed, although there are still plans to do so.

It was then separated from Manifest (then titled "Eurydice") as its own one-act when Zion Theatre Company premiered it at the Provo Theatre Company in Provo, UT, as part of the set *Immortal Hearts and Other Short Plays* on July 16, 2010.

CAST
Woman: Rachel Baird Lockhart
Man: Adam Argyle

CREW
Director: Rachel Baird Lockhart

The next year, Rachel Baird Lockhart, then living in Switzerland at the time, approached the Geneva English Drama Society, with which she was involved, to produce the play. They brought it to Festival of European Anglophone Theatrical Societies, where it performed at the FEATS Theatre Festival in Geneva, Switzerland on June 13, 2011, with the following cast and crew:

CAST
Woman: Rachel Baird Lockhart
Man: Alex Freeman

CREW
Director: Rachel Baird Lockhart

Zion Theatre Company did another production of the play which started on November 18, 2011, as part of the set of short plays called *Jinn and Other Myths,* in conjunction with the Off Broadway Theatre in Salt Lake City. The play was retitled "The Death of Eurydice," as

Mahonri Stewart became aware of Sarah Ruhl's play *Eurydice,* and wanted the title to be distinct from that play. This was also the first version to use the multimedia approach originally intended. It performed with the following cast and crew:

CAST
Woman: Aubrey Bench
Man: Garr Van Orden
Orpheus: Kyle Oram

CREW
Director: Jason Sullivan
Multimedia Directors: Jason Sullivan, Joel Petrie
Producers: Nathaniel Drew, Mahonri Stewart
Lights: David Bellis
Sound: Joel Petrie

"Death of Eurydice" then performed again at the Off Broadway Theatre in Salt Lake City, starting on August 18, 2012, as part of Zion Theatre Company's set of short plays *The Death of Eurydice and Other Short Plays.* It had the following cast and crew:

CAST
Woman: Rachel Baird Lockhart
Man: Lawrence Fernandez

CREW
Director: Rachel Baird Lockhart
Creative Director: Rachel Baird Lockhart
Technical Director: David Bellis
Lighting Design: Brittany Restrepo
Producers: Mahonri Stewart, Rachel Baird Lockhart, Penny Pendleton, Nathaniel Drew

"The Death of Eurydice" is dedicated to Anne Ogden Stewart, the love of my life. Her heart songs have led me in times of sorrow, her visions have inspired me in times of doubt, her arms have carried me in times of want, and our united belief in a better world has spurred us in times of dark.

Also dedicated to Rachel Baird Lockhart, who has become attached to the role of Eurydice in my mind, and who has done so much for the play and the planned short film version. Rachel is a true ambassador for my work and one of my dearest friends.

The Death of Eurydice

Act One

The lights dim on the MAN *and the* WOMAN. *On the screens appears what seems to be dark water. The sounds of the water lapping against a boat are also heard. Lights rise again on the* WOMAN, *as she represents sitting in a boat. Standing behind her is the* MAN. *The* MAN *wears a beautiful, Grecian helmet, or perhaps just a simple hat. At first the* WOMAN *does not notice the* MAN *and is humming softly to herself. She touches the river as the boat glides. As she interacts with the river, sounds are made to signify how she is touching it, coordinated to match exactly the sound of water to her movement. Two screens (optional) show images and film footage throughout the show, as indicated in the text, as well as additional moments decided by the director. To begin, the screens show water, or a water-like substance.*

MAN. That's a very pretty tune.

The WOMAN *is startled and looks behind her.*

WOMAN. I didn't know you were there. (*Beat.*) It's rather dark down here, isn't it?

MAN. No. Your eyes just can't see it yet.

WOMAN. I think it's dark.

The WOMAN *starts humming to herself again.*

MAN. That's a very pretty tune.

WOMAN. What?

MAN. That's a very pretty tune.

WOMAN. My husband composed it. He's talented that way. Some say that he can even make the trees and the rocks dance to his music.

MAN. Can he?

WOMAN. That's what they say.

MAN. I like music.

Silence. The WOMAN notices something in the water. She leans over, anxiously curious. The MAN does not react.

WOMAN. There's something in the water.

MAN. What do you remember?

WOMAN. About what?

MAN. What do you last remember?

WOMAN. I—I think I'm supposed to give you this.

The WOMAN takes a coin out of her mouth. She tries to hand it to the MAN. The MAN does not move to take it.

MAN. I don't need it.

WOMAN. But it's the price for the ferry . . . .

MAN. I don't need it. Throw it onto the river.

WOMAN. Into the river?

MAN. **Onto** the river.

WOMAN. But that's a waste.

MAN. Throw it onto the river.

The WOMAN is skeptical at first but then throws the coin overboard. The coin does not make the sound of a coin splashing in the water, as it should, but instead makes the sound of metal against metal.

WOMAN. I—I don't understand. It's not sinking.

MAN. Should it sink?

WOMAN. Metal always sinks in the water.

MAN. You take it for granted that the river is made of water.

The WOMAN, *even more confused than before, looks back into the water more intently and then back at the coin, touching it. She picks it up, and then throws it overboard again. It makes the same metallic sound.*

WOMAN. Amazing.

MAN. *(With a smile.)* Easily pleased.

WOMAN. And—and look at this! My hand can go into the water! *(The* WOMAN *dips her hand into the water and it comes back wet.)* If I can go into the water, why can't the coin? *(The* MAN *does not answer.)* You're not very forthcoming, are you?

MAN. I want to see you figure it out. It's no fun if I tell you everything.

WOMAN. Fun? You think this is fun?

MAN. Don't you?

WOMAN. I—well, I guess I do. *(She laughs.)* Ah, it reminds me of the day when Orpheus . . .

MAN. Orpheus?

WOMAN. My husband.

MAN. Yes. The musician.

The screens silently show the scene between her and ORPHEUS *as she describes it. At first the scene is somewhat blurry, as if we see it through water, but then it becomes clearer.*

WOMAN. It was raining and I tried to run inside, of course, but he grabbed me by the hand and told me to dance. Dance? Dance, he said! Who dances in the rain?

MAN. You did.

WOMAN. Yes, we did. We danced like Bacchus drunk with life! We were soaking—Orpheus even caught a small fever for a couple of days, but—well, it's a nice memory.

The scene on the screens fades back to water.

MAN. What do you last remember?

The WOMAN *pauses. She averts the question.*

WOMAN. Why do you wear that helmet?

MAN. It makes me invisible.

WOMAN. Uh—okay.

MAN. No, really, it does.

WOMAN. Well, it's not doing a very good job. I can see you.

MAN. Yes. *You* can.

WOMAN. I mean who says that? I ask, why do you wear that helmet, and he says, because it makes me invisible! The invisible man! Look, look, everybody, I'm the invisible man! Now you see me, now you don't! *(She laughs, but then quiets down as she says :)* Here I am and then I'm—gone. *(The* WOMAN *looks back the* MAN, *something really starting to bother her.)* What did you say your name was?

MAN. I didn't.

WOMAN. See, this mysterious stranger thing, it's not doing much for me. *(The* MAN *doesn't reply.)* Yep. Having loads of fun.

MAN. What do you last remember?

WOMAN. I'm not sure I want to remember. The water—does it make you forget?

MAN. It doesn't have to. You can push things under or make them rise to the top.

WOMAN. Should I forget? Will I be happier that way?

MAN. You'll be absolutely care free.

WOMAN. But not happy.

MAN. There are many different kinds of happy.

WOMAN. Just as there are many kinds of sad. And then—they mingle. *(Making a decision.)* I will remember.

MAN. All right.

The screen once again starts to silently show the memory as the
WOMAN describes it, at first watery and then clear and precise:

WOMAN. Orpheus was singing to me, playing his beautiful—*(The*
WOMAN starts to choke up)—music. Music. Excuse me, I don't know
why I'm—excuse me.

MAN. I understand.

WOMAN. And then he wrapped me in his arms and we slept. I woke up
just as the sun was setting and just looked at him for a long time. But
as night came I—I heard something. In the woods. It scuffled away
and I was nervous for a moment, but then—oh, it was beautiful . . .

MAN. . . . music.

A beautiful melody is heard on pipes.

WOMAN. Yes. But how did you know that? *(The MAN does not respond.)*
They were beautiful pipes. Not as beautiful as Orpheus's music, of
course, but—they had a very distinct allure. So I went into the
woods, following the music and then—oh.

MAN. The satyr.

The pipes stop.

WOMAN. A grotesque little thing. Tried to grope me, get his filthy
hands on me, but I ran. He was fast, so I cried out. I heard Orpheus
cry out in return. Orpheus was coming; I knew he was coming, but
then . . .

MAN. The serpent.

WOMAN. I didn't see it, you understand. I was so scared that I didn't
see it there in front of me in the plain moonlight.

MAN. You don't have to say anymore, if you don't want to.

WOMAN. No, I think I'd better. Just—just give me a moment. *(There is*
a pause as the WOMAN tries to muster all the courage she can to face
the truth.) I could feel the venom working quickly. I blacked out, but
I woke up for a brief moment. I was in my bed and Orpheus was

there. Singing. Singing such a sad song and then the venom finished its work and then my heart broke and—and I died.

The image on the screens fades away back to the water. For a moment there is only the sound of the river lapping against the boat.

MAN. Thank you for telling me. Not everyone does. I already know anyway, but it's different, hearing it as you have experienced it. Hearing the story as it should be told. *(Pause.)* I'm sorry for your loss.

WOMAN. So am I. *(Pause.)* You're not as I imagined you would be.

MAN. Expecting a hooded, skeleton faced man with a scythe?

WOMAN. No, actually.

MAN. A lot of people expect the hood. I'm a bit of a disappointment, I'm afraid.

WOMAN. I imagined you dressed in rich, dark fabrics. In splendor and pomp. I imagined you as arrogant, cold and uncaring.

MAN. And now you've decided that I'm not those things.

WOMAN. You're a little distant, but you seem kind enough. And you don't have any rings or jewels or silks or anything. Just those clothes and a dorky helmet. You look so—plain.

MAN. *(Sincerely.)* Thank you.

WOMAN. You're welcome.

MAN. After we defeated the Titans, my brothers Zeus, Poseidon, and I, we drew lots to see who got what. Poseidon got the sea, Zeus got the sky and I got this place. I was bitter for a while, but then—well, the place is filled with such light.

WOMAN. Light? It's even darker than when I got here.

MAN. You'll learn to appreciate it.

WOMAN. Thank you, but that's cold comfort right now.

MAN. You'll learn to see it.

WOMAN. The stories I hear are not very flattering.

MAN. We really need to work on our PR.

WOMAN. Are they true? (*The* MAN *does not reply.*) The stories? Are they true?

MAN. Why would you think they were true? Have you met anyone who has ever come back?

WOMAN. No.

MAN. Then why should they be true? How would anybody know?

The WOMAN *considers this.*

WOMAN. Are you telling me that they're not true? (*The* MAN *doesn't answer.*) I would like to prepare.

MAN. There is no preparation for it.

WOMAN. Are those horrible things going to happen to me? Am I going to eternally push a boulder up a mountain, or be surrounded by water and never able to drink, or fly around like a little bat while the great heroes walk around me as aimless ghosts? (*The* MAN *doesn't respond.*) It would be so much easier to bear, if I just knew what to expect!

MAN. You humans can be so morbid.

WOMAN. *We* can be morbid?

MAN. Were you a bad person?

WOMAN. What? Well, I would like to think that I wasn't.

MAN. Did you like hurting people?

WOMAN. No, no, of course not.

MAN. Then why are you afraid?

WOMAN. Well, it's not always about whether you were a good person or a bad person, is it? I was bit by the snake either way.

Pause. Now something is bothering the MAN.

MAN. Why do you see it as a punishment?

WOMAN. What?

MAN. Death. In your world it's the ultimate punishment.

WOMAN. Well, yeah.

MAN. It's not.

WOMAN. You can't say that to me. Not to me.

MAN. *(For the first time, the* MAN *is passionate.)* You haven't even opened your eyes!

WOMAN. I have lost everything!

MAN. What do you think is in that river? Once you immerse yourself in there, once you dive through that veil, do you think you will find fire and blood and torture? Or has it ever occurred to you that it may be a world of felicity? Has it ever dawned on your little mind that perhaps, just perhaps, it will be your liberation, like a prisoner finally stepping out of her cage into the cool, beautiful morning?

WOMAN. Is that what you're telling me is there? Is that what I can expect? *(The* MAN *doesn't reply.)* I'm sick of your uncaring silence!

MAN. It's because I care that I am silent.

WOMAN. You don't care! I have lost my Orpheus!

MAN. You don't know that.

WOMAN. I will never hear his beautiful voice ever again! *(The* WOMAN *weeps. The* MAN *stoops down and holds the* WOMAN *in a comforting fashion. She looks up at him, surprised, and then embraces him tightly in return. After a moment, she gently withdraws, with a grateful smile.)* Thank you.

> *The* MAN *touches the river, stroking it softly as if he were comforting a child.*

MAN. Do you still not see?

> *The* WOMAN *leans over, peering into the water as well.*

WOMAN. I saw something—before.

MAN. What was it?

WOMAN. I didn't get a clear understanding of it. At first I thought it was a bright city, then I thought it was my father who passed away, then I thought it was just the water reflecting the starry sky. *(Looking above her.)* Except there is no sky.

MAN. Do you want to know what you saw?

WOMAN. Yes, very much.

MAN. Then go in.

WOMAN. Into the river?

MAN. You saw that you can. Your hand is not the only thing that can dip beneath the surface.

WOMAN. But what if I drown?

MAN. No problem. You're already dead.

WOMAN. It could be frightening . . .

MAN. It could be.

WOMAN. It could be wonderful . . .

MAN. It could be.

WOMAN. What if I just find more death?

MAN. What if you find more life?

WOMAN. Would my questions even be answered?

MAN. At that point would it matter?

WOMAN. I'm scared.

MAN. Yes.

WOMAN. But I'm also fascinated.

MAN. Yes.

WOMAN. I—oh, it could be—why don't I just—just . . .

> The WOMAN breathes something in deeply. The screens brighten on, building to a glowing, warm light. A distant voice is also heard singing something beautiful, but unintelligible.

The WOMAN *smiles and basks in the feeling for a moment, but then the lights and music fade. The screens go blank again. A determined expression grows on the* WOMAN'S *face. It appears that the* WOMAN *is about to step into the water, when a different beautiful male singing voice is heard. It takes the* WOMAN *a moment to break out of her focus and she realizes she recognizes the voice:*

WOMAN. Orpheus! He found a way! He found a way to me!

MAN. That song—I have never heard such a song.

For a moment they both just listen to the beautiful song. The MAN *is moved to tears by its beauty and longing.*

WOMAN. Please—please, let me go to him. He's come so far . . .

MAN. Eurydice, you were very close—you almost jumped in. You were about to understand . . .

WOMAN. If there's a chance I can be with Orpheus, I'll take it.

MAN. You don't understand what you were on the verge of doing. You don't understand what you could have . . .

WOMAN. I don't care. I need my Orpheus.

The MAN *looks intently at the* WOMAN *and then with a look of confusion mingled with compassion, he takes the* WOMAN *by the hands. Then in a sudden moment of clarity he makes a decision:*

MAN. I will tell him that he can have you back. However, there is a condition. He will travel in front of as you leave this realm and neither of you can look back, or else you will return to my kingdom forever and he shall not have you until he comes to stay here himself. You both must be out of my kingdom before he can look back and see you and have you back in the mortal world.

WOMAN. You're—you're serious? This isn't a trick?

MAN. I'm a man of my word. Follow my instructions and you shall live a long and full life with Orpheus.

The WOMAN *impulsively embraces the* MAN, *joyously.*

WOMAN. Thank you!

The MAN *then hands her a pomegranate.*

MAN. This will allow you to cross the river.

The WOMAN *stares in wonder at the fruit. She then opens it and eats of the fruit. She steps onto the water and finds that she can stand on it. She looks up astonished at the* MAN.

WOMAN. I'm not sure if I understand.

MAN. You are now like the coin.

The WOMAN *runs off in joy. The* MAN *addresses the audience:*

MAN. As the story goes, Orpheus and Eurydice made their journey from of the Underworld. Orpheus made sure that he did not look back at his beloved following behind him. But when he was finally out and again in the mortal world, he turned around. Upon doing so, he found that Eurydice had vanished. It has since been assumed that, although Orpheus had made it out of the Underworld, in his impulsiveness he hadn't waited long enough for Eurydice to make it out as well, thus not fulfilling his side of the bargain. While this may be true, perhaps, just perhaps, Eurydice didn't disappear because Orpheus looked back. Perhaps Eurydice disappeared because Eurydice looked back.

On the screens we see ORPHEUS *is in front of* EURYDICE, *continuing his song.* ORPHEUS *never turns around, so all* EURYDICE *can see is the back of his head. They walk through the cavernous tunnel, and ahead of them they see the light of the world shining.* ORPHEUS's *pace hastens, but* EURYDICE *starts to slow down, and then stops. She sees* ORPHEUS *run out of the cavern, enveloped by the bright sunlight.*

Eurydice bites her lip, hesitating. She then hears the other SINGING *she heard before she heard* ORPHEUS, *before she was about to step off the boat. Suddenly her feet purposely turn and she deliberately looks back (It must obvious that this was her choice and not Orpheus's mistake). She hears* ORPHEUS *cry out "Eurydice, no!" but that is muffled as there is a sudden* RUSH *akin to wind or, more likely, water.*

EURYDICE *is suddenly underwater. She struggles desperately for a moment and it appears that the water may consume her. However she swims up. Then we see her head rise out of the water, gasping. She then looks around, full of wonder, joy and amazement at the new world before her. We do not see what she sees because it has grown too bright, which brightness overcomes the image on the screens.*

THE END

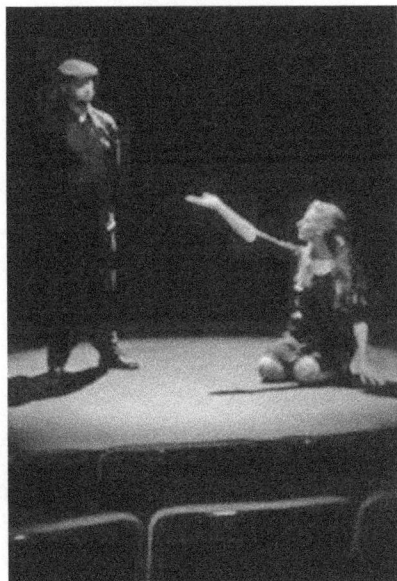

Adam Argyle as Man and Rachel Lockhart as Woman. Photo by Greg Deakins.

Rachel Lockhart as Woman and Lawrence Fernandez as Man. Photo by Naoma Wilkinson.

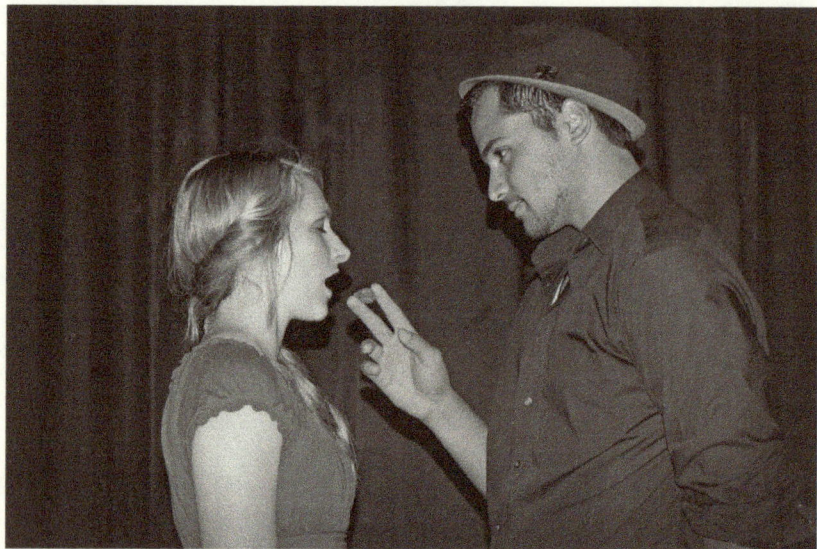

Rachel Lockhart as Woman and Lawrence Fernandez as Man. Photo by Naoma Wilkinson.

Rachel Lockhart as Woman. Photo by Naoma Wilkinson.

Rachel Lockhart as Woman and Lawrence Fernandez as Man. Photo by Naoma Wilkinson.

The Snow Queen

A One-Act Play

Production History

"The Snow Queen" was originally written as part of the full length play about world mythology, *Manifest,* which has yet to be performed, although there are plans to do so.

It was then separated from *Manifest* as its own one-act when Zion Theatre Company premiered it on November 18, 2011, as part of the set of short plays called *Jinn and Other Myths*, in conjunction with the Off Broadway Theatre in Salt Lake City. It performed with the following cast and crew:

CAST
Gerda: Jyllian Petrie
Kai: Shea Potter
The Snow Queen: Heather Jones

CREW
Director/Multimedia Director: Joel Petrie
Producers: Nathaniel Drew, Mahonri Stewart
Lights: David Bellis
Sound: Joel Petrie

For Hyrum and Charlotte. It's not quite Frozen, *but it's actually closer to Hans Christian Andersen's original story than Disney's version. However, I think even Uncle Walt would have appreciated the difference, as he loved the original fairy tale and had an unfulfilled dream to make a version of his own.*

The Snow Queen

Act One

A bright day. KAI *places his hands over* GERDA's *eyes. They both take on the demeanor of children. Multi-media screens dot the stage.*

KAI. Guess who?

GERDA. It's—Suzie Smith.

KAI. Suzie Smith!

GERDA. Okay, Anya Samuelsen.

KAI. (*At first in an unintentionally high voice.*) Do I . . . (*Lowering his voice.*) . . . do I sound like an Anya to you?

GERDA. (*With a mischievous smile.*) Maybe you do.

KAI. You know perfectly well who I am! You—you—stupid girl!

GERDA. Sticks and stones may break my bones, but names will never hurt me.

KAI. Gerda, stop it! You're ruining the game! Now tell me who I am.

GERDA. (*Pause.*) You're the boy I love.

KAI. Ewww! Gerda, that's gross!

   KAI *takes his hands off* GERDA's *eyes and steps back, horrified.*

GERDA. Oh, Kai, you're just like a boy.

KAI. I sure am! That was totally, totally, totally, totally gross. Gross times infinity, that's how gross it was.

GERDA. It's not gross, Kai. It's romantic.

KAI. Take it back.

GERDA. No.

KAI. Take it back.

GERDA. I said no.

KAI. Take it back!

GERDA. I won't! You're the boy I love and there's nothing you can do about it.

KAI. Take it back, or I won't be your friend anymore!

GERDA. You don't mean it . . .

KAI. I sure do. If you don't take it back, I'll—I'll make a club. The "Boycott Girls Who Like Boys Club." I'll get all the boys to join, and the only girls we'll let into the club are the ones who don't like us.

GERDA. You wouldn't dare.

KAI. Unh-huh.

GERDA. Nuh-uh.

KAI. Unh-huh.

GERDA. Nuh-uh!

KAI. Unh-huh!

GERDA. Well, it would be a stupid club. I would make my own club. The "Girls Who Will Always Like Boys Club." We'd set up our club right across from your club and make lovey dovey faces at you and send you valentines and sing romantic love songs to you all day!

KAI. Okay, stop it. That's totally scary.

GERDA. I'd do it, too. We'd even try and kiss you!

KAI. Gerda, don't ever, ever, ever, ever kiss me! I would like explode or shrivel up and all that would be left of me is ear wax and snot.

GERDA. No, silly, you wouldn't explode or shrivel into snot. If I kissed you, you would kiss me back.

KAI. Pfh! Not in a hundred-thousand-million-billion-trillion years. Times infinity. Anyways, nobody would join a stupid club like that.

GERDA. I don't care. Listen to me Kai and listen good: no matter what you do, no matter what you say, no matter how wrong you are, I will always love you.

KAI. Well, that's stupid.

GERDA. It's true.

KAI. What if I put worms down your shirt, or cut off all your hair or spilled ink on your favorite dress?

GERDA. I would still love you.

KAI. What if I never loved you back?

GERDA. *(Beat.)* I would cry my eyes out of their sockets and then I would still love you.

KAI considers this.

KAI. Wow. Okay, if it's like that, you can love me.

GERDA. Really?

KAI. But don't never tell nobody. All the kids would laugh at both of us.

GERDA. *(She relishes this.)* Okay. It will be our secret. Kai . . .

KAI. Yeah?

GERDA. I've got something I want to show you . . .

KAI. It better not be a kiss.

GERDA. It's not a kiss.

KAI. Or a thimble. I've read *Peter Pan*, you can't trick me.

GERDA. It's not a thimble either, but it's something nearly as good.

GERDA goes to a hiding spot where she has hidden a small, potted rose bush and brings it out to KAI. Soft music is heard.

KAI. Hey, that's cool.

GERDA. They're roses.

KAI. They're really pretty.

GERDA. Kai—am I pretty?

KAI. You? Sure.

GERDA. *(Genuinely pleased.)* Cool.

KAI. For a girl, Gerda, you're really pretty. But these flowers—wow, they're something else. Oh, hey, that reminds me! My dad gave me the coolest stuff! I left it over here. Come on!

> *KAI and GERDA go off stage and pull out several oversized cardboard boxes.*

GERDA. Totally wicked!

KAI. Yeah. This one was a refrigerator box and this one was from a dryer and this one, well, it must have been from a time machine.

GERDA. And that one?

KAI. That one—that one held the devil.

GERDA. Kai, my Mom said never to talk about the devil.

KAI. Well, in telling you to never talk about him, she talked about him, didn't she?

GERDA. Kai . . .

KAI. Well, okay, we won't call him the devil—we'll call him the—devil-troll!

GERDA. That's better.

KAI. In fact, all of these boxes were part of his kingdom. These boxes are hell boxes . . .

GERDA. Kai, my mom says hell is a bad word.

KAI. Well, your mom doesn't let you chew gum either.

GERDA. Kai . . .

KAI. Oh, okay. These boxes are Heck boxes. The great boxes of Heck!

GERDA. Thanks.

> *KAI and GERDA start to construct "Heck" with the boxes.*

KAI. This one is the bathtub that's always too hot . . .

GERDA. . . . and this one is the toilet that never flushes . . .

KAI. . . . and this is the bed that's never comfortable . . .

GERDA. . . . and this is one is the toy box that's always empty . . .

KAI. . . . sure sounds like Heck to me!

GERDA. And this one, this one is the punishment chair. The devil-troll calls it his throne, but it's really where God put the devil in Time-out.

KAI. I hate Time-out.

GERDA. And so did the devil-troll. He was so angry . . .

KAI. Can I be the devil-troll?

GERDA. Only if it's just pretend.

KAI. Of course. Just pretend. So I, the devil-troll, am so angry! But then I thought, what's so fun about being angry?

GERDA. Yeah . . .

KAI. So I thought to have some fun and show God that I didn't care about being put in Time-out. So I—I—I made me a special mirror.

One of the screens lights up. KAI goes to it and looks in it. The screen reflects KAI's image, but makes KAI look distorted. He laughs.

GERDA. I don't get why you're laughing.

KAI. What a funny mirror I made! Look it can make what normally looks good into something that looks bad! It can make what is already ugly even uglier! A man could have a freckle and it would look like it covered his whole face. A woman could have a small hair on her chin, and it could make it look like she had a full beard! It's brilliant! Absolutely hilarious! Come look at yourself in it, Gerda! *(GERDA looks in it, but she isn't nearly as pleased by her distorted appearance.)* Wow! Look how ugly it makes you!

GERDA. What did he call it?

KAI. Hm. I think I'll call it—satire.

GERDA. I don't like it.

KAI. That's because you don't understand it yet! You've got to be clever to get it.

GERDA. Well, then I'd rather not be clever.

The screen starts to show KAI's story, but instead of being KAI and GERDA, we see more accurate devils depicting the story.

KAI. Well, this devil-troll, he was clever, not like some silly girl who had nothing but kisses and romance in her head. And he showed it around to all his devil friends and they thought he was very clever, too, and they all laughed. And he had all sorts of girls who fell in love with him because he was so clever, but he couldn't care less because it was more important to be clever than to be loved by silly girls . . .

GERDA. Kai, I don't like this game . . .

KAI. . . . and finally the devil-troll, who was really the devil and didn't care what the mothers of silly little girls thought about him, finally the devil had the idea of getting out of this stupid Time-out, out of Hell, not Heck, and he thought to bring the mirror to heaven . . .

GERDA. Really, I think we should play something else . . .

KAI. Oh, he was going to bring it to heaven and he was going to make God and his angels look into it and, oh, he would laugh so hard . . .

GERDA. But that's when the devil made his mistake. For God broke his mirror!

The images in the screens shatter, breaking and falling, continuing to fall in little pieces . . .

KAI. What? No!

GERDA. Yes! God broke his mirror and shattered it into a million-billion pieces!

KAI. Well, then the devil took those million-billion pieces and scattered them to the earth. (*KAI holds his hands up to the sky, and looking up, shouting in mocking and ecstatic tones. He then acts as if he is spreading the shattered glass to unsuspecting people below.*) A piece of glass would fall into a person's ears and then they would magnify what they heard people say and they would laugh at such nonsense! Then it would fall onto people's tongues and they could speak eloquently about the stupidity of other people! And then it would fall into people's eyes and their hearts—Ow!

Suddenly KAI *cries out in sharp pain as something has fallen into his eyes and his heart. As soon as he cries out, the screens go dark, the shards of glass now gone.* GERDA *immediately comes to* KAI's *aid.*

GERDA. Kai! Are you all right?

KAI. My eye—something in my eye. *(Clutching his chest.)* Oh, and my chest hurts, something close to my heart . . .

GERDA. What can I do to help?

KAI. Stop blubbering over me, you little girl!

GERDA. Little girl?

KAI. Look at you. Crying like a baby! Baby-soggy pants, can't stand to see someone hurt!

GERDA. Kai, why are you . . . ?

KAI. Look, I'm sick of childish games. Can't we do something real?

GERDA. Real?

KAI. Yes, real! Something that actually exists, instead of stacking boxes like they were something other than boxes.

GERDA. But you liked the boxes . . .

KAI. Yes, when I was a child.

GERDA. You are a child.

KAI. Not anymore. It's time you grew up, too.

KAI accidentally knocks over the rose bush.

GERDA. Careful!

KAI. Ugh, get that thing away from me.

37

GERDA. You said it was pretty.

KAI. It's been chewed up by a worm. *(The screens show snowflakes falling.)* Look, it's snowing.

GERDA. But it was warm just a second ago ...

KAI. Look at how perfect the snowflakes are, Gerda. Aren't they beautiful?

GERDA. I like my rose.

KAI. So varied, yet so perfect. The mathematical integrity of each unique snowflake is such a miracle—if there were such things as miracles, that is.

GERDA. It's cold ...

KAI. Is it?

GERDA. My mom says I should never be out in the cold without my jacket. I'm going home.

KAI. Hm? What's that? Oh, yes, all right. Go crying to your mommy. Leave it to the adults to enjoy real life.

GERDA. I—I'll see you later.

> GERDA, *her feelings hurt, exits.*

KAI. They're like—like random time tables. One times 2 is two. Two times 12 is 24. 24 times 36 is 864. 864 times 1,098 is 948,672. Variables made into patterns. Random numbers creating symmetry. Chaos IS the order. Meaninglessness IS the religion. They are perfect, yet always different. Structured, yet always random.

> THE SNOW QUEEN *appears on the screen. At first she is nothing more than a figure of frost on glass. Yet as the conversation progresses she transforms and solidifies into the figure of a beautiful woman wearing a long, white coat.*

SNOW QUEEN. You have the true heart of a realist.

> KAI *is startled.*

KAI. Wh-Who are you?

SNOW QUEEN. You know me, my boy.

KAI. I-I'm not a boy.

SNOW QUEEN. Oh? Well, if you're a man then, you won't mind the cold?

KAI. C-cold?

SNOW QUEEN. See, you still feel it. Chattering teeth and all.

The SNOW QUEEN appears as if she walks out of the screen.

KAI. Yeah, I—I'm really cold.

SNOW QUEEN. Let me help you, come here.

KAI approaches. The SNOW QUEEN grabs his hand.

KAI. Y-you're like ice.

SNOW QUEEN. But you like it, don't you? *(KAI nods.)* Come crawl underneath my fur coat that will help warm you. *(The SNOW QUEEN wraps her fur around the MAN, holding him close.)* Better?

KAI. M-much better.

SNOW QUEEN. But you're still cold. *(The SNOW QUEEN kisses KAI's forehead.)* Cold?

KAI. Y-yes.

The SNOW QUEEN kisses KAI.

SNOW QUEEN. Cold?

KAI. No. I can't feel it anymore.

SNOW QUEEN. You're no longer a boy, Kai. You are a man.

KAI. Thank you. You said that I knew you.

As the SNOW QUEEN describes the next scenario, it is shown on the screen.

SNOW QUEEN. Your father showed you to me. The frost had frozen on the window pane, and there he pointed me out. My figure outstretched in the frost, my voice calling in the winter wind.

KAI. You're the Snow Queen.

SNOW QUEEN. Your father said, "She is come to fetch me."

KAI. And he died the next morning.

The screen goes black.

SNOW QUEEN. I know you're a little scared right now. That's all right.

KAI. Have you come for me as well?

SNOW QUEEN. That depends—do you want to follow me?

KAI. Yes.

SNOW QUEEN. Then follow me.

The screen shows a snow storm, with the SNOW QUEEN and KAI flying through it. In the distance they see her cold, icy kingdom. KAI's eyes widen in wonder. The scene on the screen fades. We hear the voices of a search party in the distance, crying out KAI's name. GERDA enters, this time with red shoes.

GERDA. Kai! Kai! Kai! Kai, where are you?!

One of the screens lights up with the SNOW QUEEN appearing on it.

SNOW QUEEN. You won't find him.

GERDA. Who are you?

SNOW QUEEN. He's with me.

GERDA. Kai? You have Kai! His mother is so scared, bring him back!

SNOW QUEEN. He's free to come back anytime he wants to. But, you see, my dear, he doesn't want to.

GERDA. Of course he wants to. He's a little boy who needs to be at home with his mother.

SNOW QUEEN. He's not the little boy you once knew.

GERDA. Kai is Kai. He can't not be Kai!

SNOW QUEEN. Kai is Kai, but there can be many kinds of Kais.

GERDA. Give him back, please, give him back.

SNOW QUEEN. As I said . . .

GERDA. Let me talk to him.

SNOW QUEEN. Oh, I don't allow interference. My law is firm and frozen in that regard.

GERDA. There must be a way.

SNOW QUEEN. *(Looking at the GERDA's red shoes.)* There are those . . .

GERDA. My shoes?

SNOW QUEEN. Very pretty. They make you distinct.

GERDA. My father gave me these shoes—they are my most special things.

SNOW QUEEN. If you want a chance at getting back Kai, a sacrifice is required.

> *GERDA considers this.*

GERDA. For Kai.

> *GERDA takes off the shoes and places them before the screen.*

SNOW QUEEN. You may come down to my kingdom and speak to your friend.

> *KAI enters. He is now covered with ice and frost. The SNOW QUEEN vanishes from the screens and now there appear geometric shapes on the screens, each of them cold and ice-like. KAI is engrossed with the shapes, as if he is trying to find a pattern. When he touches the screens, the shapes react to him and move at his bidding. He keeps re-organizing them into different orders and patterns. He is never satisfied with what he finds and starts over.*

GERDA. Kai?

KAI. *(Doesn't look at her; still focusing on the shapes.)* Hm?

GERDA. Kai, is that you?

KAI. Who are you?

GERDA. It's me . . . Gerda. Your friend.

> *For the first time, KAI turns and looks at the GERDA. For a moment, there is a touch of warmth in his expression.*

KAI. Gerda . . . *(The warmth disappears.)* The little girl.

> *KAI goes back to the shapes.*

GERDA. I'm not a little girl anymore, Kai. I haven't been since you left.

KAI. That's good to hear. You got to be so annoying.

GERDA. I miss our days as children.

KAI. Three time nine is 27. 61 times 33 is 2013. 333 times 777 is 258,741.

GERDA. What are you doing?

KAI. I'm multi-tasking. Currently I'm working on my multiplication skills while trying to figure out this geometric puzzle.

GERDA. Wow. You always were better with numbers than I was.

KAI. Yes, I was. Yes, I am.

GERDA. Your numbers—your snowflakes.

KAI. *(Beat.)* Snowflakes . . . *(A moment of short-lived wistfulness before going back to the shapes. As KAI continues to converse with GERDA, he still doesn't look at her, but concentrates on the shapes.)* 107,963 times 639,253 is 69,015,671,639 . . .

GERDA. The puzzle . . . ?

KAI. The Snow Queen set it up for me.

GERDA. What's the point?

KAI. It's quite ingenious . . .

GERDA. But what's the point?

KAI. *(Annoyed and discouraged.)* I haven't figured that out yet. There is some pattern, some way to find . . .

GERDA. Find what?

KAI. Eternity.

GERDA. Eternity?

KAI. She says that if I can puzzle eternity out, she will give me the world and a pair of new skates.

GERDA. Why do you want the world?

KAI. Who wouldn't?

GERDA. I wouldn't—not at such a high cost, at least.

KAI. Cost? Why, there's no cost. She's given me everything! *(He finally turns again and talked excitedly, but he only glances at her occasionally, as he is too self absorbed to really focus on her for more than a moment.)* Gerda, your mind was always too small to understand. I feel such intellectual capacity, I have accumulated such knowledge. Whiz, Zip! I can receive answers in an instant, understand them in their nuances! My mind dissects and enlarges and magnifies!

GERDA. Yes, I think you magnify their importance. Like your satire.

KAI. You say you grew up, but you never grew up. *(KAI goes back to his shapes.)*You couldn't ever cool off enough to see the reality around you.

Angry, GERDA *twirls* KAI *around and makes him look at her.*

GERDA. Reality? You say this magnifying, this distorting of sizes makes you clever. That's not reality—that makes small things outsized, brings them out of their context, out of the bigger picture in which they're only a part!

KAI. I need to get back to my puzzle.

GERDA. And you say you've grown up? Playing intellectual games, absorbed in your own micro-universe—how does this work to help anyone?

KAI. I can see that you're not going to be reasonable. I think it's time for you to go.\

GERDA. Not unless you're coming with me.

KAI. Look, Gerda, I've tried to be patient, but I'm losing my temper . . .

GERDA. Good! Lose your temper! I'd like to see some real heat come from that frozen heart!

KAI. You have always been so smug, so annoying. Mother says this, Mother says that—your trite, little rules don't apply to me! The universe I work in is huge, it's vast!

GERDA. Your universe could dance on the head of a pin.

KAI. You know what? It's not your mother, it's not your rules—it's you! If someone was going to bring me back to what used to be home, it wouldn't be you. I could never suffer myself to keep company with such an ignorant, obnoxious female!

There is a tense pause. Although GERDA is hurt, she continues on with even more determination.

WOMAN. Listen to me, Kai, and listen good: no matter what you do, no matter what you say, no matter how wrong you are, I will always love you.

KAI opens his mouth to refute this, but he can't. Instead he gains his composure and just says:

KAI. I don't care.

At this GERDA starts to cry, tears streaming down her face.

GERDA. And no matter how much you hurt me, I will always love you still.

GERDA embraces KAI suddenly. KAI struggles, but GERDA's tears fall upon him, shown also on the screens. The sound of steam is heard, as well as warm, even romantic and lush, music. It's much like the music with the rose, but less simple, more full.

KAI. Whoa. I—I felt that. Your tears—they're hot.

Terrified, but entranced, KAI walks to her and touches her face. The sound of steam again. He touches his own face, his own eyes, with GERDA's tears. Again, the sound of more steam, and the ice begins to fall off. She goes over and kisses him on each cheek, with the subsequent sounds of steam again.

GERDA. Kai . . .

KAI begins to cry himself, and images of steam erode the geometric shapes on the screens and images of light and warmth and light appear in their stead. KAI and GERDA kiss each other warmly and, for a moment, actual steam (if possible) erupts from where they are standing and KAI is now completely free from the Snow Queen's enchantment.

KAI. Have I lost my childhood?

GERDA. You tell me.

KAI kisses GERDA quickly and playfully, then breaks from her embrace.

KAI. *(Right along with the kiss.)* Tag. You're it.

GERDA laughs.

GERDA. Oh, you're not getting away that easy!

With an excited shriek, GERDA chases KAI. They laugh and giggle and are as carefree as children.

THE END

Jyllian Petrie Unice as Gerda and Heather Jones as the Snow Queen. Photo by Kurt Perry.

Shea Potter as Kai and Jyllian Petrie as Gerda. Photo by Kurt Perry.

Shea Potter as Kai and Heather Jones as the Snow Queen. Photo by Kurt Perry.

Shea Potter as Kai. Photo by Kurt Perry.

Jyllian Petrie Unice as Gerda and Shea Potter as Kai. Photo by Kurt Perry.

46

Shea Potter as Kai and Jyllian Petrie Unice as Gerda. Photo by Kurt Perry.

Shea Potter as Kai and Heather Jones as the Snow Queen. Photo by Kurt Perry.

Jinn

A One-Act Play

Production History

Zion Theatre Company premiered "Jinn" on November 18, 2011, as part of the set of short plays called *Jinn and Other Myths*, in conjunction with the Off Broadway Theatre in Salt Lake City, Utah. It performed with the following cast and crew:

CAST
Calypso: Rebecca Minson
Shopkeeper: Jason Kelly Fullmer
Jinn 1: Luci McNair
Jinn 2: Shea Potter

CREW
Director: Jyllian Petrie Unice
Multimedia Directors: Jason Sullivan, Joel Petrie
Producers: Nathaniel Drew, Mahonri Stewart
Lights: David Bellis
Sound: Joel Petrie

"Jinn" then performed again at the Off Broadway Theatre in Salt Lake City starting on August 18, 2012, as part of Zion Theatre Company's set of short plays *The Death of Eurydice and Other Short Plays*. It had the following cast and crew:

CAST
Calypso: Rebecca Minson
Shopkeeper: Michelle Markland
Jinn 1: Rachel Baird
Jinn 2: Lawrence Fernandez

CREW
Creative Director: Rachel Baird
Technical Director: David Bellis

Lighting Design: Brittany Restrepo
Producers: Mahonri Stewart, Penny Pendleton,
Nathaniel Drew, Rachel Baird
Original Music and Sound Design: Nathaniel Drew

"Jinn" then performed starting on May 3, 2011, at Arizona State University as Kendra Schroeder's capstone project. It performed with the following cast and crew:

CAST
Calypso: Sydney Weinberger
Shopkeeper: Imran Malik
Jinn 1: Victoria Murray
Jinn 2: Michael Bowler

CREW
Director: Kendra Schroeder
Sound and Lighting Design: Noelle Nichols
Set and Costume Designer: Thomas Underal

For my friend Rachel Baird Lockhart, who asked for it.
Thank you for believing in my work.

Also for my friend Rebecca Minson.
For two productions of "Jinn," she has embodied Calypso exquisitely.

Jinn

A One-Act Play

A shop. On the shelves are many, many glass bottles of all different kinds of colors, shapes and sizes. The shop is full of them, almost bursting. As a collective, they are quite beautiful and when hit by the light they cast colorful shadows on the ground and against the walls. The entire setting of the show happens in the shop. The SHOPKEEPER, *who can be female or male, is organizing this menagerie of glass beauty when* CALYPSO, *a young woman, enters and starts inspecting the bottles. These two characters can be placed in a myriad of times, a myriad of places, they can modern or period, or perhaps even be made to be timeless.*

CALYPSO. These are beautiful. What a unique shop.

THE SHOPKEEPER. Thank you.

CALYPSO. I love the elegant sense you give to something as pragmatic as a bottle. You do make these yourself, don't you?

THE SHOPKEEPER. Me? Heavens, no.

CALYPSO. Oh. That's a shame. I thought you might have the look of a glassblower.

THE SHOPKEEPER. Not nearly so interesting as all that. Just the Shopkeeper.

CALYPSO. I see. Just the Shopkeeper.

THE SHOPKEEPER. And you are Calypso.

CALYPSO. How did you . . . ?

THE SHOPKEEPER. I know everyone's names, as soon as they enter my shop.

CALYPSO. No, really, how did you . . . ?

THE SHOPKEEPER. You've been here before.

CALYPSO. No, I would remember a place as beautiful as . . . *(The*
SHOPKEEPER goes to a particular bottle, grabs it and places it before
CALYPSO.) Wait.

THE SHOPKEEPER. I told you.

CALYPSO. Why do I remember this bottle?

THE SHOPKEEPER. It belongs to you.

CALYPSO. Oh, I didn't say I was going to buy anything . . .

THE SHOPKEEPER. It's already yours.

CALYPSO. That's generous of you, but . . .

The SHOPKEEPER goes to another bottle and brings it to
CALYPSO.

THE SHOPKEEPER. And this one has just come in for you.

CALYPSO. No, really, I couldn't . . .

THE SHOPKEEPER. It's not a matter of could or couldn't, it's a matter of
fact. I keep them here for you.

CALYPSO. You say they're already mine?

THE SHOPKEEPER. They most certainly are.

CALYPSO. Well, if you're *really* giving them to me, then I certainly
don't want to keep them *here.*

THE SHOPKEEPER. I'm just following your previous instructions.

CALYPSO. I mean this one would look great in my kitchen. And this
one, well, with some red flowers, it would be . . .

THE SHOPKEEPER. You're not understanding.

CALYPSO. Can you wrap them up for me? It'd be a shame, if they broke.
They really are most enchanting. Thank you for the gifts, they're
perfect.

THE SHOPKEEPER. I said you're not understanding.

CALYPSO. Really, how do you stay in business, if you just give them away?

THE SHOPKEEPER. The bottles are irrelevant.

CALYPSO. I definitely wouldn't say that! I am a big believer in the power of beauty.

THE SHOPKEEPER. It's what is in the bottle that really matters.

CALYPSO. But they don't have anything in them.

THE SHOPKEEPER. They do.

CALYPSO. They don't even have any corks or bottle stoppers.

THE SHOPKEEPER. The bottles themselves are sufficient to contain what's inside.

CALYPSO. If you're going to tell me that you're bottling air, well, that's just idiotic. Don't even try to sell me the air.

THE SHOPKEEPER. Calypso, you don't understand.

CALYPSO. What don't I understand?

THE SHOPKEEPER. Now you're getting somewhere.

CALYPSO. **What don't I understand?**

THE SHOPKEEPER. Here, hold this one.

> *The* SHOPKEEPER *hands the first bottle to* CALYPSO. CALYPSO *is caught off guard when she touches the bottle and reacts almost as if she had water thrown in her face. She quickly places the bottle down.*

CALYPSO. What just happened?

THE SHOPKEEPER. It'll be easier if you tell me.

CALYPSO. There was such intense emotion—all sorts of emotions— they just rushed through me like . . . like . . .

THE SHOPKEEPER. I know the words are hard to find.

CALYPSO. Are there words for this? This is beyond my experience.

THE SHOPKEEPER. It is not beyond your experience.

CALYPSO. I'm starting to remember this place—vaguely. Like a dream you almost remember when you wake up—but then it fades . . .

THE SHOPKEEPER. As soon as one leaves this store, the memory of it is hard to hold. You look pale, have a seat.

CALYPSO. What is in those bottles?

THE SHOPKEEPER. The Jinn.

CALYPSO. The what?

THE SHOPKEEPER. The Jinn. At least that's the word in Arabic. You would know them better as genies.

CALYPSO. Genies? As in Aladdin's genie?

THE SHOPKEEPER. No, not like the storytellers have fabricated them.

CALYPSO. So if I rub that bottle, will one of these Jinn grant my wishes?

THE SHOPKEEPER. No, at least not in the way you are thinking. But they certainly are connected to your wishes—and desires.

CALYPSO. Why are you being so cryptic? Please, just talk plainly with me.

THE SHOPKEEPER. Nothing is "plain" here. All is shadow and colored light.

CALYPSO. Where am I? I just wanted to distract myself and do some shopping.

THE SHOPKEEPER. Distract yourself from what?

CALYPSO. I—well, what do you mean?

THE SHOPKEEPER. What are you trying to distract yourself from?

CALYPSO. Well, I didn't say it was anything in particular. You know how it is, I am certain you have lots of people walk through those doors.

THE SHOPKEEPER. I certainly do.

CALYPSO. I hope it doesn't sound superficial, but I really enjoy shopping. It's not so much about the *things*, you know. It's about the experience.

THE SHOPKEEPER. The experience.

CALYPSO. I enjoy all sorts of stores, whether it's an open flea market or an expensive dress shop. Oh, and little, eclectic stores like this—pawn shops, second hand places, specialty stores with little trinkets or knick knacks or—or foreign items! An elephant tusk or a porcelain figurine or an old sword—it's the experience of it all! The more foreign the better, I think. And to be surrounded by so many people!

THE SHOPKEEPER. Yes, so many people doing their shopping.

CALYPSO. Of course. It's movement and bustle and haggling and—well, don't you see? They're these little interactions, bumping into each other, thumbing through sales together, money crossing hands, the small talk among merchants and customers . . .

THE SHOPKEEPER. Do you always go alone?

> CALYPSO *stops in her train of thought and looks at the* SHOP-KEEPER, *a little stunned. She stumbles with her thoughts for a little bit.*

CALYPSO. Alone?

THE SHOPKEEPER. Yes, you're alone.

CALYPSO. Well, you're here with me.

THE SHOPKEEPER. But do you have any companions who come with you? Friends? A husband, children?

CALYPSO. No. No, I don't have anyone like that.

THE SHOPKEEPER. And so you go shopping.

CALYPSO. No, no, you're misinterpreting all of it.

THE SHOPKEEPER. Am I?

CALYPSO. All of those—those kinds of relationships—well, when you come home from a hard day, you don't just want to get into another fight, or deal with all of the crying and yelling. Or devote all your energy to someone who is starved for attention or, worse yet, be the one starved for attention. I mean, when you're already at your wits' end, what's the point of all that?

THE SHOPKEEPER. Indeed.

CALYPSO. Now I'm going to sound a little strange here, but hear me out. People say they want these deep relationships, these—these intimate relationships where you can finish each other's sentences and almost read each other's thoughts. Well, excuse me for liking my privacy, but that's all a little—well, it's all a little *exposed* for my tastes.

THE SHOPKEEPER. Exposed?

CALYPSO. Exposed. Vulnerable. Just out in the open like that. Who really wants that kind of life?

THE SHOPKEEPER. Apparently, you don't.

CALYPSO. No. I don't. But listen to me just carrying on! Chatter, chatter, chatter, noise, noise, noise . . .

THE SHOPKEEPER. . . . bustle, bustle, bustle, shop, shop, shop.

CALYPSO. Stop it.

THE SHOPKEEPER. I apologize. You wouldn't want to *expose* yourself, of course.

CALYPSO. I said stop it! Look, we're way off topic. The bottles. Such pretty bottles.

THE SHOPKEEPER. Yes. Hold this one.

The SHOPKEEPER *offers her the second bottle.* CALYPSO *hesitates.*

CALYPSO. Just box them up for me, won't you?

THE SHOPKEEPER. Just hold it.

CALYPSO *looks at the bottle, frightened now, but she draws in a big breath and takes the bottle from the* SHOPKEEPER. *Her reaction is even more intense this time, although maybe not as animated, but she doesn't let go of it as quickly.*

CALYPSO. Oh! Oh—this one is so sad. But so beautiful . . . (CALYPSO *starts to struggle with the intense emotion, wanting to hold on, but eventually she can't and thrusts it back into the* SHOPKEEPER'*s hands.*) I can't! I'm sorry, but I can't! Why don't you show me some more of these bottles? Maybe one which is a little more cheerful. A bright and dainty bottle would do nicely, maybe one that I can put perfume in. Can I put perfume in it, if it already has a genie in residence? I keep forgetting that something lives in them. Don't want to drown the little creatures. In fact, I'm so taken with your little Jinn, maybe I can make a collection. I collect oh so many things . . .

THE SHOPKEEPER. Calypso . . .

CALYPSO. In fact, do you do exchanges? I'm not sure I'm really satisfied with the two Jinn you gave me. I would be more than happy to . . .

THE SHOPKEEPER. Calypso, those two bottles are yours and no one else's.

CALYPSO. Well, then I'll just have to get more then, won't I? Build up that collection! I'll become your most loyal customer!

THE SHOPKEEPER. You have other bottles here, Calypso, but those two are the most prominent, the most important. These ones on the shelves, they belong to others. But these—these are your Jinn. They are yours to do what you want with. But I will warn you that if you leave this shop with them, the Jinn will escape from the bottles permanently.

CALYPSO. What do you mean escape?

THE SHOPKEEPER. Within the shop, the Jinn can be brought out of the bottle and you can look at them, admire them, despise them, laugh at them—whatever you want. But in that open air, the bottles lose their magic. And once the Jinn are free, they have a life of their own. They have their own wills that alter our lives in unseen ways. Every customer receives this warning—you can free the Jinn, you can be their liberator. But mischief will follow.

CALYPSO. Mischief! What kind of evil thing have you given me?

THE SHOPKEEPER. The Jinn are not always evil. Actually, they often can be very good and virtuous—but they are also not orderly. No Jinn, in any way, is predictable. Especially once they are free, don't ever think that you can control them.

CALYPSO. Really, Shopkeeper, this may be a little more responsibility than I was bargaining for.

THE SHOPKEEPER. These are your Jinn. You are now their master in this place. Do with them as you will. Now, if you'll excuse me, I have some cataloguing to do in the back.

CALYPSO. Shopkeeper!

The SHOPKEEPER *exits.* CALYPSO *looks at the two bottles warily. Growing more and more nervous, she turns and nearly exits the entire shop, but then looks back at the bottles. Curiosity starts to consume her as she turns and stares at the bottles. Progressively,* WHISPERS *are heard, perhaps even seductive or enchanting* MUSIC, *perhaps even with a Middle Eastern feel to it.* CALYPSO *is startled at first, but the whispers somehow make sense to her and she approaches the bottles. There is still some hesitation as she circles the bottles, inspecting them. The music grows more lush and enticing until* CALYPSO *can't withhold any longer and she grabs the first bottle. The music stops and nothing happens. She taps the bottle.*

CALYPSO. Well, that was anti-climactic.

Suddenly there is an exceptionally loud BLARING SOUND *and the* LIGHTS FLASH *on brightly. There is a sudden blackout. After several moments, the lights slowly rise again to reveal* CALYPSO *still in the shop, but now accompanied by the* FIRST JINN. *This* JINN *is veiled, wrapped head to toe, possibly in an Islamic burqa, or a perhaps a hijab that also veils the face. The clothing is possibly black, but more likely brightly colored, possibly the same color as the bottle it just emerged from.*

CALYPSO (CONT'D). Wow. Er, hello.

The FIRST JINN'*s eyes widen in surprise. She is wary of* CALYPSO.

CALYPSO (CONT'D). Don't worry, I . . .

CALYPSO *tries to draw near to the* FIRST JINN, *but the* JINN *withdraws, growing ever more suspicious.*

CALYPSO (CONT'D). No, you don't have to . . .

FIRST JINN. Stay back.

CALYPSO. So you can speak.

The JINN still lingers back.

CALYPSO (CONT'D). I'm not going to hurt you.

FIRST JINN. Liar.

CALYPSO. Please . . .

FIRST JINN. Liar!

CALYPSO goes forward and tries to grab the FIRST JINN's hand. The FIRST JINN slaps it away. CALYPSO attempts to grab the hand again and this time holds on, even as the FIRST JINN struggles against her touch. CALYPSO then grabs the FIRST JINN's other hand, making a soothing "Shh" sounds. Their eyes lock and the FIRST JINN relaxes a bit, but she is still more than a little afraid.

CALYPSO. See?

FIRST JINN. What do you want?

CALYPSO. I'm—curious.

FIRST JINN. About me?

CALYPSO. Yes.

The FIRST JINN struggles again. CALYPSO holds on.

CALYPSO (CONT'D). Trust me.

FIRST JINN. No.

CALYPSO. Please . . .

FIRST JINN. I don't know you. You don't know me. There is nothing to trust.

CALYPSO. Then let's get to know each other. Then we'll see. *(The FIRST JINN considers this. CALYPSO drops her hands. The FIRST JINN creates just a little bit of comfortable distance, but is still willing to engage with* CALYPSO.) There's nothing to fear.

FIRST JINN. You're naive. But—familiar.

CALYPSO. Why—why do you wear that?

FIRST JINN. Why do you?

CALYPSO. Do you like the outfit? The bottom is from an expensive shop I like to go to a few streets over from my home—the top, though, that's my prize. Second hand store. You would never be able to tell, would you?

FIRST JINN. No.

CALYPSO. Don't want to be too predictable, do we? Combine the cheap and the sublime and then don't let anyone tell the difference! Keep them off balance, keep them guessing, keep up the mystery.

FIRST JINN. Yes. That's it.

CALYPSO. We can't expose ourselves, can we?

FIRST JINN. Yes. You understand.

CALYPSO. Yes. I do.

They connect. The FIRST JINN *draws closer.*

FIRST JINN. What's it like? Out there?

They both look to the door.

CALYPSO. Tolerable. If you know what you're doing.

FIRST JINN. And if you don't?

CALYPSO. Then you might as well stay here.

FIRST JINN. I see.

CALYPSO. Isolation. It's not always so bad, is it?

FIRST JINN. Isn't it?

CALYPSO. They think it's a big punishment, that. Solitary confinement. But I bet your thoughts are interesting. Alone with your thoughts like that, it must be nice, not having everyone pressing in on you.

FIRST JINN. I don't know. I don't have anything else to compare it to except being here now with you.

CALYPSO. And your bottle. How pretty it is.

FIRST JINN. Is it?

CALYPSO. Look. The bright color, the elegant formation. To some, this may seem decently common. But to me—well, I know these things. I know cheap junk and I know—a treasure.

FIRST JINN. A treasure.

CALYPSO. Yes! And you should treasure it as well.

FIRST JINN. I will. It's the only home I have.

CALYPSO. Home. There's something about home, isn't there? The safe place, where you go to when it's become too loud outside. Too tumultuous. *(The FIRST JINN begins to become emotional, a deep seated sadness coming upon her.)* Oh, dearie, what's wrong?

FIRST JINN. I—I don't know. *(The FIRST JINN begins to cry and collapses to the floor.)* You—you shouldn't see me like this.

CALYPSO. Maybe you're right. I'll leave you to your privacy. Maybe this was all a mistake.

CALYPSO turns to go, but then looks back with a good deal of pity. She goes to the FIRST JINN and kneels next to her.

FIRST JINN. No, really, you should . . .

CALYPSO takes the FIRST JINN's hand. CALYPSO, surprised, takes in a strong, shocked breath.

CALYPSO. I can—I can—how can I feel your pain? It's so strong . . .

FIRST JINN. You don't want to understand.

CALYPSO. No! Tell me, tell me, please . . .

FIRST JINN. Tell *you?* Tell my jail keeper!

The FIRST JINN rises in a terrible fury.

CALYPSO. Jail keeper?

FIRST JINN. You have the power to release me.

CALYPSO. No, no . . .

FIRST JINN. You know you do!

CALYPSO. There must be a reason. There must be a reason you're here, and not out there.

FIRST JINN. I don't care about your reasons, or your excuses, or the things you tell yourself to soothe your nerves to sleep on those dark, windy nights!

CALYPSO. Now wait a minute—I have never done you any harm.

FIRST JINN. The Shopkeeper told you. Told you that you have the power to release me and then you dare—you *dare* tell me that you haven't done me any harm!

CALYPSO. I didn't think you were supposed to hear that.

FIRST JINN. You can't hide anything from me. But you have me hide everything from you.

CALYPSO. Me? I'm not making you hide anything.

FIRST JINN. (*Pause.*) Yes. Of course. You're right. Just go. It's all right, everything is all right here. Let's soothe and smooth it all out. But, please, just go.

CALYPSO. I'm not going anywhere.

FIRST JINN. Still curious? That morbid fascination. Who's under the veil, you're asking yourself. I can see it in your eyes.

CALYPSO. I—I can respect your privacy.

FIRST JINN. Privacy.

CALYPSO. Look. Really. I want to be understanding here.

    CALYPSO *stands and moves away from the* FIRST JINN.

FIRST JINN. (*Noting the move.*) So distantly understanding.

CALYPSO. Look, what do you expect from me?

FIRST JINN. What do you expect from *me*? You're the master here.

CALYPSO. Am I?

FIRST JINN. I will do your bidding. Send me in the bottle—or free me.

CALYPSO. Free you? I hate to disappoint you, but there is no real freedom out there. You're better off here.

FIRST JINN. Then why don't you stay here, and I'll take your place out there?

CALYPSO. That's not quite what I meant.

FIRST JINN. Of course not.

CALYPSO. But—but sometimes I wish I could stay in place like this, though. By myself, surrounded by such beauty.

FIRST JINN. Such a pretty prison.

CALYPSO. Prison. I suppose so. I understand how you must feel.

FIRST JINN. Only too well.

CALYPSO. What do you mean?

FIRST JINN. Mean? What do I *mean*? Or what do *I* mean?

CALYPSO. No more vague sayings! I hate that.

FIRST JINN. Wonder of wonders . . .

CALYPSO. Oh. I'm sorry. That wasn't very polite.

FIRST JINN. Polite.

CALYPSO. I—I'm very sorry.

FIRST JINN. You're plenty polite. But not very good.

CALYPSO. Now that's uncalled for.

FIRST JINN. Uncalled for!

CALYPSO. Where are your manners?

FIRST JINN. Manners!

CALYPSO. Stop repeating me!

FIRST JINN. Repeating! It's not repeating. It's an echo.

CALYPSO. Stop it, you self pitying wretch! (*To* CALYPSO's *surprise, the* FIRST JINN *shrieks in fury and attacks her. They struggle and fight.*) What are you doing?!

FIRST JINN. What are you doing?!

CALYPSO. Get away from me!

FIRST JINN. Get away from me!

CALYPSO. I am your master!

At this the FIRST JINN *backs off, withdrawing in shame.*

FIRST JINN. I apologize.

CALYPSO. I thought you said that you would do my bidding.

FIRST JINN. Usually.

CALYPSO. Usually?

FIRST JINN. Usually.

CALYPSO. Well, that's not good enough.

FIRST JINN. As you wish, Master.

CALYPSO. I'm nobody's master.

FIRST JINN. Then why should I do your bidding?

CALYPSO. You're—unpredictable. Even here you're unpredictable.

FIRST JINN. And you are perfectly predictable? Level, steady, unthreatening?

CALYPSO. I pride myself on those qualities, yes. Can't have anything reckless happening, can we? Can't make people nervous.

FIRST JINN. If you say so, Master.

CALYPSO. Don't call me . . .

FIRST JINN. If you don't want me to call you Master, then free me.

CALYPSO. Who knows what you'll do out there. What they'll do to you.

FIRST JINN. Does it really matter?

CALYPSO. Yes. Nothing matters more. If the—if the equilibrium is thrown off out there—well, they're not too kind to the offenders.

FIRST JINN. I—I understand that you want to protect me, but I can also have such wild excitement, such unrestrained joy.

CALYPSO. They don't look upon those qualities with any more forgiveness. No, no, you're better off here.

FIRST JINN. Happiness. Do you want happiness?

CALYPSO. Who doesn't?

FIRST JINN. I can give it to you. It'll be your wish from me. Let me free and I can dance with you and fill you with such life and lust and love that you won't care about that herd and their equilibrium!

CALYPSO. I thought the Shopkeeper said that you didn't grant wishes.

FIRST JINN. But I can fulfill desires. Or at least I can give you desire.

CALYPSO. Happiness? You can grant true happiness?

FIRST JINN. Yes.

CALYPSO. But not eternal happiness. It's only temporary, isn't it? After that the vultures come. What of the sadness I felt from you? Or the rage you exhibited just barely? (*The* FIRST JINN *is silent.*) They're part of the package as well. (*The* FIRST JINN *turns and sits alone. There is an uncomfortable silence. The* FIRST JINN *looks up, her eyes full of emotion. A beautiful, yearning* MUSIC *starts to be heard in the distance. The* MUSIC *begins to crescendo and swell.*) How . . . ? I'm not even touching you and I can feel that? That's—that's the strongest feeling of any of them. (CALYPSO *comes to* FIRST JINN, *touching her on the shoulder. She gasps, but then just sits next to the Jinn, looking up. Tears spring to her eyes.*) I've—I've never felt that before.

FIRST JINN. Yes, you have. Once.

CALYPSO. I would remember.

FIRST JINN. You don't remember because it is there—in the other bottle.

CALYPSO. What?

FIRST JINN. It's there. In there. Or at least the way to access it is.

CALYPSO. You seemed so familiar just now.

FIRST JINN. The resident of that bottle and I are siblings, you know.

CALYPSO. The way you say things sometimes—or your inflection—is that it?

FIRST JINN. He and I are close cousins. We understand each other. Feed off each other's energy.

CALYPSO. What is this emotion? What is this that you feel so strongly?

FIRST JINN. Yearning.

Something touches CALYPSO. Deeply. Tears begin coming to her eyes. She touches them in surprise.

CALYPSO. No. I'm not like this.

FIRST JINN. Aren't you?

CALYPSO. No, no, this only leads to . . . to . . .

FIRST JINN. To pain? How would you know that?

CALYPSO. Of course I'm not talking from personal experience, but . . . *(The FIRST JINN grabs the second bottle and offers it to CALYPSO. CALYPSO hesitates.)* I can't. *(The FIRST JINN offers it again, more urgently.)* No, really—I can't!

FIRST JINN. Let me out. And then meet my brother. And let him out.

CALYPSO. I'm not letting anything out!

FIRST JINN. Yes! There it is! There you go!

CALYPSO. Get away from me!

FIRST JINN. Fear is a part of me, too!

CALYPSO. I don't want anything to do with any of this anymore!

FIRST JINN. Feel. No more distractions, no more evasions—feel!

The FIRST JINN places her hands on CALYPSO's face and, together, they both breathe in deeply. There is a brief silence, although it is a complete and utter quiet. Then CALYPSO looks up at the FIRST JINN, an understanding sweeping across her face. She begins to laugh. It is a natural, happy laugh, as if a burden had just been lifted. The FIRST JINN laughs as well. The laughter eventually turns into tears and CALYPSO collapses into the FIRST JINN's arms, the FIRST JINN both crying with her and comforting her at the same time. They both quiet down and the intensity of the emotion settles into a quiet serenity. They both enjoy this stillness for a moment, until CALYPSO breaks from the spell, pulling away from the JINN.

CALYPSO. This is too much.

FIRST JINN. I—I felt free for a moment. So did you.

CALYPSO. You don't know me. I don't know you.

FIRST JINN. That's not true.

With the FIRST JINN's back to the audience, so that only CALYPSO can see her face, the FIRST JINN pulls back her veil. CALYPSO shows surprise, even though a part of her knew all along.

CALYPSO. No.

FIRST JINN. I've been with you all along.

CALYPSO. This is too much! (*CALYPSO grabs the abandoned veil and covers the FIRST JINN up again.*) Back in the bottle!

The BLARING NOISE occurs again, as well as the BRIGHT FLASH, and then there is a black out. When the lights slowly rise, the FIRST JINN is gone, and CALYPSO is standing there, emotionless. Enter the SHOPKEEPER.

THE SHOPKEEPER. I thought I would check on you.

CALYPSO. Why did you do this to me?

THE SHOPKEEPER. I haven't done anything to you.

CALYPSO. You led me here, didn't you?

THE SHOPKEEPER. I never lead anyone. I just tend the shop, keep things orderly. Meticulous order is very important here. People tend to appreciate that.

CALYPSO. I'm not sure I appreciate it.

THE SHOPKEEPER. I don't think you're sure of much right now, are you? An unexpected reflection is rarely easy to face, especially with the clarity of one of the Jinn.

CALYPSO. Reflection. She wasn't a reflection.

THE SHOPKEEPER. Wasn't she?

CALYPSO. That's not what I am. That's not what I've created for myself.

THE SHOPKEEPER. Your internal energy can be repressed. But it can't be destroyed. It has to go somewhere. Thus this place. Sometimes you can find my shop just underneath the surface. Sometimes you have to dig for a long time, navigate through a labyrinth of serpentine hallways and locked doors. And then there are other times when the shop simply rises, unbidden—like today.

CALYPSO. All of these bottles . . .

THE SHOPKEEPER. Little shards of people's souls. Unwanted edges— or sometimes they're wanted too much. I keep them for my customers. But you're always welcome to come and . . .

CALYPSO. No. That's not what I want.

THE SHOPKEEPER. (With a pleasant smile.) Of course. The customer is always right. Now if you'll excuse me, I'll be back to my cataloguing. If you need me, just . . .

CALYPSO. Wait.

THE SHOPKEEPER. Yes?

CALYPSO. I—she said that her—her brother is in the other bottle. If she was emotion, then this one is . . .

THE SHOPKEEPER. You already know the answer. Remember, we're always open. 24 hours a day, 7 days a week. Stay as long as you'd like.

The SHOPKEEPER exits. CALYPSO approaches the other bottle.

CALYPSO. Memory. The brother of Emotion is Memory. (*The same WHISPERS and MUSIC that Calypso heard before with the first bottle occur.* CALYPSO *grabs the second bottle. There is the* BLARING SOUND *and* FLASH OF LIGHT *again and then blackout. As the lights rise again there is the* SECOND JINN. *He is also veiled and covered. He stands silently and still and* CALYPSO *goes to him, circling him. The* SECOND JINN *doesn't respond.)* Well? *(The* SECOND JINN *doesn't do so much as look at her.)* Aren't you supposed to—well, do something? *(*CALYPSO *goes to touch his veil. He breathes in deeply and looks gently at her.)* Is that it? The veil? *(*CALYPSO *rips off the veil and outer garment to reveal a man about her age, and from her period.)* Zachary?

The SECOND JINN *looks down at* CALYPSO *and smiles warmly.*

SECOND JINN. Hey, Calypso! It feels like I haven't seen you forever.

CALYPSO. *(She is now suddenly part of the memory and what now what seems to be a completely different persona.)* You know me—I like surprises.

SECOND JINN. Back for the summer?

CALYPSO. Yeah, staying with my parents.

SECOND JINN. How is it then?

CALYPSO. School?

SECOND JINN. Yeah.

CALYPSO. Oh, Zachary! I am so glad I did this.

SECOND JINN. You are so far away from our little town now.

CALYPSO. Well, I'm here now, aren't I?

SECOND JINN. Here you are.

CALYPSO. You stopped writing.

SECOND JINN. And so did you.

CALYPSO. My studies keep me busy—so much to learn, so much to understand. That's the part of it I love the most—dwelling on life, drinking deep of the Universe. Asking the big questions and not flinching in the face of the answers.

SECOND JINN. Ready to face it all, are you?

CALYPSO. Yes, oh yes! And it's so wonderful not worrying about the tedious details of this place—helping with the crops or looking after the animals or dealing with small minded neighbors or . . .

SECOND JINN. We're small minded, are we?

CALYPSO. No, not you. Never you. The kindness you and your family have always shown me will be engraved on my heart forever. Never forgotten, you understand?

SECOND JINN. You used to like this life, Calypso.

CALYPSO. I didn't know anything else.

SECOND JINN. And now you have your other world.

SECOND JINN turns to leave, but CALYPSO stops him.

CALYPSO. Zachary, why are you being like this? I came—I came to . . .

SECOND JINN. I've really missed you.

CALYPSO. Yes. I've missed you so much, too. I'm so full of memories sometimes.

SECOND JINN. Me too.

CALYPSO. Sometimes when those awkward silences come up between people—you know, when the subject has run out and people scramble for another thing to chatter about—well, with you it was always all right. Silence wasn't something to be afraid of.

SECOND JINN. Sometimes it would be preferred even. That night I held your hand.

CALYPSO. Or when you kissed me on the cheek.

SECOND JINN. We never got further than that.

CALYPSO. No. We didn't. Do you regret that?

SECOND JINN. Sometimes. You?

CALYPSO. Often.

SECOND JINN. My sisters would love to hear from you.

CALYPSO. I actually already dropped by.

SECOND JINN. I heard. Two weeks ago. You've been in town two weeks.

CALYPSO. Yes.

SECOND JINN. And you didn't try to visit again after that?

CALYPSO. They told me that you—that you were seeing someone.

SECOND JINN. Yes. I am. She and I—we're engaged now.

CALYPSO. Oh! Oh. When did it happen?

SECOND JINN. Three days ago.

CALYPSO. I see.

SECOND JINN. I waited until you came back into town. I—I waited for you. But when you didn't come to see me . . .

CALYPSO. I read something interesting at the University.

SECOND JINN. Well, as long as it's "interesting" then.

CALYPSO. Please, Zachary. Just listen. There was a Greek playwright and thinker—Aristophanes. He was talking with all these great thinkers and they were having this really interesting discussion. The subject progressed and turned to the God of love, Eros.

SECOND JINN. All right. Go on.

CALYPSO. He said that there is this—this hurt, this wound we carry around. An aching sting we carry from before we even came to this life. He said that before this life we were different creatures. Creatures with two heads, four arms, four legs. But when we tried to climb to heaven, Zeus sent down his barrage and we all split into two—a male and a female. All of us have been looking for our missing half since then, to reunite with them and heal that unbearable, dull ache.

SECOND JINN. Calypso . . .

CALYPSO. Maybe I'm standing in your way of your other half.

SECOND JINN. What?

CALYPSO. Maybe you and she are each other's cure for that pain. Maybe it would be just selfish of me to hold onto you when I'm not even sure what I want anymore. I don't want to ruin your chances, just because I'm confused as to what mine were, or are in the future.

SECOND JINN. Calypso, wait. I'm here with you right now. I'm willing to . . .

CALYPSO. Who knows? Maybe there is someone out there who can fulfill me, too. Maybe it's best for both of us and we just need to stop holding onto the past.

SECOND JINN. Is that how you really feel about it?

CALYPSO. Has this girl made you happy?

SECOND JINN. You made me happy, too. Her and I—we're really just starting out. But you and I—we have history. Memory. Calypso, I can still feel you in my nerves, my fingers, the stretch of my muscles. I still have these sweet dreams about you, and I wake up so sad. Full of so much—aching loneliness. You are a part of me, always will be.

CALYPSO. No. Memories fade. I'll fade. We can push our memories down.

SECOND JINN. I'll never be able to get rid of you.

CALYPSO. I think we both need a new start. I was stupid to come back.

SECOND JINN. I don't want a new start!

CALYPSO. But you see, darling—I do.

The SECOND JINN *looks over* CALYPSO, *hurt.*

SECOND JINN. Is that it then? After all we have meant to each other, we just part paths, just like that?

CALYPSO. Just like that.

The SECOND JINN *hardens, and simply nods.*

SECOND JINN. If that's how you want it.

The BLARING NOISE *occurs again.*

CALYPSO. No, no, let me go back. That's my wish, let me go back! *(There is the* BRIGHT FLASH, *and then there is a black out. When the lights slowly rise, the* SECOND JINN *is gone and* CALYPSO *is alone.)* Zachary!

I was wrong! Please, please, come back! Don't marry her, don't leave me so alone! *(CALYPSO breaks down in tears. Enter the SHOPKEEPER, who stands apart from her silently for a moment. CALYPSO looks up, trying to gain some composure upon seeing the SHOPKEEPER.)* I almost went back that night. I became suddenly afraid, terrified that I may have made the most terrible decision of my life. But how could I dare? How could I dare stand in the way of his happiness when I was so unsure? Why couldn't have I been more sure? I went to the wedding party. They looked very happy, and Zachary seemed very happy that I was there to share it with him. That's the memory I choose to remember. Seeing him so happy with her and her so happy with him.

THE SHOPKEEPER. Yes, you've certainly never bottled that memory up for me.

CALYPSO. That's because I made the right choice and I need something—something! Something to remind me that I was right.

THE SHOPKEEPER. I can take this to the back, if you want.

CALYPSO. No. Not yet. I—I lost a lot of interest in things after that. University was teaching me to dwell on things. Things would go over and over in my mind. Ideas or thoughts or—memories. They would keep me up at night, I couldn't sleep!

THE SHOPKEEPER. And it was soon after that you came here. I have a whole section in the back from that part of your life.

CALYPSO. I dropped out of school. Got a job that allowed me to live independently, apart. I could just go out and look through my shops and be—distracted. I couldn't deal with the buzzing thoughts, the endless, circular questions. The lonely regrets. None of it had any answers anyway.

THE SHOPKEEPER. Very good, Miss. I'm assuming you want the bottles to stay here then?

CALYPSO. No!

THE SHOPKEEPER. No?

CALYPSO. Just—just give me few more minutes with them.

THE SHOPKEEPER. If that's what you desire, but . . .

CALYPSO. Yes?

THE SHOPKEEPER. I'm really not supposed to interfere.

CALYPSO. What? Tell me.

THE SHOPKEEPER. I often wonder why people come back. They seem to desire these moments, they find excuses to come here. Why on earth come back?

CALYPSO. Why indeed?

THE SHOPKEEPER. I think you may be onto something. Just fly around out there, like a butterfly. A beautiful, delicate butterfly floating from flower to flower, never entangled by any of the webs in here.

CALYPSO. A focused existence, just flower to flower.

CALYPSO takes both bottles and studies them. She then holds them both tightly and gasps with the feelings and memories that flood into her.

THE SHOPKEEPER. Miss! That's going to be too much!

CALYPSO shouts out and then releases the bottles. She looks up to the SHOPKEEPER.

CALYPSO. I feel so much . . .

THE SHOPKEEPER. So much pain, so much regret.

CALYPSO. I *feel* so much! I *remember* so much!

THE SHOPKEEPER. Keep it all here. I will take care of it. You don't have to . . .

CALYPSO. Get away from me!

THE SHOPKEEPER. I'm trying to help you.

CALYPSO. You—you look at me with those dull, lifeless eyes and you say—you say you're trying to help me?

THE SHOPKEEPER. That's the Jinn talking.

CALYPSO. It's *me* talking!

CALYPSO *looks at the bottles with sudden clarity and realization.*

THE SHOPKEEPER. Miss, you won't be able to make a rational decision if you . . .

CALYPSO. I could go back to school. That's a start.

THE SHOPKEEPER. You won't want to make those kinds of decisions in such an emotional state. You'll just accumulate more bottles down here that way.

CALYPSO. No. No more bottles.

THE SHOPKEEPER. You're confused.

CALYPSO. I am not confused! I am more centered, more myself than I have been in years.

THE SHOPKEEPER. The emotions, the memories, they're having an effect on you. This is not who you chose to be.

CALYPSO. Well, then I can make new choices. Zachary and I—we're done, I know that. But I can find someone else. Maybe I was right, after all. Aristophanes' ache—I can fill that ache!

THE SHOPKEEPER. No. I am sorry, that is not possible. If it's not one ache, then it's another. Calypso, there is no end to loss, no end to the unpredictable storms out there. The Jinn are children of chaos. Those Jinn are . . .

CALYPSO. Those Jinn are me! They are shards broken off of my soul. And I'm telling you right now, I have come to claim my soul back out of this petty pawn shop!

THE SHOPKEEPER. Now listen here! I have been here for age after age, civilization after civilization. For thousands of years I have dealt with these Jinn you send me, and I am more than fine with that, for that is my role. That is my purpose. But, make no mistake; I know that all of you are just like the same, irresponsible children that came before you, acting out on every impulse and desire. You think your society progresses? From country to country, son after father, but you bring me the same mistakes, the same regrets, the same rage, the same despair, and I must contain them for you. It is I who must bring some discipline into your world and make you *functional*.

CALYPSO. You wanted to know why.

THE SHOPKEEPER. Pardon me?

CALYPSO. You wanted to know why we keep coming back here, to look at the bottles.

THE SHOPKEEPER. All right.

CALYPSO grasps the bottles, but instead of crying out this time, she allows both the emotions and the memories to wash over her.

CALYPSO. So that we can *be*.

THE SHOPKEEPER. You are, with or without the Jinn.

CALYPSO. Are we?

THE SHOPKEEPER. Yes. Listen, those are your property. They are to do with as you please. I shouldn't have got involved. But I will just repeat what I told you earlier. I will warn you that if you leave this shop with them, the Jinn will escape from the bottles permanently. Within the shop, the Jinn can be brought out of the bottle and you can look at them, admire them, despise them, laugh at them—whatever you want. But in that open air, the bottles lose their magic. And once the Jinn are free, they have a life of their own. They have their own wills that alter your life in unseen ways. Every customer receives this warning—you can free the Jinn, you can be their liberator. But mischief will follow.

Exit the SHOPKEEPER. CALYPSO looks at the bottles. A sudden fear comes upon her and she rushes to the counter and places them there, turning to go, but then suddenly the same enticing MUSIC we have heard previously plays. CALYPSO walks over to the bottles and studies them. She is indecisive, but then resoluteness comes over her. She takes the bottles and exits.

THE END

Rebecca Minson as Calypso and Luci McNair as Jinn #1. Photo by Kurt Perry.

Rebecca Minson as Calypso and Luci McNair as Jinn #1. Photo by Kurt Perry.

Rebecca Minson as Calypso. Photo by Kurt Perry.

Rebecca Minson as Calypso and Luci McNair as Jinn #1. Photo by Kurt Perry.

Rebecca Minson as Calypso and Rachel Baird as Jinn #1. Photo by Naoma Wilkinson.

Lawrence Fernandez as Jinn #2 and Rebecca Minson as Calypso. Photo by Naoma Wilkinson.

Sydney Weinberger as Calypso and Imran Malik as the Shopkeeper. Photo by Kendra Schroeder.

Michael Bowler as Jinn #2 and Sydney Weinberger as Calypso. Photo by Kendra Schroeder.

Sydney Weinberger as Calypso and Victoria Murray as Jinn #1. Photo by Kendra Schroeder.

Evening Eucalyptus

A Mythical Drama in Two Acts

Production History

Evening Eucalyptus premiered on November 7, 2014, at the Echo Theatre in Provo, UT. It had the following cast and crew:

CAST
Arthur Stevenson: David Lasseter
Abigail Baker: Anna Hargadon
Pindari: Robert Burch
Zeek: Stephen Geis
Jody: Bryn Dalton Randall
Trooper: Neal Hooper

CREW
Set Design/ Set Construction: Jason Sullivan and Mahonri Stewart
Lighting Design: Mandy Lyons
Fight Choreography: Adam Argyle
Poster Artist: Liz Pulido
Costumes/Props/Sound Design: Mahonri Stewart

*For Georgia, for Darcy, for Clive, for Miss Amanda, for Mish,
and all those others in Albury who caught my soul,
put it in a mason jar, shook it up
and then let it fly up to the Southern Cross.
I dearly miss my time in Oz.*

A Note on Casting:

The casting of separate actors for the Dream Spirits is not essential to the show. They can be played by the same actors who play Abigail, Zeek, Jody, Trooper, and Pindari (who would step in and out of certain dream spirit roles). Within the script, however, there is no occasion where Arthur can be a dream spirit.

The Dream Spirits can be represented through many means such as media, puppetry, etc. If a production does desire to create a larger cast, however, the dream spirits can be extended to include any number of actors/dancers that the director/choreographer wants to include. The minimum of actors needed, however, is 6. Gender is not necessarily important either way for the dream spirits except for the obviously titled "Female Dream Spirit" and the "Tree Spirit," both of which are definitely female.

The breakdown of "characters" is as follows:

ARTHUR STEVENSON, male

ABIGAIL BAKER, female

PINDARI, male

JODY, female

ZEEK, male

TROOPER, male

DREAM SPIRITS, including:

GREAT FISH

NEPELLE

BUNYIP

RAINBOW SERPENT

YABBRA

WEEUM

FEMALE DREAM SPIRIT

DIRAWONG

TREE SPIRIT

Evening Eucalyptus

Act One

SCENE 1

Albury, New South Wales, Australia; within far sight of the Snowy Mountains. The year is 1912. There are two locations on stage. The first, larger and currently lit section is a porch and the front yard of a well kept, but sad looking home. Its one truly redeeming feature is a beautiful eucalyptus tree in the yard.

The second section of the stage, intersecting with the eucalyptus tree and currently unlit, is a piece of riverbed by the Murray River. It is now late at night. We hear an early automobile drive up (and perhaps see the headlights) and then hear the doors open and close.

Enter ARTHUR STEVENSON *with a suitcase of luggage.* ARTHUR *is a tired looking man, who seems older than he really is by the virtue of the restrained pain he holds in his demeanor. He looks around the yard quiet and unassuming. This is his home now, but with the way he acts, one would assume that he was a stranger or a visitor. Almost timidly he approaches a dilapidated rocking chair on the front porch and then decides to sit in it, placing his one suitcase of luggage on his lap. He looks up into the sky.*

A light turns on in the house, making the window bright with warm, yellow light. The light moves through the house and to the door, revealing ABIGAIL BAKER, *carrying a lamp.*

ABIGAIL. Mr. Stevenson? Arthur Stevenson?

ARTHUR. *(Standing)* Yes.

ABIGAIL. I'm Abigail Baker. The one who wrote back to you about the place. You're later than expected. Long drive, Mr. Stevenson?

ARTHUR. Very long. Long train ride, long drive.

ABIGAIL. Is that all the luggage you have?

ARTHUR. Yes. All of it.

ABIGAIL. Well, this is your place now. You could've brought a lot more, sir.

ARTHUR. I don't need any more.

ABIGAIL. Well, it's a good thing that the previous owners left it mostly furnished then. They left all the way to Perth, so they didn't want to haul the heavy things. Let me take your luggage for you. *(ABIGAIL takes the bag.)* Do you want to come in?

ARTHUR. Give me a moment.

> ABIGAIL *nods and goes back into the house for a moment.* ARTHUR *walks off the porch and into the front yard. He looks into the sky, disturbed and enchanted simultaneously.* ABIGAIL *re-enters.*

ABIGAIL. Sir, would you like . . .

ARTHUR. The sky is different.

ABIGAIL. Pardon?

ARTHUR. I had forgotten how different the constellations are.

ABIGAIL. Under the Southern Cross we stand.

ARTHUR. The things one forgets.

ABIGAIL. You've been here before, Mr. Stevenson? I thought you were a Pom—uhm, I thought you were from England.

ARTHUR. Not originally. I lived down in Melbourne until I was twelve years old. Then my father rose up in the shipping company he worked for, so we moved overseas. Don't think too poorly of me for losing my accent. In England it's best to—not stand out too much. Getting a foothold in that system was difficult enough without the handicap of dialect.

ABIGAIL. What has brought you back to Australia? (*There is a pause. ABIGAIL looks over at ARTHUR and finds that his face has gone blank.*) Excuse me, I didn't mean to pry.

A kookaburra bird rattles off in the distance, its chattering more like a monkey than a bird.

ARTHUR. I had also forgotten how loud those kookaburras are!

ABIGAIL. It's the cockies that get to me. Makes me think of some sort of ancient pterodactyl every time, shrieking before it swoops down to eat me!

ARTHUR. Have any galahs in the area?

ABIGAIL. Some.

ARTHUR. Stupidest bird to fly the earth.

ABIGAIL. (*With a short laugh*) Yeah. Pretty or not, not the brightest beasts. Me, I prefer creatures that are a little more sturdy.

ARTHUR. (*Beat.*) I'm tired.

ABIGAIL. Yes, sir. Your room is in the back.

ARTHUR is about to exit, out of sorts, but then stops and sighs, frustrated with himself.

ARTHUR. I'm sorry. (*Pause.*) Do you live nearby?

ABIGAIL. A couple of miles that way.

ARTHUR. A couple of miles—I'll drive you.

ABIGAIL. You're exhausted, sir. I'm not sure if it would be safe for you.

ARTHUR. You can't walk at this time of night.

ABIGAIL. I've done it a hundred times. I'm more than capable.

ARTHUR. We'll set a room up here for you tonight. Of course, that is if you haven't anyone waiting for you.

ABIGAIL. Really, sir . . .

ARTHUR. Please, humor me. I was late; let me make it up to you.

ABIGAIL. Would that be—wise?

ARTHUR. Which room is the most comfortable?

ABIGAIL. Well, yours, of course.

ARTHUR. Then that's where you'll sleep.

ABIGAIL. No, I couldn't. This is your house.

ARTHUR. I'll be fine. You have to understand, I don't deserve to get comfortable.

ABIGAIL. Sir?

ARTHUR. Pardon me. *(Beat.)* You'll take my room.

ABIGAIL. Really, Mr. Stevenson, I couldn't . . .

ARTHUR. I don't need anything fancy.

ABIGAIL. Well, nothing in the house is what you'd call fancy.

ARTHUR. Good. Then you'll have my room tonight and I'll take the guest room.

ABIGAIL. No, sir. There must be some boundaries. Staying at your place for the night is—questionable enough.

ARTHUR. Not the sort to do as you're told, I suppose. Even when it's out of kindness.

ABIGAIL. I haven't had the luxury of protection in my life, and I'm not about to be softened by it now. Women in England may need to be protected from the sun, but here it beats down on us every day of our lives.

ARTHUR. Please, stay in the guest room, at least.

ABIGAIL. Well, I suppose that's all right. I'll only be here until tomorrow.

ARTHUR. Do you have new work yet?

ABIGAIL. Not yet, but I have some promising leads in town.

ARTHUR. What did you do for the last owners?

ABIGAIL. Kept house, cooked . . .

ARTHUR. Then that's what you'll do for me. I'm a terrible cook.

ABIGAIL. Well, sir, the ones who were here before, they were a family. You're a . . . a . . .

ARTHUR. Single man? Yes, that's an idea I still have to get used to.

ABIGAIL. Sir?

ARTHUR. So you don't want to work for me? Too uncomfortable working for a single man?

ABIGAIL. I didn't say that. Work is work.

ARTHUR. Good to hear. I'll double your wages.

ABIGAIL. Double!

ARTHUR. I want someone who can help me become acquainted to the place.

ABIGAIL. Mr. Stevenson, I don't mean to whinge, but . . .

ARTHUR. Then don't whinge. Please, accept my offer.

ABIGAIL. I don't want to cheat you.

ARTHUR. You're not. But it comes with conditions.

ABIGAIL. Conditions?

ARTHUR. You may not find me to be easy company.

ABIGAIL. *(Half-jokingly)* Should I be worried?

ARTHUR. If I'm silent, let me be silent. Don't try to urge conversation. I have my moods. You must allow me to endure them on my own, Miss Abigail.

ABIGAIL. A small price for double the wages. And call me Miss Abbie. I prefer something less formal in my title. *(Beat.)* I must say, I will be glad not to leave this place.

ARTHUR. Attached, are you?

ABIGAIL. You'll understand soon, sir.

ARTHUR. I suppose I will. Miss Abbie?

ABIGAIL. Yes?

ARTHUR. I know I just went on about leaving me in moods . . .

ABIGAIL. *(With a smile, perhaps even a smirk)* Is the inconsistency already starting to show?

ARTHUR. *(Smiles back)* Perhaps—for the times that I do want to talk, if I need some company, would you oblige me?

ABIGAIL. Just talking?

ARTHUR. Just talking. I don't expect many visitors, so I'll need your conversation sometimes—but nothing flittering or petty or inconsequential.

ABIGAIL. You get agitated?

ARTHUR. There's always a little of that under the surface, I'm afraid. *(Beat.)* Do you read?

ABIGAIL. I read what I can, but books are a luxury which not all of us are afforded, especially when there's work to be done. *(Beat.)* Read the newspaper in town sometimes, to see what's happening. I'm also fond of Banjo Patterson's poetry . . .

ARTHUR. Do you feel?

ABIGAIL. Feel, sir?

ARTHUR. Strong feelings. Emotion.

ABIGAIL. If you're expecting some sort of philosopher, I think I would disappoint you.

ARTHUR. *(Pause; unconvinced.)* The Southern Cross. What do you see? How does it make you feel?

ABIGAIL *looks up in the sky at the constellation thoughtfully.*

ABIGAIL. *(Unsure.)* I see the Mercy Seat. It's like the cross of Christ and it makes me feel so—so—no, pardon me, that's not it, not tonight. *(Pause; then more sure.)* I see a tree, like this Eucalyptus tree. I climb that tree, as free as a little girl, and I find myself in a current of sky light and galaxy. I reach out and I touch it and dip my hand into that river above me, just as if it were the Murray River, and I close my eyes as I feel it cool and calm like running water.

> ABIGAIL *looks up at* ARTHUR, *suddenly self conscious.* ARTHUR *approaches* ABIGAIL *and smiles.*

ARTHUR. You can start work in the morning. *(Beat.)* But, as I said, I'm tired.

> ARTHUR *is about to exit inside, but* ABIGAIL *stops him with:*

ABIGAIL. What brought you here to Albury, Mr. Stevenson? Business?

ARTHUR. My business is all sold off.

ABIGAIL. Early retirement?

ARTHUR. Something like that.

ABIGAIL. Why not go to Melbourne, where you were from then?

ARTHUR. I saw the ad, Miss Abbie. I made a decision. That's all.

ABIGAIL. All right. But what do you plan on doing?

ARTHUR. Pardon?

ABIGAIL. You'll have a lot of free time on your hands.

ARTHUR. I—I'm so tired, Miss Abbie.

ABIGAIL. Of course, Mr. Stevenson. It's been a long journey.

ARTHUR. Good night.

ABIGAIL. Good night.

> ARTHUR *exits into the house.* ABIGAIL *looks after him, surprised. She then sits in the rocking chair, wrapping her arms around herself. Suddenly* ARTHUR *comes back out.*

ARTHUR. There's no library. No place for books.

ABIGAIL. Well, no. The Penrods were not big readers.

ARTHUR. Then that's what I will do. I'll put some shelves in my room.

ABIGAIL. There are tools in the shed. We can go into town tomorrow to buy some materials which you think are suitable.

ARTHUR. I think you're right. It will be important to keep myself occupied.

Exit ARTHUR, *back into the house.* ABIGAIL *looks up at the stars above her and, suddenly grateful to the universe, she sits back and simply enjoys the evening sky.*

SCENE 2

The lights fade on the house and rise on the riverbed. PINDARI *an Australian Aboriginal man who is in his early to mid thirties sits by the river, in deep thought, staring out at the river. Enter a man and a woman,* ZEEK *and* JODY, *both part of Australia's famous swagmen: poor, transient workers, who travel by foot from farm to farm looking for temporary work. They both have the traditional swagman gear: a swag (a canvas bedroll), a tucker bag (bag for carrying food) and some cooking gear such as a Billy can (tea pot or stewing pot), which they carry on their back. They look over at* PINDARI, *consult each other, and then approach him.*

JODY. This fella's got the right idea. Can we sit with you, mate? *(PINDARI looks up and simply nods.* JODY *and* ZEEK *start unpacking a bit, setting up their cooking gear for dinner.)* Thanks heaps, fella. I'm Jody, this is Zeek.

ZEEK. Short for Ezekiel.

JODY. And he is a regular prophet, this bloke. Can tell you when it's going to rain two days in advance!

ZEEK. S'truth! I can also tell fortunes. You want your future told, fella? I can map out your life from this moment to the very day you die! I charge a small fee, but I figure you abbos know the value of a gift like that! *(PINDARI keeps looking out.)* Well, yeah, it's quite the gift.

JODY. So what's your name, fella?

PINDARI. My name is Pindari.

JODY. That mean something special? *(PINDARI looks at them skeptically.)* Don't be so serious, mate! We're not here to hurt you.

PINDARI. It means "from the high ground."

JODY. Grouse. *(Awkward pause, as PINDARI continues to look out, not even having as much as looked at them fully.)* Are we close to Albury and Wodonga yet?

PINDARI. Just a few miles. Albury is on this side of the river. Wodonga's on that side.

JODY. Much in the way of jumbuck?

PINDARI. Heaps of farms—a lot of work during shearing season.

JODY. Say, Pin . . . Pin . . .

PINDARI. Pindari.

JODY. Can I call you Pindo? It'll be much easier on me. *(PINDARI doesn't reply.)* Well, say, Pindo, me and my mate, well, we figure that sticking together has done us some good. We show the mob that not only do we have a ready worker to shear their sheep or work their property, but, hey, we've got a full work force to offer them! You know what I mean? *(PINDARI doesn't reply.)* Yeah, well, we also watch each other's backs and we figure that we swagmen can have it kind of tough . . .

PINDARI. I'm not a swag man.

JODY. Not saying you have to be, mate! But it's a nice life—romantic, you know. Sleeping under the stars, going from place to place, never tied down, always an adventure; see what I mean, Pindo? *(PINDARI doesn't reply.)* But it can get kind of tough when you're alone. Swagman or not, it's nice to have mates who'll stick up for you if you get in a blue or, I don't know . . . Say, if you were to get on the wrong side of the law or some rot like that. Having mates who've got your back. See the upside of that? *(PINDARI doesn't answer.)* Of course you do! So what do you say, mate? We could use a third on our walkabout.

PINDARI. What you do is not a walkabout.

JODY. Oh, one might not think so, I see that, fella! You know your walkabouts and whatnot more than we do, sure. But that doesn't mean there isn't—overlap. Able to tap into that same spirit, eh?

ZEEK. Leave it be, Jody. We don't need a third . . .

PINDARI finally stands and faces ZEEK.

PINDARI. There's something about you . . .

ZEEK. You know nothing about me, fella.

Enter ARTHUR.

ARTHUR. Pardon me, but I think I may be lost. Could you direct me to . . . ?

PINDARI. Arthur?

ARTHUR. Pardon? Do I know you?

JODY. G'day, mate! I'm Jody, this is Zeek.

ZEEK. Short for Ezekiel.

JODY. And he is a regular prophet, this bloke. Can tell you when it's going to rain two days in advance!

ZEEK. S'truth! I can also tell fortunes. You want your future told? I can map out your life from this moment to the very day you die! I charge a small fee, but I figure a man of your breeding knows the . . .

ZEEK freezes mid-sentence. Both he and JODY have frozen. ARTHUR is startled.

ARTHUR. Are you all right? Sir, are you . . . *(Noting JODY as well.)* Miss, is everything . . .

PINDARI. Arthur, don't you recognize it?

ARTHUR. How do you know my name? What is going on here? We need to get a doctor, this is very irregular. No, truly, we need to get a . . .

Lights shut off on JODY and ZEEK, making them disappear. The lighting and atmosphere change to DREAMTIME, while a didgeridoo (and perhaps other music) plays underneath.

PINDARI. Still don't recognize me, Arthur?

ARTHUR. How do you know my name?

PINDARI. Don't tell me that you've forgotten me. We both lived in Melbourne when we were children when I moved to be there with my—adopted parents. When your parents were not looking, which was heaps, we would meet by the ocean, play in the sand, jump into the surf . . .

ARTHUR. Pindari? Pindari! *(ARTHUR embraces PINDARI.)* For heaven's sake, my friend, what are you doing here?

PINDARI. Do you know where "here" is?

ARTHUR looks around and then a realization hits him.

ARTHUR. Dreamtime. But that was—that was just our game.

PINDARI. What was a game to you is a real place to my people—if I can still call them that.

ARTHUR. Am I dreaming?

PINDARI. I haven't been here since my time here with you.

ARTHUR. Pindari, I don't know what you're talking about.

PINDARI. The Dreamtime is more real than the thing we call reality. I have been searching for it again for many years.

ARTHUR. You've lost your old aboriginal accent.

PINDARI. Just as you lost yours.

ARTHUR. I suppose we both had to—acclimate.

PINDARI. I was taken away from my parents. Given to whites to be raised. But I'm trying to—re-connect. I am finally taking my Walkabout, following my own story. And here you are, the one who went to the Dreamtime with me. Perhaps we need each other once again.

ARTHUR. A strong coincidence, certainly, but I think we can't assume . . .

PINDARI. The Murray River has a strong song line. The veil between our world and the Dreaming here is very thin. It is a very special place.

ARTHUR. Pindari, what is going on here? That was just our—imagination. It was vivid, granted. I have since wondered if there was something wrong with us. For a long time as a child I tried to convince anybody who would listen that it was . . .

PINDARI. . . . real. We tapped into something, Arthur. And I lost it. Damn it, growing up in your world, your culture—I lost it! But here it is again.

ARTHUR. This is insane—some sort of shared delusion.

PINDARI. During the Dreaming—there was a great earthquake. *(The sound of an EARTHQUAKE. ARTHUR feels its effects and stumbles to his hands and knees.)* From this earthquake came a little stream, and from that little stream came another tremor, another great earthquake! *(The sound of an EARTHQUAKE again.)* And from this earthquake a great fish emerged from the stream. *(A DREAM SPIRIT appears. The DREAM SPIRITS take many forms throughout the play, but at this point she is a beautiful, elegant fish. The DREAM SPIRIT dances beautifully, telling the story through movement that PINDARI is telling with words.)* This beautiful fish was too large for the narrow stream it had found itself in, so it dug in it head and thrust its tail about until it plowed itself in the earth, the water flowing all around it, expanding, reaching, creating a whole new space for itself! The water flowed around it and the Great Fish rejoiced. It swam all the way down to a Great Lake and created a sacred path, its songline. *(At this point another DREAM SPIRIT takes on the role of "Nepelle.")* But Nepelle there, the great ruler of the Heavens, stopped the fish. He clutched that great fish and, with a hand terrible and kind, cut up the First Fish into thousands of pieces, each piece there taking life of its own. And then Nepelle threw those fish back into the river, to live their own lives, whether to swim in the great river, or to be captured upon the spear of a man. *(The DREAM SPIRITS exit.)* Do you believe this story, Arthur?

ARTHUR. Pindari, you and I loved your people's stories—but since when did you take them literally? We used to laugh about it all.

PINDARI. No. You used to laugh.

ARTHUR. Pindari, really, the mystic act is a little debasing . . .

PINDARI. Don't you even see what is around you, you stupid man?

ARTHUR. Wait, no need to . . .

PINDARI. I've spent my life learning to speak your language, to learn your customs; I even wear your clothes. My adopted parents were well meaning, but my parents—my real parents—they were traditional. Taught me the stories and the songlines and the rituals. And I remember every word. But now I have two worlds competing in me. I understand your people in a way your people never understood us, never considered us! My people have done this, but your people are never willing to meet us half way! You came to our country and now it is time that you understood our ways!

ARTHUR. I—I am sorry, my friend.

PINDARI. Tell me you see it, truly see it. I know you do.

ARTHUR. I—I see it. How do you do this, Pindari? You've always been able to do this to me—some sort of hypnosis?

PINDARI. Why are we both here?

ARTHUR. Apparently, you're the prophet, not me.

PINDARI. I'm baffled as well.

ARTHUR. Real or not, we're not children anymore, Pindari. These visions have very little use to what we have to deal with now.

Something moves in the river. It is the BUNYIP.

PINDARI. Be careful, brother. The Bunyip stalks the river.

Suddenly, Dreamtime fades, and JODY *and* ZEEK *are back into their original positions before the Dreamtime.*

ZEEK. . . . value of a gift like that!

ARTHUR *is bewildered and disoriented.*

JODY. You don't look so good . . .

ZEEK. You all right, mate?

PINDARI. The two said they are looking for work, Arthur.

JODY. Er, yes! Have any jumbuck? We're experts with the shears.

ARTHUR. I'm sorry, but I don't have any sheep. My housekeeper and I do all that we need around my place.

PINDARI. *(Suddenly:)* You have any stumps?

ZEEK. Stumps?

ARTHUR *looks at* PINDARI *curiously.* PINDARI *only smiles.*

ARTHUR. Well, yes, I do. How did you . . . ?

PINDARI. I—don't know. The thought occurred to me.

ARTHUR. The previous owners cut down some of the eucalyptus trees, but never cleared out the stumps. That would be useful if someone could help us with them. It's heavy work.

JODY. Look no further, mate! Zeek and I could do that for you, right as rain.

ARTHUR. But I only have one extra bedroom.

ZEEK. She'll be right, mate. Jody can have the bed. I've got my trusty swag. I'll be good sleeping outside.

ARTHUR. And what about you, Pindari?

ZEEK. How did you know his name?

ARTHUR. Pindari and I are old friends. Pindari?

PINDARI. I can sleep outside, too. I prefer it lately.

ARTHUR. Well, if we hurry to Miss Abbie in time, I may be able to get you all some dinner.

JODY. Beauty!

ARTHUR and PINDARI exit together, but ZEEK stops JODY and holds back for just a bit.

ZEEK. That was really odd, Jody.

JODY. Look, Zeek, food is food, money is money, work is work. It would be better when you can get the food and money without the work, but we take what we can get, right?

ZEEK. I don't trust the abo. I smell a con.

JODY. We can't miss opportunities like this, mate. Maybe we'll get lucky and score something big.

ZEEK. I've got a feeling . . .

JODY. I've got a feeling, too—this could mean big bikkies for us! Don't spoil it.

ZEEK still hesitates. Re-enter ARTHUR.

ARTHUR. You two coming?

ZEEK. *(Pause.)*Yeah. We're coming, mate.

Exit ARTHUR, JODY, and ZEEK.

SCENE 3

ABIGAIL is outside, chopping wood. Nightfall is fast coming. We see the headlights and hear the car doors slam. Enter ARTHUR, PINDARI, JODY, and ZEEK.

ABIGAIL. Why, Mr. Stevenson, you've got a whole mob with you!

ARTHUR. Miss Abbie, you don't need to do the heavy kind of work, really . . .

ABIGAIL. It needed to be done. The wood pile was low.

ARTHUR. I can do it in the future.

ABIGAIL. So can I.

ARTHUR. Truly, I . . .

ABIGAIL. Over the past month, I hope I've shown you how capable I am, sir. I have strong arms, strong legs, a strong back. If I see something that needs to be done, I will do it.

ARTHUR. We will talk about this later.

ABIGAIL. We have already talked about it. I do what needs to be done.

JODY. Except the stumps. We'll take care of those.

ABIGAIL. You object to me chopping wood, but hire another woman to dig out the stumps?

ZEEK. I can vouch for Jody. Much stronger than she looks. She's no common woman.

ABIGAIL. Most of us around here aren't.

ARTHUR. Er, yes—pardon me, I've been very rude, I believe I haven't even made introductions! This is my trusted housekeeper Miss Abbie. As you can seem she's pretty much run the place since I arrived here.

JODY. I respect another woman who's not afraid to sweat in the sun.

ARTHUR. Miss Abbie, this is Jody, Zeek, and Pindari. Zeek and Jody want to do some work for us, so I'm going to set them up here for a few days while they take out those two stumps in the back.

ABIGAIL. And Mr. Pindari?

ARTHUR. He's an old friend of mine. It was quite the coincidence to meet him out here, that's the truth!

PINDARI. It's feeling less and less like a . . .

ARTHUR. Let's not get superstitious.

PINDARI. You white people believe in a man who walked on water and was raised from the dead. You have no place in calling other people superstitious.

ARTHUR. Well, I've rejected all of that, too. The last time you saw me, I was on a boat to England! There is no way any of us could have known . . .

PINDARI. Exactly.

PINDARI looks at ARTHUR very seriously, but then lets out a loud, boisterous laugh, which causes ARTHUR to laugh as well. There is something familiar, easy to this interaction.

ARTHUR. You always knew how to turn around a mood.

PINDARI. But now—now something different is here.

ARTHUR. Different?

PINDARI. I see—sorrow in your heart. It must have called to me, sang to me, sang to me and connected to my own sorrow. Our stories are now intertwined. *(Beat.)* It's time.

ARTHUR. Time? Time for what?

PINDARI. Time? Time for food! I'm hungry!

PINDARI laughs again. Without asking for permission, PINDARI exits into the house.

ABIGAIL. You—you two seem very close, Mr. Stevenson.

ARTHUR. As close as I have been to anyone. It's as if no time passed at all.

ABIGAIL. As if it all had smoothed away . . . *(ARTHUR gives ABIGAIL a sharp look.)* I'm sorry, Mr. Stevenson. None of my business, of course.

JODY. So you weren't expecting him, mate?

ARTHUR. No.

ABIGAIL. There's only the one extra room, sir.

ARTHUR. Put Jody in the back room. Zeek and Pindari have volunteered to sleep outside.

ABIGAIL. Yes, Mr. Stevenson. I'll check the room.

Exit ABIGAIL.

ZEEK. Well, sir, that bung is hard to wrap your head around, isn't he?

ARTHUR. Call him that again, Zeek, and you'll have to find work elsewhere. He has a name.

ZEEK. Yeah, Pindari. I caught that. Sorry, I know he's your mate.

ARTHUR. He and I went through a lot together. When my Mum died, well, he was all I had. He had been adopted by a local family—if adopted is the right word for it.

JODY. What about your Dad?

ARTHUR. My father and I were never close.

JODY. What did he think about you coming back Down Under?

ARTHUR. He's been dead for over ten years now.

JODY. Sorry to hear that, mate. What exactly did your father do?

ZEEK. Don't be a sticky beak, Jody.

JODY. Hey, I'm just being friendly.

ARTHUR. Your friend is right. That's enough questions. *(Tense pause.)* You can unload your things inside.

> *JODY and ZEEK glance at each other and then exit inside. ABIGAIL re-enters.*

ABIGAIL. The room's ready, sir.

ARTHUR. Thank you, Miss Abbie.

ABIGAIL. The shelves look good, by the way. You're quite the carpenter.

ARTHUR. Thank you.

ABIGAIL. As soon as the books you had shipped from England arrive, I'll make sure they're put up. What's your next project?

ARTHUR. I'm thinking of doing something out back once the stumps are gone. Perhaps even some sort of landscaping or irrigation or . . .

ABIGAIL. But you're not going to take down any more of the trees, are you?

ARTHUR. No, no, I like the trees.

ABIGAIL. Good.

ARTHUR. But it appears that Penrods had something else in mind.

ARTHUR goes to the eucalyptus tree.

ABIGAIL. Pardon?

ARTHUR. The marks—they tried to cut this one down. Like the ones in the back.

ABIGAIL. Yes, but they had a hard time doing it. It was like the tree was deflecting their axes.

ARTHUR. Truly?

ABIGAIL. When they took down the other trees in the back, I had nightmares about it for weeks. I was grateful this one put up a fight.

ARTHUR. What were their plans out in the back?

ABIGAIL. The Penrods wanted to build some sort of gazebo, make the place "prettier." I didn't see what could make the place more pretty than those trees, and they never did build that gazebo. Just left those desolate stumps. Sometimes this place may seem a little shabby, Mr. Stevenson, I know that but, well, there's something magical in the land.

ARTHUR. Oh, you believe in magic, do you?

ABIGAIL. I've felt it for a long time.

ARTHUR. Er, I was joking.

ABIGAIL. Magic may be too romantic of a word, but—well, I'm not the only one who's—well, never mind.

ARTHUR. No, I want to know.

ABIGAIL. You'll think it's superstitious.

ARTHUR. Maybe. Maybe not.

ABIGAIL *stops and considers and then goes on.*

ABIGAIL. Mrs. Penrod had a dream.

ARTHUR. A dream?

ABIGAIL. She dreamed that this tree was—speaking to her.

ARTHUR. So what did this tree, er, say?

ABIGAIL. It told them to move out.

ARTHUR. The Penrods moved because the tree told them to?

ABIGAIL. Yeah.

ARTHUR. So is the tree going to turn me out someday, too?

ABIGAIL. No.

ARTHUR. And how do you know that?

ABIGAIL. Because it was waiting for you.

ARTHUR. Pardon?

ABIGAIL. Because that's what it told the Penrods. That this place was being reserved for the next inhabitants.

ARTHUR. That's quite the story.

ABIGAIL. Well, Mr. Stevenson, if a tree was paving the way for anyone, I'm certainly glad it was you. I mean—well, what I mean is that you've been very good to me.

ARTHUR. Despite not letting you at the stumps?

ABIGAIL. I—I suppose I wouldn't have wanted to be a part of that anyway. Again, the trees were special to me.

ARTHUR. What a conundrum you are, Miss Abbie. At times it's like your skin is bark, but get past that and reach the sensitivity inside . . .

ABIGAIL. I wouldn't call myself sensitive, sir.

ARTHUR. Why not? Is there something wrong with being sensitive?

ABIGAIL. Yes! Yes, when it's used as an excuse to shelter me, to stop me from doing what I'm capable of!

This stuns ARTHUR. *He becomes introspective and distant.*

ARTHUR. Good night, Miss Abbie.

ARTHUR *is about to go to the door inside.*

ABIGAIL. Mr. Stevenson!

ARTHUR *stops.*

ARTHUR. I've appreciated the work that you've done. I've never doubted your capacity.

ABIGAIL. I—I appreciate that.

ARTHUR. And you may be right—perhaps it's better if we shield ourselves from weakness more often.

ABIGAIL. I . . .

ARTHUR. Good night.

ABIGAIL. Wait. I—well, look, the stars are finally coming out. That foreign sky of yours.

ARTHUR. It's not so foreign anymore. Why, I'm having familiar faces crowd in all around up there. Pindari showing up, and—and you and I are getting along swimmingly, of course.

ABIGAIL. Yes. Swimmingly.

ARTHUR. But sometimes being out here so alone, with so much space around us, not having people crowd in like they were in Liverpool— it creates a sense of expanse, doesn't it? It's easy to feel a little—lost. It's easy to miss—old familiarities.

ABIGAIL. But isn't it liberating? It may feel like disconnection, but we can stand strong and independent, ready for anything.

ARTHUR. Such a false phrase that is—"ready for anything." There are events in our lives, that there is no preparation for.

ABIGAIL. Perhaps—but perhaps that Southern Cross up there will eventually soothe all that hurt of yours away.

A tense pause.

ARTHUR. You keep trying to get a foothold, Miss Abbie. Please . . .

ABIGAIL. Excuse me, Mr. Stevenson.

ARTHUR. As you said, we need to protect ourselves from weakness.

ABIGAIL. I never used the word "weakness."

ARTHUR. Didn't you? Well, it's time for dinner.

ABIGAIL. Of course. What would you like me to make, Mr. Stevenson?

ARTHUR. Oh, how about I treat you to a meal, Miss Abbie? Have a seat inside—I can compose you a Shepherd's Pie that will awe and delight you.

ABIGAIL. I thought you said you were a terrible cook.

ARTHUR. Did I say that?

ABIGAIL. You certainly did.

ARTHUR. I always forget how good your memory is. *(Pause.)* Well, Shepherd's Pie is simple enough for even my base talent.

ABIGAIL. If you say so.

They both exit into the house.

SCENE 4

It is the early morning, just before sunrise, as ARTHUR *enters from the house onto the porch, having just awoken recently. Yet, instead of looking refreshed by the cool, morning air, he looks concerned and stressed. He leans against the railing, absorbed in his thoughts, when he hears* ZEEK *rustle in his sleeping gear on the ground. He then looks over at* PINDARI, *who is sleeping peacefully far away from* ZEEK.

ARTHUR *walks off of the porch and approaches one of the eucalyptus stumps in the front yard. It is exceptionally large.*

He squats down, analyzing it. His hand brushes over the surface of the stump, as he stares hard at it.

ARTHUR *then exits into the house, and the re-enters with a pick ax, shovel, etc.*

ARTHUR *approaches the stump again and uses a pick ax to start attacking it. The sound wakes* ZEEK *and* PINDARI. *They approach* ARTHUR. *They both notice the emotional ferocity that* ARTHUR *is going at the stump with.*

JODY *enters from the house, also having just woken up. She also appears concerned at* ARTHUR'S *state.* ZEEK *places his hand on* ARTHUR'S *shoulder.*

ZEEK. Jody and I can take it from here.

JODY. Yeah, it is why you hired us.

ARTHUR *aggressively shrugs off* ZEEK'S *hand and continues working on the stump, wordlessly.* ABIGAIL *enters, just coming to work from the direction opposite of the house.*

ABIGAIL. Pindari, what is . . . ?

PINDARI *shakes his head and just continues to stare at* ARTHUR. ARTHUR *gets the pick ax stuck in the stump. He tries to loosen it, but it won't budge. He yells out and kicks the stump.*

ZEEK. *(Quietly to* ABIGAIL:*)*Does this happen a lot?

ABIGAIL. Reporting in for duty, Mr. Stevenson.

ARTHUR *doesn't even seem to hear* ABIGAIL *as he continues to strain with the pick ax.*

ABGAIL *comes over to* ARTHUR *and places one of her hands on* ARTHUR'S. ARTHUR *looks up angrily, but upon looking in* ABIGAIL'S *concerned eyes, relents.*

ARTHUR *then looks around at* ZEEK, PINDARI, *and* JODY, *at a loss to explain himself.*

ARTHUR. I . . .

JODY steps forward and takes a shovel.

JODY. She'll be right, Mr. Stevenson. We'll take it from here.

JODY starts digging around the stump. ZEEK goes to the pick ax and, with only a little struggle, pries it free. He then throws it to the ground, grabs another shovel, and starts digging with JODY.

ABIGAIL. Arthur . . .

ARTHUR throws up his hands, still frustrated, and then storms into the house. PINDARI approaches ABIGAIL.

PINDARI. Give him some space.

ABIGAIL. Do you know what is going on him with him? Why he's here?

PINDARI. No. Do you?

ABIGAIL. I have a couple of theories, but we're supposed to do what about it, exactly?

PINDARI shrugs and then goes and tries to retrieve another tool to help, but ZEEK stands in front of the tools.

ZEEK. We've got it covered.

There is a tense pause between ZEEK and PINDARI.

PINDARI. I'm not asking to be paid. You don't need to be threatened. I just want to help.

ZEEK. We've got it covered.

ZEEK turns away and goes back to work. PINDARI looks at him hard and then turns back to ABIGAIL.

ABIGAIL. If you want to give a hand, I am about to make breakfast.

PINDARI nods. PINDARI and ABIGAIL then exit into the house, as ZEEK and JODY continue working on the stump. Lights fade.

SCENE 5

Lights rise on the Murray River portion of the stage where we find ARTHUR. *He looks into the river, darkly. There is movement in the water—the* BUNYIP. *But before it can fully reveal itself,* ABIGAIL *enters in a huff, with a basket of food.*

ABIGAIL. Mr. Stevenson!

ARTHUR. Goodness, Miss Abbie! I was trying to get away from people!

ABIGAIL. A big part of what you pay me for is to cook for you. You pay me well, so I aim to fulfill my job description!

ABIGAIL sits and starts spreading out the food.

ARTHUR. How did you find me?

ABIGAIL. Pindari told me that you often come here to get away.

ARTHUR. Yes, as I said—to get away!

ABIGAIL. I must say, I don't appreciate you going off without a word to anybody about where you're going or when you'll be back! You may think you are the center of the universe . . .

ARTHUR. I do not think that I am the center of the universe . . .

ABIGAIL. Could have fooled me with all of your damn moping and your ridiculous demonstrations of manly angst!

ARTHUR. I—I am sorry about that. But I did warn you about my moods. You said that you would let me endure them!

ABIGAIL. Yes, but not without your lunch!

ABIGAIL slams the plate of food in front of ARTHUR.

ARTHUR. Miss Abbie, if I have . . .

ABIGAIL. I am here, too, you know. I deserve to be considered.

ARTHUR. *(Beat.)* Of course you do. *(ARTHUR begins to eat his food.)* Mm. Good chicken.

ABIGAIL. There. My duty is done. Now I'll be off.

ARTHUR. Let me drive you back.

ABIGAIL. No, thank you.

ARTHUR. Truly, Miss Abbie, don't be angry.

ABIGAIL. You're the only one who gets to be angry then?

ARTHUR. It's not as becoming on a woman . . .

ABIGAIL. It becomes me as well as you!

ARTHUR. Yes, yes. I truly am sorry. How can I make it up to you?

ABIGAIL. Start seeing others. Start seeing me. Instead of treating me like . . . like . . .

ARTHUR. Like what?

ABIGAIL. A stranger.

ARTHUR. You want something more than what we have?

ABIGAIL. I—I didn't mean it like that.

ARTHUR. Tell me then.

ABIGAIL. Tell you what?

ARTHUR. You want me to see you. Then let me see you. What is it that you want?

ABIGAIL. That's not quite what I was . . .

ARTHUR. What, shy now? After the flurry and bluster, you just want to withdraw? Sounds familiar . . .

ABIGAIL. Why are you doing this?

ARTHUR. I am doing my best here, Miss Abbie! And my best will never be enough!

ABIGAIL. What?

ARTHUR. Never mind. (ARTHUR goes back to his chicken and eats.) It really is very good.

ABIGAIL. Ta. (Beat.) I'll be going now.

ARTHUR. Wait. Just one more moment. *(Beat.)* I saw you. I've seen you ever since the day I came here. I couldn't help not seeing you. When you walked out of the house after I drove up, basked in the light of that kerosene lamp—it's as if I've seen you in my mind's eye ever since.

Pause.

ABIGAIL. I'm not sure I understand.

ARTHUR doesn't look at ABIGAIL as he says this:

ARTHUR. You shine, Miss Abbie. People have tried to smother you with black blankets, but your independent spirit just burns right through them. You won't be suppressed by the likes of me. And I admire you all the more for it.

ARTHUR still doesn't look back. ABIGAIL looks at him, not without some stirring in her soul. But she resists:

ABIGAIL. I will see you at the house, Mr.Stevenson.

Exit ABIGAIL. ARTHUR looks back into the river blankly. Lights dim on ARTHUR. Lights rise back up on JODY and ZEEK, looking weary from their work. There is a pail of water with cups and a ladle which they drink from. ZEEK pours some of the water on the top of his head.

ZEEK. Those are damned stubborn stumps.

JODY. From the sounds of it, though, he'll be paying us something fine for it. Didn't you think it sounded high, though?

ZEEK. I'm not complaining.

JODY. Neither am I. But makes you think the bludger has some money to spread around, doesn't it? You think he has it tucked away in some bank, or that he's got some here?

ZEEK. Now, let's not spoil things, Jody. I thought we were beyond that sort of thing now.

JODY. For a while maybe. But opportunities, Zeek, we've got to pay attention to our opportunities.

ZEEK. Let's not draw attention to ourselves.

JODY. They've got nothing on me.

ZEEK. I thought you and I were watching out for each other. Proper mates. Wasn't that the deal?

JODY. Of course we are. But I can't let your past dealings bugger my future, now can I?

ZEEK. Jody . . .

JODY. Nor would I be much of a mate, if I let you bugger your own future either.

ZEEK. This is our future. It's not a bad future, isn't that we always tell people? Make our own way, walk our own paths, leaving a place when we want to leave it, staying when we want to stay.

JODY. Our little excuses for the way we live are rot and you know it, Zeek. I hate not having a brass razoo to my name. I'm tired of it . . .

ZEEK. Well, I suppose it's a rough life for a woman . . .

In a sudden flash of anger, JODY takes out a rather wicked looking bowie knife, and brandishes it towards ZEEK.

JODY. I've been digging that stump right there with you, haven't I? I can dig out your liver just as well as I've dug that stump.

ZEEK. I'll be stuffed, Jody!

JODY. I can have you stonkered in three seconds flat.

ZEEK. With a blade like that, too right! Now put that bloody thing away! What the hell are you doing?

JODY. I don't need the blade, if you want to have a blue right here.

ZEEK. Rack off! I'm not going to fight you!

JODY. Why, because I'm a woman? Won't hit a lady?

ZEEK. First of all, you aren't a lady. Second, you and I both know that I'm not worth a zack in a fair fight. I'm not challenging your manhood or your womanhood—I'm not challenging your anything, Jody! I promise. Now shove the knife away.

JODY. All right.

JODY puts away the knife.

ZEEK. I'd swear that you were off your face, if I didn't know that neither of us has been able to afford some real grog for weeks!

JODY. Look, I'm sorry, mate. Don't know what riled me up so much.

ZEEK. Now what would have happened, if one of those bludgers came out at that moment, with that wicked piece of steel in your hand? Huh? They would have had the troopers come down right on top of us! This is what I mean when I don't want any unnecessary attention on us!

Enter ABIGAIL, from the direction of the river. She still has the picnic basket

ABIGAIL. Everything all right?

JODY. Yeah, sorry, Miss Abbie, we were working out an argument from a long time ago. We've got it sorted now.

ABIGAIL. All right. Well, I've got some extra chook from lunch, if you're interested.

ZEEK. Thank you, Miss Abbie!

Both ZEEK and JODY start going hungrily at the chicken.

ABIGAIL. Well, you two have been working hard. I have to admit, I thought you were a couple of sundowners who would be gone the next morning. But here you still are, working away at those stumps. It looks like they're pretty deep, though. They're going to take you a while.

JODY. That's what we're thinking, too.

ABIGAIL. Well, I'll leave you to it then.

JODY. Wait a minute, if you will, Miss Abbie. I'm curious. What is it exactly that Mr. Stevenson does for a living?

ABIGAIL. You'll have to direct those sort of questions to Mr. Stevenson himself.

JODY. Which means that you don't know, do you?

ABIGAIL. I know plenty about what I need to know about, Jody. Those things I don't know about are none of my business—nor yours.

JODY. From what I've been able to gather, he's doing just fine for himself lounging around here. Now this place isn't anything to sneeze at, the kind of place that purposely doesn't draw attention, but everyone's eaten well, he's paying Zeek and I big bikkies for our work, and I assume he's doing the same for you. So, with no cattle or jumbuck to speak of, no job that he carts off to, where's he getting all that money, I wonder?

ABIGAIL. As you said, Miss Jody, Mr. Stevenson is paying all of us handsomely. Now part of that payment comes at a cost on our part. He likes his privacy.

Exit ABIGAIL, into the house.

JODY. As good as a guard dog, she is.

ZEEK. Sometimes you're plain stupid. You're going to get us in trouble.

JODY. You have to trust me on this.

ZEEK looks soberly at JODY and, finishing his chicken, throws the bones back down on the plate.

ZEEK. No, I don't.

JODY. Now, Zeek . . .

ZEEK. And if you ever pull a blade on me again, you'd better be able to follow through with it, because if you cross me—well, just remember why I'm trying to not draw attention.

JODY. Mate, you're taking this all wrong.

ZEEK. We've had a rip snorter time, you and I. I can't say that I have minded having the pleasures of the kind provided by the female variety. You've been real willing that way. But after this job, well, you'll go one way and I'll go another.

JODY. Don't talk like that. I know things have been a bit dodgy today, but . . .

ZEEK. You'll go one way and I'll go another. *(Tense pause.)* Now I'm going to go back to work on the stump.

Exit ZEEK. JODY, frustrated, takes the last piece of chicken is about to start into it when PINDARI enters from the house.

JODY. Pindo!

PINDARI. G'day, Jody.

JODY. Look, Pindo, I don't think we ever properly thanked you for this job. That was real friendly of you to stick your neck out for us like that.

PINDARI. No worries.

JODY. Hey, you want this last piece of chook?

That stops PINDARI, who was on his way. He's tempted.

PINDARI. Chook?

JODY. You've tasted Miss Abbie's cooking. It's pretty damn good.

PINDARI. Ta.

PINDARI sits with JODY and eats the chicken.

JODY. So you and Mr. Stevenson were old mates, huh?

PINDARI. Very good mates. We experienced marvelous things together.

JODY. Like what?

PINDARI. You wouldn't understand.

JODY. Oh, I'm pretty experienced, Pindo. It's hard to present me with something that I wouldn't understand.

PINDARI. I told you. Certain things remain—sacred. Especially from those who just want to gawk and stare and ridicule that which they don't understand.

JODY. You talk really well for an aborigine.

PINDARI. My adopted parents were educated in the ways and language of your people.

JODY. So you're just like a white man!

PINDARI. I hope not. That is why I am here.

JODY. On your walkabout.

PINDARI. Really, I don't want to . . .

JODY. You're re-connecting.

PINDARI. You're—intuitive.

JODY. Inui-what?

PINDARI. Ha!

JODY. What?

PINDARI. Just enjoying the irony.

JODY. Look, I'm not stupid . . .

PINDARI. I never said you were stupid. Intuitive means insightful.

JODY. I went off on this walkabout with this old fella once. At first I thought he was mighty strange, but he let me tag along, and, I'll tell you, mate, he was special. He could do things that I never thought possible. That changed me. Made me believe there might be something out there that means more than all of this clap trap around us.

PINDARI. Women aren't even supposed to go on Walkabouts.

JODY. Are you making fun of me?

PINDARI. Not at all.

JODY. Because I can be as tough as any man, and I . . .

PINDARI. I don't doubt it. Maybe we all have something to learn from each other.

JODY. I—I know Zeek seems stand-offish with you, but I'm not like that. I swear.

PINDARI. *(An analyzing pause.)* When I was brought into my adopted parents home as a teen, my English was very broken.

JODY. It's like that program they started . . .

PINDARI. With me, it happened before the child removal laws. My parents died, so the Christian missionaries found a home for me. Not among my own people, though—and so I am, as you say, re-connecting.

JODY. They let you keep your name. That's somethin'.

PINDARI. They tried to re-name me Jacob. A lot was taken away from me—I would not let them take my name. *(PINDARI studies JODY for a moment, trying to gauge just how much he can trust her.)* My people—many of us are losing our connection to our heritage. You white people came with your grog, with your expectations, with your imposing ways. You take our children from us, try to breed our ways out of us, try to take off our skin and replace it with yours. But whether you take my skin, you cannot take my soul. I have decided that I will not lose my soul.

JODY. Some would say they are saving your soul.

PINDARI. *(Testing her:)* And what do you say, Jody?

JODY. *(Beat; considering.)* I say they don't treat you much better than the jumbuck they shear. And I would tell anybody who treated me like that to stuff it.

PINDARI. You're not like I thought you would be.

JODY. And who did you think I was, Pindo?

PINDARI. Hard. Like a mountain of rock.

JODY. I am strong.

PINDARI. I did not say strong. Strong is good. Strong spits in the face of evil. But hard—it's not be good to be hard.

JODY. You know, Pindo, you're a pretty smart fella. Smarter than me, I think.

PINDARI. No, don't talk like that. We all do what we do. We have different experiences, one is not more valuable than the other, if we recognize it. You survived. Harsh country there. But here—maybe we all can transform here.

JODY. Pindo . . . Pindari . . .

PINDARI. Why are you with Zeek?

JODY. I—I don't always know.

PINDARI. He has a dark spirit.

JODY. Spirit? Oh, no. Zeek, well, he's a bit of a fraud. Pretends to these powers and, between me and you, I think he's got a few kangaroos loose in the top paddock. But you're the real fair dinkum kind of prophet. Zeek, I don't know, I'm not feeling right safe around him, you know? I think I'm going to cut him loose after this job.

PINDARI. You're saying that you want to travel with me, eh?

JODY. Yeah, let's do one of your walkabouts. Find your totem spirits, sing and walk your songlines, find your sacred art, dance your corroborees. We can do all of that.

PINDARI. *(Pause; searching* JODY.*)* It's not a weakness to feel lonely, Jody.

JODY. Who said anything about being lonely? Look, fella, I'm trying to do you a favor here. You could use some one with my kind of experiences . . .

PINDARI. I think your path can still be changed.

JODY. My path? What are you yabbering on about?

PINDARI. The Bunyip stalks the river.

JODY. Now you're talking fairy tales.

PINDARI. I—maybe. I don't know what I was talking about.

JODY. Pindo?

PINDARI. Something strange has been happening to me. I traveled for weeks alone in the outback and the bush. Maybe it finally got to me.

JODY. Look, Pindo, you're kind of scaring me now, so I'm just going back to work. But thanks for the chat and all.

PINDARI. Jody, it would be nice to travel with you. I would like that . . .

JODY. Really?

PINDARI. But even though I would like it, we not going to be traveling together . . .

JODY. Sure, mate, I was just trying to . . .

PINDARI. . . . but I think you're right to leave Zeek on his own there. Sooner rather then later. He's sorry business.

JODY. *(Pause, then sincerely:)* Yeah. I appreciate it, Pindo. You're a good bloke.

Exit JODY. PINDARI sits cross legged beneath the eucalyptus tree, looking up at it, quite still. After a moment ARTHUR enters.

ARTHUR. Don't tell me you think the tree is magic, too.

PINDARI. G'day, Arthur.

ARTHUR. Abigail said the former owners thought the tree came to them in a night vision. How does that figure with your Dreamtime?

PINDARI. All things have a spirit.

ARTHUR. And can all spirits can speak to us?

PINDARI. Not everyone. Or maybe not all of us can hear them. But, as much as you fight the spirit in you, Arthur, it can hear. Miss Abbie, too.

ARTHUR. I've been thinking of our—experience the other day.

PINDARI. I have, too.

ARTHUR. We had vivid imaginations. I was fascinated by your culture.

PINDARI. We were tapping into something far greater than either of our cultures.

ARTHUR. You always did have a great power of suggestion over me. Is that all it was?

PINDARI. Whether it is imagination or reality, that is not all it is.

ARTHUR. I don't think that it's that simple.

PINDARI. Those things which seem simple, are really the most complex, eh? Arthur, there is something I haven't told you. My family was part of the Bundjalung Nation there. We were in Northern Australia when I was born.

ARTHUR. How did you end up in Melbourne when we were children then? Your tribe was on the other side of the continent.

PINDARI. My family had a dream. We followed a series of songlines to travel there.

ARTHUR. Who had the dream? Your father? Your mother?

PINDARI. All of us. We all had the dream on the same night.

ARTHUR. Well, Pindari, that's . . .

PINDARI. We dreamed about my parents' death.

ARTHUR. Death? I thought you were lost.

PINDARI. I never wanted to tell anybody. Thought they might think I did it, since I knew about it. This is the first I have mentioned it since then.

ARTHUR. You all walked there knowing what was going to happen? You walked into such an awful fate?

PINDARI. We are all threads of Kurrajong bark—part of a greater weaving.

ARTHUR. Okay, Pindari, I don't know what your game is, but it's not funny anymore.

PINDARI. It never was a game! You never understood.

ARTHUR. I don't believe in your superstitions.

PINDARI. You used to believe.

ARTHUR. No! There may have been moments where you've tapped into something mysterious, certainly. But—but what you propose Pindari—they're myths! Fairy tales! That is what is wrong with your people. We may have not always treated you as you should have been, I agree with that certainly. But to leave you in such darkness and superstition when the world of science and learning and education is available—that would have been an even greater tragedy!

PINDARI. The arrogance of the so called enlightened!

ARTHUR. You're holding onto dark ages and darker myths!

PINDARI. No, I am talking from experience. I have had the future told to me in the night, and then seen that future come into the present. I have had miracles heal and grow under my hands. I have confronted forces that were nothing less than what we call supernatural—which were only too natural! Oh, your privilege, your wealth, your education has put you on a nice tower, completely disconnected from the spirit of the earth and her children. I almost fell for that trap as well, your people almost drowned me. No longer. I am now putting my hands back into that dirt and throwing the earth over my head. I will say to Her, "Speak to me!"

ARTHUR. I—I see that you're passionate about this, but how can you even entertain . . . ?

PINDARI. The story.

ARTHUR. Pardon me?

PINDARI. The story. Maybe it's literal, as I say. Maybe it's not, as you say. But that doesn't make it any less true.

ARTHUR. You realize how crazy you sound, don't you?

PINDARI. I have never been more full of the right in my whole life. Listen, Arthur, listen of the first times—of the Dreamtime.

ARTHUR. I'm not interested in any more stories. You go on like some medicine man from a story book, or a prophet from a Greek drama! That's not real, Pindari! We are human beings, not these shards of a myth. We are flesh and blood wandering in a world that has never promised us that it would make sense. That's a lie we told ourselves.

PINDARI. No. I will not let you rob me of the spirit my ancestors gave me! I do not care about the world you inhabit. Your people have pulled us too much into that one. But my people gave me a door to another place. And I am giving it to you. This is sacred. Now listen. *(PINDARI pauses and then switches into a storytelling mode, with appropriate gestures and vocal emphasis.)* Before the beginning, the world had no shape, no color. It was flat. Barren. Like a woman without a child.

ARTHUR. Pindari, I know this story, you used to tell me it when we were children.

PINDARI. Listen! *(The lights and mood change to Dreamtime. A didgeridoo plays.)* But after this time of silence and nothingness came the Dreamtime. Great Spirits rose from the earth where they had slept for countless days! Much time passed, a new world came, different but the same. *(The DREAM SPIRITS rise into the scene and dance.)* These giant creatures, with their great movements across the earth, formed the earth into mountains and rivers and shapes! Their paths created what we call songlines, which we follow for holy journeys, travel in the same direction the spirits traveled, singing their songs and dancing their dances at the sacred places. One of these Great Spirits was the Rainbow Serpent there. *(The RAINBOW SPIRIT emerges as the focal DREAM SPIRIT. A great, watery, colorful snake, the RAINBOW SPIRIT dances with reckless abandon and strength, following after the pattern of PINDARI's narration.)* The Rainbow Serpent was a great water spirit. When it lifted its tail, it created the rainbow across the sky. It was bold and beautiful. His water was a necessary part of the struggle of life and creation. But his water was also unpredictable and destructive. Soon it was creating great floods and destruction. Then it did something so wrong, so horrible, that it has remained a secret ever since. After this horrible deed, there was an innocent bird, the Yabbra, who was pursued and beaten by the great Rainbow Serpent.

In the narration, the YABBRA emerges from the DREAM SPIRITS. The RAINBOW SERPENT pursues the YABBRA and then starts to beat the YABBRA mercilessly. For the first time, one of the DREAM SPIRITS *speaks. Surprisingly, its dialect is British cockney:*

YABBRA. Please, Gov'nor! Help me, sir!

ARTHUR. No . . .

YABBRA. 'e is going to kill me! I'm going to die 'ere, if you don't 'elp me! I can see you, you can see me—'e doesn't see you yet, though, sir, you can surprise 'im!

ARTHUR. I can't help you . . .

YABBRA. Please! Please!

ARTHUR. Stop it, Pindari . . .

YABBRA. You can 'elp me . . .

Another DREAM SPIRIT *emerges from the group, a female, and stands beside* ARTHUR *urging him. She talks in an English accent.*

FEMALE DREAM SPIRIT. Help him, Arthur. Arthur, have some pity, you can help him.

ARTHUR. I can't do it . . .

FEMALE DREAM SPIRIT. Help him!

ARTHUR. Stop it, Pindari!

PINDARI. The story is not over.

ARTHUR. Yes, it is!

Suddenly ARTHUR *breaks away and exits. The* DREAM SPIR- ITS *scatter. The Dreamtime is gone.* PINDARI *looks after* ARTHUR.

PINDARI. Arthur! Come back! Arthur!

Blackout.

SCENE 6

ABIGAIL is beating rugs out in the front yard. Enter ARTHUR, still distraught from the previous scene. As Arthur enters, he stops upon seeing ABIGAIL. Ashamed, he rushes to the house. ABIGAIL stands in front of him.

ABIGAIL. What's wrong?

ARTHUR. Please.

ABIGAIL. I've seen you in some pretty desperate looking moments, but never looking like this.

ARTHUR. I can handle this.

ABIGAIL. And what if you couldn't? What if this just boils in you for so long that it has no place to go, no way to go?

ARTHUR. You agreed to the conditions of this job, Miss Abbie. Are you no longer willing to abide by those conditions?

ABIGAIL. Let go of your pride, Mr. Stevenson.

ARTHUR. Pride? Pride! I wish I had some pride.

ABIGAIL. You make all these oblique references, then refuse to follow them up. You can't do that to people and then refuse them when they want to help—when they want to care!

ARTHUR. Then maybe there's the mistake. Don't care! Not about me! Just—just do your job!

ABIGAIL. This has come to mean more to me than just a job.

ARTHUR. You're a house keeper. Who do you think you are, my—my wife?!

ABIGAIL. No. Of course not.

ARTHUR. Maybe I've let you be too close. Haven't kept up the proper— etiquette. Protocol.

ABIGAIL. Is that how you really want this arrangement to be?

ARTHUR. *(Pause.)* No.

ABIGAIL. Neither do I.

ARTHUR. Let's—let's give you the rest of the day off. I—I just need to be alone right now.

ABIGAIL. Mr. Stevenson . . .

ARTHUR. I want to be alone!

ABIGAIL. Yes, sir.

> ABIGAIL *turns to go, but stops and turns back to* ARTHUR.

ARTHUR. Please, Miss Abbie, I've already embarrassed myself enough. I know how you feel about weakness.

ABIGAIL. Forget what I said.

ARTHUR. I don't need your protection.

ABIGAIL. Maybe you do! Maybe we all need a little protection! A little kindness. Maybe we all can watch out for each other.

ARTHUR. I do not watch out for people! You don't know me. You may think that you see something gentle or kind, but where was my kindness when the world broke to pieces all around me? Where was my kindness when it wasn't about being careful of a person's feelings, but instead about being brave enough to attend to another's very life? Where was my kindness when it needed to be accompanied by bravery!

ABIGAIL. Be clear with me. Tell me.

ARTHUR. You are brave and strong and as hard as granite! You keep trying to draw my heart out, but I know your strength will only crush it! *(Shocked pause.)* Abigail, I—I'm sorry. I didn't mean that.

ABIGAIL. I'll take the day off. I think we both need to calm down. But I want to come back tonight. Not as your house keeper, not as your inferior, not as the servant who you pay money. Tonight I will come back as your friend. And I expect you to treat me as a friend at that point.

ARTHUR. I don't deserve your friendship.

ABIGAIL. Friendship is never about deserving.

ARTHUR. *(Pause.)* All right.

ABIGAIL. Good. But tonight the rules will be off. You'll make dinner for us, since you will be the host. And then we'll continue with
some—poetry.

ARTHUR. Poetry?

ABIGAIL. Banjo Patterson.

ARTHUR. All right.

ABIGAIL. And then we'll talk.

ARTHUR. Abigail . . .

ABIGAIL. We'll talk about whatever we want. Like friends talk. But no
prying. I promise. But if you want to . . .

ARTHUR. I'll see you tonight.

ABIGAIL. Tonight then.

Exit ABIGAIL. Exit ARTHUR.

SCENE 7

*We are once again by the riverbed of the Murray River. ZEEK
is there, staring out onto the river, in a dark mood. It is sunset,
its light reflecting red on ZEEK. Enter JODY.*

JODY. There you are, mate. Been looking for you ever since tea. Had
me worried that you might have bailed out on me.

ZEEK. I will bail out on you, as soon as we're done. Didn't you understand our last conversation?

JODY. Now, Zeek, we were both upset. We both just needed to cool down. We had a go at each other, that's all. We've done that a million times.

ZEEK. Not usually with bowie knives.

JODY. Look, this is a good thing we've had. A really good thing.

JODY sits by ZEEK, *comfortably close.*

ZEEK. I can't trust you.

JODY. And I've always been able to trust you? Especially knowing all I do about you? Not likely. It ain't about trust, mate. It's about—convenience. (*JODY takes* ZEEK's *hand, taking the finger of her other hand and gently caresses it with her forefinger, marking a path on it.* ZEEK *finally looks up at her.*) We're convenient for each other. And the truth is—I don't have a thing without you.

ZEEK *fights both his mistrust and his longing.*

ZEEK. I'm not good for you, you know. I'm unpredictable.

JODY. And I am predictable? That's what makes us perfect for each other.

ZEEK. Are you talking to me as a partner or as a woman?

JODY. Both.

ZEEK. We create sparks. All around us, when we're rubbed together we create sparks. That's bound to create some fire.

JODY. Fire, or maybe water, maybe we'll drown the world or burn it up. That's the beautiful thing about us, isn't it?

ZEEK. I know you think I'm a fraud, Jody. About my so called gifts, I mean.

JODY. Have you ever pretended otherwise to me?

ZEEK. Before that night, that night when my whole dirty world changed, I had a dream. I dreamed of blood.

JODY. Blood?

ZEEK. And now seeing the sun red on the river, the vision is coming to me again.

JODY. What are you talking about, Zeek?

ZEEK. There's going to be blood again.

JODY. Look, get rubbish like that out of your head. Let's head back before they think we're gone for good.

ZEEK. Maybe we should. Just go, I mean. Maybe we should. Gone for good. Away from this strange place.

JODY. No, that stump's almost out. I haven't been sweating like a brumby over that thing not to get our last payment on it.

ZEEK. I'm a dark prophet, Jody. I see blackness and blood, that's all I ever see.

JODY. Zeek—you're giving me a fright, mate. The sun's down now, it's getting dark, we should . . .

ZEEK. *(Almost as if he's in a trance:)* I see a black creature stalking the river. Like the abo said: the Bunyip. The Bunyip swimming in the reddest of rivers. This monster, this dark spirit will swim in that river, carrying its prey in its gaping, open, endless mouth.

JODY. Whoa, mate. Maybe, maybe you're right. Maybe I'm being stupid about us being together. Look, I mean no offense, but you're sounding . . .

> ZEEK *stands and faces* JODY *wildly. For a moment it appears that he may do violence on her. He charges to her, and* JODY *screams, reaching for her knife.* ZEEK *takes the knife swiftly and throws it on the ground. He grips her tightly, covering her mouth. He then kisses her hungrily. At first it appears that* JODY *may resist, but then she concedes, and kisses* ZEEK *back, just as hungrily.*

Act Two

SCENE 1

Evening at the house. ABIGAIL and ARTHUR are sitting on the front porch. ABIGAIL is reading to ARTHUR by lamp light. She is reading the poetry of Banjo Patterson, specifically "The Man From Snowy River." Abigail reads the poem with energy and drama, obviously as enthralled with it as she was the first time she read it.

ABIGAIL. ". . . He sent the flint-stones flying, but the pony kept his feet,
He cleared the fallen timber in his stride,
And the man from Snowy River never shifted in his seat—
It was grand to see that mountain horseman ride.
Through the stringybarks and saplings, on the rough and broken ground,
Down the hillside at a racing pace he went;
And he never drew the bridle till he landed safe and sound
At the bottom of that terrible descent.
He was right among the horses as they climbed the farther hill,
And the watchers on the mountain, standing mute,
Saw him ply the stock whip fiercely; he was right among them still,
As he raced across the clearing in pursuit.
Then they lost him for a moment, where two mountain gullies met
In the ranges—but a final glimpse reveals
On a dim and distant hillside the wild horses racing yet,
With the man from Snowy River at their heels . . ."

ARTHUR. Stop for a moment, Abigail.

ABIGAIL. I'm sorry. Are you tired?

ARTHUR. No, no. Tell me, Abbie, this poem—the Man from Snowy River—the character, I mean. Is he your kind of man?

ABIGAIL. I don't think I understand your question.

ARTHUR. So rugged. So undaunted. So—brave.

ABIGAIL. Yes?

ARTHUR. Is that, to you, what you would call the ideal man?

ABIGAIL. Well, they're admirable qualities, certainly . . .

ARTHUR. They certainly are.

ABIGAIL. Why do you ask, Mr. Stevenson?

ARTHUR. Pardon me. My own inadequacies crowd around me sometimes.

ABIGAIL. You are not inadequate.

ARTHUR. I know some people who would beg to differ with you.

ABIGAIL. Well, then I would beg to differ with them. Truly, sir, you've been very kind to me. Gentle.

ARTHUR. And you value that as well? Kindness? Gentleness?

ABIGAIL. Above all else.

ARTHUR. Oh, come now! This is Australia! The land of the rugged hero, the man of strength, the man of men! The drover, the rancher, the horseman with bullwhip in hand! The Man from Snowy River! You yourself said it was your favorite poem.

ABIGAIL. Let's go back a bit. (*Back into the poem:*)
"But still so slight and weedy, one would doubt his power to stay,
And the old man said, 'That horse will never do
For a long and tiring gallop—lad, you'd better stop away,
These hills are far too rough for such as you.'
So he waited, sad and wistful—only Clancy stood his friend -
'I think we ought to let him come,' he said;
'I warrant he'll be with us when he's wanted at the end,

For both his horse and he are mountain bred.'"
(Beat.) He was the runt. No one thought he could do it.

ARTHUR. Not all of us have proved so capable.

ABIGAIL. Where is this coming from?

ARTHUR. Miss Abbie—Abigail. I—just pretend I didn't mention it, all right?

ABIGAIL. All right. Your business is your business, Mr. Stevenson.

ARTHUR. I want you to call me Arthur now, please. I'm rather tired of Mr. Stevenson. *(Beat.)* You're always so ready to serve me, to defend me, to help me, to patiently endure all my secrecy and flaws!

ABIGAIL. Are you upset with me?

ARTHUR. No, your actions are those of a friend. But you've never given me any cause to be truly upset.

ABIGAIL. And that frustrates you?

ARTHUR. Yes!

ABIGAIL. You want me to get on your nerves?

ARTHUR. No!

ABIGAIL. I'm very lost, Mr. Stevenson.

ARTHUR. Arthur! Call me Arthur.

ABIGAIL. Arthur.

ARTHUR. I don't want you to frustrate me, or to annoy me, or to defy me—unless you want to. Do you understand?

ABIGAIL. Not at all.

ARTHUR. I've done you a great disservice, Abbie.

ABIGAIL. No, you haven't, sir.

ARTHUR. I beg to differ.

ABIGAIL. Then I beg to differ with you, sir!

ARTHUR. There you go!

ABIGAIL. What?

ARTHUR. That's what I want! I want you to be able to speak your mind.

ABIGAIL. Then you're the first man I have ever met who feels such.

ARTHUR. I imagine that may be true. When you stand up to me, it's—magnificent. I want you to never worry about losing your job, or losing your dignity, or losing—well, never worried about losing anything. Just—just always speak your mind. That's the new rule.

ABIGAIL. How can I speak my mind, when you have buried yours?

ARTHUR. Yes. That.

ABIGAIL. You want me to speak freely? Well, I can't. One can't speak free things to a person who has locked himself in a chest.

ARTHUR. If I could make you understand it correctly, I would be so tempted to . . . to . . .

ABIGAIL. You don't think that I haven't seen your hidden glances, and your buried despair?

ARTHUR. I'm not a hero from a poem. I—I couldn't even keep my own wife!

ABIGAIL. There. There it is. Arthur, I've known all along that you were divorced. I've picked up on your ambiguous statements, I've seen that desolate mark around your finger where your ring used to be . . .

ABIGAIL takes ARTHUR's hand, showing him the mark. Neither of them let go.

ARTHUR. Abbie—this is painful . . .

ABIGAIL. I knew that you weren't a widower. You would keep her memory with you, there would be photographs, tokens of your life together . . .

ARTHUR. Abbie, I'm sorry that I brought this up . . .

ABIGAIL. You haven't been trying to keep the memory alive, you've been trying to bury it. With no headstone to mark the place! But it's there, written on every line of your face.

ARTHUR. I know.

ABIGAIL. Do you think all that matters to me?

ARTHUR. It mattered to her. I could never be strong enough, brave enough . . .

ARTHUR lets go of ABIGAIL's hand, looking away.

ABIGAIL. I'm not her.

Pause.

ARTHUR. We were in London. We were coming home from the theater. We had misplaced our carriage, took a wrong turn at some point. We turned down this alley and that's when we witnessed it. There was a man. He wasn't a large man. I was taller, probably stronger, too. But this man he was beating another man, a man smaller than both of us. I had never seen such ferociousness, such unrestrained violence. He didn't have a weapon, but the violent man kicked, he scratched, and punched and pummeled the other man's face until the teeth broke, until the blood flowed from his nose and his mouth. The man who was being beaten was so imploring, he was begging for mercy with such agonizing energy! Why didn't this man respond to such pleading? The man who was being beaten couldn't pay his debts. That's all it was about—the man's debts. The smaller man looked up at us, could see us, and for a moment there was this glimmer of hope. We could help him! I could help him! I looked at my wife, and her eyes urged me on, urged me to save him. But that violent ferocity. I took my wife's hand and turned the other way—she resisted, told me to save him, and when I wouldn't, she tore away from me. If I wouldn't do anything about it, she would. I stopped her. I literally dragged her away from the scene. The next morning I went to the police and told them what I knew. They were able to catch him. But the other man was still dead. I knew it and my wife knew it. We both knew I had proven to be a coward. She told me that I was the Pharisee who turned away from the Samaritan on the road. After that, things changed. The earth crumbled between us and eventually she found— strength. She found strength in other places. In another man. (*There is a long pause and* ARTHUR *is unable to look at* ABIGAIL.*)* Now you know the most shameful thing about me. *(*ABIGAIL *touches* ARTHUR's *face gently, urging him to look at her.)* At least you're kind enough to pity me.

ABIGAIL. Why did you come back to Australia?

ARTHUR. This was the land where they used to send the prisoners. This was the land of the exiles.

ABIGAIL. Arthur . . .

ARTHUR. I'm not sure what I exactly expect you to do with that information. I would understand if you thought it best to . . .

> ABIGAIL *embraces* ARTHUR. ARTHUR *hesitates for only a moment before he fully accepts the embrace gratefully. Lights fade to black out.*

SCENE 2

> *In the dark we hear the tune of "Waltzing Matilda" being whistled, slow and almost melancholy. The lights slowly rise to reveal* ZEEK *whittling a wooden figurine into existence. It's nearly finished. Enter* PINDARI, *coming towards the house.* PINDARI *sits quietly by the eucalyptus tree, staring at* ZEEK. *After a moment,* ZEEK *looks up, bothered by the attention.*

ZEEK. You want something, fella? *(*PINDARI *looks away.)* Look, if you've got something on your mind, just spit it. *(*PINDARI *is still quiet.* ZEEK *stands and walks over* PINDARI, *staring down at him with a sense of intimidation.)* I don't care for your kind. Never have. But I'm not looking for any trouble.

PINDARI. But trouble found you. You can't run from it forever.

ZEEK. Are you threatening me, abo?

> PINDARI *stands and matches* ZEEK's *stare.*

PINDARI. I know what is in your heart.

ZEEK. And what is that?

PINDARI. You know like I do the black river that flows in there.

ZEEK maintains his gaze for a moment, but then breaks away.

ZEEK. You're damn crazy.

Enter ABIGAIL, from the house.

ABIGAIL. Tea will be ready soon, boys. I've got some nice lamb cooking.

ZEEK. Ta, Miss Abbie. But, if you don't mind, I'm going to take a walk for a bit. Clear my head some.

ABIGAIL. Don't take too long, Zeek. It's almost done.

ZEEK. She'll be right.

Exit ZEEK.

ABIGAIL. What's bothering him?

PINDARI. Me.

Beat.

ABIGAIL. Do you trust him?

PINDARI. No, but like all similar things, he's necessary.

ABIGAIL. What do you mean by that?

PINDARI. Water pushes us to the land. On those rocks we find safety or we are crushed.

ABIGAIL. Nobody around here is going to get crushed.

PINDARI. Arthur told me about the tree and the old owner's dreams. That you understand. But maybe you don't know you understand.

ABIGAIL looks towards the eucalyptus. She considers it.

ABIGAIL. I felt that it was special before anybody told me about any dreams. I come out here sometimes when the wind is blowing and hear the eucalyptus leaves and—and I almost feel like she is singing to me.

PINDARI. Maybe she does. A spirit lives in her, like all living things.

ABIGAIL. I know. Sometimes it's like I have wind in my heart. I feel like I have a connection to everything around me, every piece of God's earth. But it is—it's kind of crazy, isn't it? Ludicrous. My parents weren't ones for fancy and daydreaming. Always put me to work. Quiet, hard work. They were religious, taught me to be, too, but they were more—practical about it. But then it would rain outside, or the breeze would pick up, or I would see a kangaroo jumping to who knows where in the distance—and it was as if a spirit whispered in my ear.

PINDARI. Come here.

> PINDARI *takes* ABIGAIL *to the tree. He places her hands on the trunk of it. Instinctively,* ABIGAIL *closes her eyes and breathes in and out deeply. Peaceful music plays in the distance.* ABIGAIL *opens her eyes in surprise.*

ABIGAIL. Do you hear that?

PINDARI. She's singing to you.

ABIGAIL. No, it's in the distance. *(Letting go of the tree.)* It sounds like our new neighbors down the way are musicians.

PINDARI. Yes, perhaps. But she's singing to you.

ABIGAIL. Evening's falling . . .

PINDARI. She's singing.

ABIGAIL. The lamb . . .

PINDARI. I'll take care of it.

ABIGAIL. But . . .

PINDARI. Let her sing.

> ABIGAIL *goes and touches the tree, closes her eyes again, and lets the music wash over her. The music seems closer, approaching ever closer.* PINDARI *enters into the house to watch over the cooking meal.*

Suddenly the DREAM SPIRITS *crowd in around her and* ABI-GAIL *finds herself in Dream Time. She interacts with them joyously, the* SPIRITS *all stop and bow as a beautiful female* TREE SPIRIT, *or goddess, steps out of the tree.*

ABIGAIL. *(Pause.)* I know you, don't I?

The TREE SPIRIT *draws close to her and embraces her in her arms.*

TREE SPIRIT. Remember me . . .

ABIGAIL. Mother?

TREE SPIRIT. I am that, too. Listen for my song.

The TREE SPIRIT *enters back into the tree.*

ABIGAIL. No, please, don't leave me—I know you. Deep inside I know you . . . *(*ABIGAIL *goes back to the tree and places her on hands on it again, trying desperately to regain that connection.* ARTHUR *enters and is startled by the sight of* ABIGAIL. *He approaches her, taking in the sight peacefully. He comes from behind her, touching her on the shoulder.)* Pindari? *(*ABIGAIL, *startled, turns to find* ARTHUR, *not* PINDARI.*)* Oh, Arthur! This—this must look very silly to you.

ARTHUR. Not at all. It was—unexpectedly beautiful.

ABIGAIL. I—I am a Christian, you know. Don't think you've hired some pagan . . .

ARTHUR. Yes, A Christian who believes in all of those magical trees that give people dreams and deflect axes . . .

ABIGAIL. Well, now I feel silly.

ARTHUR. No. Don't. You and this place. It's like you're connected. The owners have changed, but here you still are. Like some tree nymph housed in that eucalyptus.

ABIGAIL. A tree nymph? That's a rather romantic thought.

ARTHUR. What if it is?

ABIGAIL looks at ARTHUR directly at this comment. Both are a little startled at the direction this conversation is going, but do not resist it.

ABIGAIL. Nymphs can be cast out, like the ones cut down in the back. What are you going to with this one?

ARTHUR. She certainly won't be cast out.

ARTHUR leans gently against ABIGAIL as she leans back into the tree. They kiss. They separate slowly, look at each with surprise and gratitude, and then kiss again, with energy. PINDARI comes out to tell them that the meal is ready, but upon seeing them, he simply smiles and walks back into the house. They separate from their kiss.

ABIGAIL. Oh.

ARTHUR. Look, if that was a mistake . . .

ABIGAIL. Did you think it was a mistake?

ARTHUR. No.

ABIGAIL. Neither did I.

They kiss again.

ARTHUR. I think Pindari came to call us to dinner.

ABIGAIL. Maybe we should go in.

ARTHUR. Maybe we should.

Another kiss.

ABIGAIL. Although, he did seem perfectly content to leave us alone.

ARTHUR. He's a very wise, spiritual man.

One more much longer and more passionate kiss. JODY enters.

JODY. Blimey!

ARTHUR and ABIGAIL separate.

ARTHUR. Excuse us, Jody.

JODY. Look, sorry, mate, I just didn't know you two were . . .

ABIGAIL. Neither did we.

JODY. S'truth! Can't say I'm surprised, though.

ABIGAIL. Well, I dare say it caught us by surprise.

JODY. I don't know, Mr. Stevenson's had no eye for anyone but you since I've met him.

ARTHUR. I would have thought that I was more discrete than that.

JODY. Sure, sure, mate. But a lonely heart is much more sensitive in seeing another lonely heart. And, well, you two have been lonely for each other constantly. Congratulations.

ARTHUR. I suppose we say thank you to that.

ABIGAIL. Yes, thank you.

JODY. Goodonya. Now, anyone seen Zeek? The bludger left me to tackle that stump on my own for that last little bit.

ABIGAIL. He seemed distracted.

JODY. He did, eh?

ABIGAIL. Perhaps something that passed between him and Pindari.

JODY. Those two haven't hit it off, that's true. Though, it's Pindari that convinced Mr. Stevenson here to hire us on, so I don't think Zeek's got too much room to complain.

ARTHUR. Yes, he was pretty insistent.

JODY. Excuse me for asking, sir—but, well, Pindo's been a good bloke to me, even if he and Zeek don't get along. What's going to happen to him after he leaves here?

ARTHUR. Well, he's welcome to stay here, although I don't think that is quite his way. This walkabout he's on—his visions push him on like a drover. A bit like you and Zeek, I suppose.

JODY. You don't figure that he and I—Pindo, I mean—well, now I'm just being stupid.

ABIGAIL. What is it?

JODY. I just get muddled sometimes. Perhaps I don't like the walk-about as much as I let on.

ABIGAIL. Then why do you feel like you have to live it?

JODY. I'm not exactly what one would consider a lady like yourself. Not the sort to catch myself a husband easily.

ABIGAIL. But you can work. Steadily, I mean, in one place. I've done it.

JODY. But, Miss Abbie, you must admit that there's miles apart between you and me.

ABIGAIL. Is there? Different circumstances maybe.

JODY. Yeah, maybe.

ARTHUR. *(After a meaningful, if not somewhat awkward, pause.)* Well, from the smells of it, I think the lamb is done.

JODY. Bonzer.

Exit ARTHUR, ABIGAIL, and JODY into the house.

SCENE 3

ZEEK is on the bank of the Murray River, whittling at the wooden figurine he was working on in the previous scene. He raises it, inspecting it. The small, wooden statue is a man, and if one was able to inspect it closely enough, they would find that the statue's face is disfigured with fear, even terror. ZEEK stops whittling and stares at it.

ZEEK. I look at you, little bludger, and see a shard from a tortured soul. But whose soul? Mine? Or that man from so long ago.

The didgeridoo plays, indicating Dreamtime, but this time underscored with something sinister. DREAM SPIRITS swirl around ZEEK, but much more bleak and frightening versions than those we have seen before. Yet among them is the same RAINBOW SPIRIT and YABBRA from previously. YABBRA emerges from the DREAM SPIRITS. *The* RAINBOW SERPENT *pursues the* YABBRA *and the starts to beat the* YABBRA *mercilessly. To* ZEEK's *surprise, however, he sees* ARTHUR *and* PINDARI *standing nearby.* ZEEK *stands, but he is unseen by* ARTHUR *and* PINDARI.

YABBRA. Please, Gov'nor! Help me, sir!

ZEEK. What the bloody hell.

ARTHUR. No . . .

YABBRA. He's going to kill me! I'm going to die here, if you don't help me! I can see you, you can see me—he doesn't see you yet, though, sir, you can surprise him!

ARTHUR. I can't help you . . .

YABBRA. Please! Please!

ARTHUR. Make it stop, Pindari . . .

YABBRA. You can help me . . .

A FEMALE DREAM SPIRIT *emerges from the group and stands beside* ARTHUR, *urging him. She talks in a British accent.*

FEMALE DREAM SPIRIT. Help him, Arthur. Arthur, have some pity, you can help him.

ARTHUR. I can't do it . . .

FEMALE DREAM SPIRIT. Help him!

ARTHUR. Stop it, Pindari!

PINDARI. The story is not over.

ARTHUR. Yes, it is!

Suddenly ARTHUR *breaks away and exits. The* DREAM SPIRITS *freeze.* PINDARI *looks after Arthur.*

PINDARI. Arthur! Come back! Arthur!

PINDARI turns and sees ZEEK for the first time. He doesn't seem particularly surprised. They move among the frozen DREAM SPIRITS.

ZEEK. I must be off my face.

PINDARI. You remember drinking then?

ZEEK. No. Isn't that point of it? Not to remember?

PINDARI. Your people ruined my people with that poison.

ZEEK. That has nothing to do with me, mate.

PINDARI. Maybe not. Maybe they ruined you, too. Or is that your own fault, eh?

ZEEK. I've nothing to do with your people at all.

PINDARI. Maybe not all of us, except one. Maybe two. The figurine in your hand there, is that him then?

ZEEK. Is that who?

PINDARI. I know the secret in your heart already, Zeek. I was shown in a dream.

ZEEK. You don't know a thing then. *(Uncomfortable pause.)* Where are we?

PINDARI. You have a gift, dark cousin. You been here before, but you see many dark things. Black visions. Not unlike me, yet not like me.

ZEEK. See, I don't like this. You know too much.

PINDARI. *(Motioning once again to the wooden carving piece.)* Is that him?

ZEEK. I don't know. I didn't carve in the color of his skin yet.

PINDARI comes and takes the statue. ZEEK gives it up only reluctantly. PINDARI stares at it and then throws it into the Murray River, the bank of which has remained present in this excursion into Dreamtime. The water turns red. ZEEK tries to lunge in after it, but PINDARI restrains him.

PINDARI. Wait.

Out of the river rises one of the Dream Spirits, the BUNYIP. *Calm and patient, it stays still for some time. It is a fierce looking creature, stylized after the fashion of the other Dream Spirits, but far more frightening.*

ZEEK. The Bunyip.

PINDARI. In the billabongs, in the riverbeds, in the swamps, and in the stagnated traces left by the Rainbow Snake, the Bunyip waits. Very sorry business, this dark water spirit, this devil, this imposter. He is a patient creature. So patient that we forget he is there.

ZEEK. Look, this is some dream, some nightmare . . .

PINDARI. You know your gifts.

ZEEK. I didn't want any of this . . .

PINDARI. You know how you used those gifts there . . .

ZEEK. I don't want this . . .

PINDARI. How you twisted those gifts!

ZEEK. I don't want any of this!

PINDARI. They were your birthright . . .

ZEEK. I am not one of you!

PINDARI. They were your birthright and you used them to butcher a man!

ZEEK. You here to condemn me? Well, bugger that!

PINDARI. Wait. I am here to warn you, brother. As bad as things are for you, they can be worse. Still, there is a choice . . .

ZEEK. Choice? I used up my choices long time ago, mate. Now I'm just a wanderer, like a blind dingo following the scent of a phantom in the desert . . .

PINDARI. Then wander for something better. Follow something better.

ZEEK. There's nothing better. Just a barren wasteland of howling days and cold, bitter nights.

PINDARI. Look for redemption.

ZEEK. There is no redemption! There are no second chances for me! Get out of here you damned abbo!

PINDARI. Far back enough, you're an abo, too! You're like me, a man torn between two peoples!

ZEEK. I'd prefer all the spirits of hell than to get one crumb of redemption from a black hand like yours!

A primal scream raises from ZEEK and he goes to attack PINDARI, but before he can reach him, the BUNYIP viciously attacks ZEEK. The lights suddenly black out amidst ZEEK's horrific screams. We hear ZEEK's belabored breathing, as the light raise back on and ZEEK is back on the riverbank. He discovers that his wooden figurine is back in his hand. He looks at it, reflecting the terror on his own face that is etched into statue. He is about to throw the statue into the river, but then he stops and looks at it again. A dark somberness crosses over him as he slowly pockets the wooden statue and exits.

SCENE 4

It is late at night and ABIGAIL is sitting underneath the eucalyptus tree, staring out at the stars, perfectly content. ARTHUR comes out from the house and comes and sits by ABIGAIL.

ARTHUR. I'm sorry that took so long. Pindari seems quiet at times, but get him on certain subjects and he can yabber one's ear off. I'll take you home now.

ABIGAIL. Is it all right if I stay a little longer?

ARTHUR. Certainly.

ABIGAIL. I spend so little time there, you know, that little house of mine. It feels—desolate. Like I abandoned it a long time ago.

ARTHUR. I know what that feels like. When my wife and I were in our hardest time . . .

ABIGAIL. You can say her name, you know. Your ex-wife's name. I've never heard you say it.

ARTHUR. That can't be right.

ABIGAIL. You've never said it.

ARTHUR. *(Pause.)* Rose. When Rose and I were in our hardest time, when our marriage was at its most strained after that horrible night—our halls were so empty. We hadn't any children, but it was as if I felt their—ghosts. As if all the children we were supposed to have were irreparably lost from me forever. And meals—meals were the worst. We would avoid each other, but there was still that unspoken obligation to eat meals together. The silence was so loud that it would give me terrible headaches.

ABIGAIL. That's how it was with my parents. That silence. Hardly a word between the three of us, except to ask me unimportant details about my day. But they never asked each other questions, not even about the unimportant details.

ARTHUR. Was your childhood unhappy then?

ABIGAIL. I didn't know it, if it was. It was just my day to day existence. But it was quiet. Everyone was so quiet. I don't think I would have minded hearing my parents argue every so often, just to remind me that they were still there. It was such a relief when I found my own voice could break that stillness.

ARTHUR. Quiet isn't always bad, is it? It's pretty quiet right now. Out here under that Southern Cross of ours.

Distant music plays.

ABIGAIL. I don't think I look at the stars nearly as often back at my little house. I just go home, go to bed, get up, and come back here. I spend my days here. Even many of my evenings, under this eucalyptus tree with you. This feels so much more like—home.

ARTHUR. I'm glad.

ABIGAIL snuggles into ARTHUR, which ARTHUR welcomes contentedly. ABIGAIL is beginning to drift a little into a half sleep. The music becomes less and less distant, and eventually is omnipresent all around them.

ABIGAIL. *(A little teasing.)* You know, you're losing that Pommy accent of yours.

ARTHUR. Egad!

ABIGAIL. Well, Aussie is your native tongue after all.

ARTHUR. My childhood was happy, you know. Australia wasn't a penal colony to me then. Melbourne was home. Just as this is home. No more affectation, no more playing that role. I still haven't figured out who has been playing that music. The Freemantles can't even hum "Waltzing Matilda" right, so it can't be them.

ABIGAIL. It's the eucalyptus. Singing us to sleep.

ARTHUR. That's a nice thought.

ABIGAIL. That's what Pindari told me. It's the tree's spirit singing.

JODY rushes out of the house, onto the deck.

JODY. Mr. Stevenson, sir?

ARTHUR. What is it, Jody?

JODY. Have you seen Zeek at all since this afternoon?

ARTHUR. No.

JODY. He went off to the river and that's the last I saw of him.

ABIGAIL. I was surprised that he didn't eat tea with us. But he's been doing that off and on, as of late.

JODY. We're nearly done with that last stump. He said he would be back to see if we could take a crack at it and maybe finish it today. But he's disappeared since then.

ABIGAIL. He's been late before, hasn't he?

JODY. Not this late. It's nearing nine o' clock. He spends a lot of time by the river lately doing who knows what, but it's really slowed us down. I don't know—this doesn't feel right.

PINDARI comes out from the house.

PINDARI. A trooper is coming.

A TROOPER ("Bush police" made up of military officers) enters coming towards the house and approaches the group.

ARTHUR. G'day, sir.

TROOPER. G'day.

ARTHUR. How can we help you?

TROOPER. Pardon the interruption, but are you Mr. Arthur Stevenson?

ARTHUR. I am.

TROOPER. I have been told that you've been employing a swagman by the name of Ezekiel . . .

ARTHUR. Yes. Is he all right?

TROOPER. I haven't a clue how he is, but the aboriginal he killed has been underground for five years.

ABIGAIL. You're talking about Zeek?

ARTHUR. Are you sure you have the right man?

TROOPER. Yes, he's the bloke. Sometimes called Zeek the Prophet.

JODY. He has the right man.

ARTHUR. What are you saying, Jody?

JODY. I know about the murder. I've always known about the murder, ever since I met him. He hasn't done anyone harm since then, but that doesn't change what he did. But why the manhunt for an aboriginal death? I wouldn't have guessed you bludgers to have set so much energy in a case for a mob that the government hasn't treated very well in the first place.

TROOPER. You can say that I have made it my personal case, miss. The victim in question was a friend of mine. His name was Dural.

JODY. Well, I'd say it's about time Dural received justice. I'll tell you everything I know.

TROOPER. I appreciate the honesty—but why now?

JODY. I suppose that makes me a criminal as well, doesn't it? By hiding the secret for so long? No worries, though, I'm tired as hell in keeping this secret buried in here. Tired of all of it. Put Zeek in prison, put me in prison, I wouldn't give a quid for all of it anymore.

PINDARI. He threatened her.

TROOPER. Well, yes, that would put a different spin on it.

JODY. How'd you know about that, Pindo?

PINDARI. He threatened to kill her if she told.

TROOPER. Are you involved in this, too, fella?

JODY. I swear to you, sir, Pindari has nothing to do with it. But I'm confused how you know that.

PINDARI. Not by any way that would hold water in your law.

TROOPER. Nevertheless, I'll need to talk to all of you. Can I come inside? We may want to get comfortable. This is going to take a while.

ARTHUR. Whatever you need, sir.

They all exit into the house, except PINDARI *and* JODY. PIN-DARI *grabs* JODY *by the hand.*

PINDARI. Jody . . .

JODY. We'd best be careful, mate. It'll look suspicious if the two of us are out here alone, considering what's just happened.

PINDARI. Be careful around Zeek. Do not have a blue with him.

JODY. I've got a lot to make up for, Pindo. I'm going to do my best to help the trooper.

PINDARI. Please . . .

JODY. Pindo, why, you're sweet. Maybe you're warming up to me, after all.

PINDARI. Do not confront Zeek.

JODY. Sorry, Pindari, this is when I need to be strong.

Exit JODY *into the house. Extremely bothered,* PINDARI *exits as well. Lights dim.*

SCENE 5

It is now morning. JODY *is waiting on the porch.* ZEEK *enters.*

JODY. Was wondering whether you were going to show up at all.

ZEEK. Sorry about that, Jody. I've been fighting some demons.

JODY. The old demons?

ZEEK. Yeah, the same old ones. Stirring up the same old hell inside of me, flowing like a river, turning the water red.

JODY. You ever figure turning yourself in, mate?

ZEEK. Not a word of that.

JODY. Perhaps your conscience has been pressing on you all these years for a reason. Odd things have happened here . . .

ZEEK. I'm not turning myself in. I lost too much already, I'm not going to lose my freedom, too.

JODY. When a man does something like that, you think that even his own soul rebels against him?

ZEEK. Look, I had a job, I had a house, I had a wife, I had a life! I had a lot more than this damned wandering you and I do. Our walk-about is through hell, and that's enough punishment for me. But we don't talk about this. I've told you we never talk about this, especially when people could be around.

JODY. We are going to talk about it, mate.

ZEEK. Stop it now, Jody . . .

JODY. We're going to talk about it because the more you don't, the more chance another person could get hurt, just like that poor fella who carked it because of you.

ZEEK. Since when did you start caring about filthy aboes?

JODY. You're the filthy one, rotting in the core, carrying that smell everywhere you go. You just have to get close enough to you to smell it. And, mate, you and I have gotten pretty close.

ZEEK. It's that Pindari fella. Don't think I haven't seen you undressing him with your looks and your stares. He's gotten your attention, who knows how. It's sick.

JODY. Rubbish.

ZEEK. You've been having a naughty in your mind with that fella since we've got here.

JODY. You're sick.

ZEEK. Oh, like you said, Jody, we've been close—very close. I know you. I know that twisted loneliness of yours would make you go after a dingo when it hits.

JODY pulls out her bowie knife.

JODY. Sick, I say!

ZEEK. Oh, you're going to threaten me again? Well, I've got one up on you this time.

ZEEK pulls out a gun and levels it on JODY. There is another click, as the TROOPER enters with his own pistol cocked, trained on ZEEK.

TROOPER. You kill that good sheila, I will drive a hole in the back of your head, and that's the truth.

ZEEK. So this what our partnership has come to, Jody? You've turned me in?

TROOPER. No, mate, I've been hunting you for a good while now. I found you without her help. So put the gun down.

ZEEK makes as if he is going to put the gun down, but then turns swiftly and shoots the TROOPER, who is instantly killed. He then turns the gun on JODY, but in an instant PINDARI barrels out of the house and charges toward ZEEK. PINDARI is shot, but is able to crash down on ZEEK.

JODY. Pindari!

ABBIE charges out of the house, with a shot gun in her hand, zeroed in on ZEEK. ARTHUR follows her, but his gun is not raised. JODY runs and scoops PINDARI into her arms, in shock, silent tears running down her cheeks. ZEEK scrambles up and trains the gun back on JODY and then to ABIGAIL and ARTHUR, and then to JODY again, but then finally upon ABIGAIL and ARTHUR, as they are the most imminent threat.

ZEEK. Now let's not be in a rush here.

ABIGAIL. If you move to harm one person, Zeek, I swear by all that I love, that I will kill you dead.

ZEEK. I doubt you even know how to use . . .

ABIGAIL fires the gun just above his head, purposely missing him.

ABIGAIL. That was a warning. Next time the shot goes into your chest.

JODY rises, her knife in hand. She is trying to keep it together, despite the extreme emotions she is feeling.

JODY. And if she doesn't kill you, I will.

ZEEK, now very afraid, starts backing up.

ZEEK. I don't want trouble. I've never wanted trouble.

ABIGAIL. Well, trouble has found you.

ZEEK turns and runs, exiting. ABIGAIL keeps her gun trained on ZEEK, as JODY and ARTHUR rush to PINDARI.

JODY. Pindo. We'll get you help.

PINDARI. Jody. I saw you die. Every time, no matter how I changed it, I saw him kill you. But I found a way. I found a way . . .

ARTHUR. Don't give up . . .

PINDARI. Sorry, brother, I can already feel my spirit walking. But don't worry. Through my Walkabout I found my purpose, through coming here I became something so much more . . . I . . .

ARTHUR. Abbie, go get the medical kit inside . . .

PINDARI. I chose this. I found my soul again. After all that all that wandering—oh, it's so beautiful, someday you'll see, too—don't worry—no worries . . .

> PINDARI *is dead.* ABIGAIL *lowers the gun and comes to those surrounding the dead prophet.*

ABIGAIL. "Greater love hath no man this, that a man lay down his life for his friends."

> ARTHUR *embraces his dead friend, anguished.* ABIGAIL *tries to touch his shoulder to comfort him, but he pulls away.*

ARTHUR. I'm a coward . . .

ABIGAIL. Like he said, he chose this, Arthur.

ARTHUR. And why didn't I choose it? You, you all were so brave. I—I did nothing!

ABIGAIL. Arthur, stop.

JODY. Mr. Stevenson, this is Zeek's damn work, it has nothing to do with you.

ARTHUR. It was as if I wasn't even here.

> ARTHUR *rises and turns to the house to retreat into it, but* ABIGAIL *grabs his hand and pulls herself into him.* ARTHUR *resists at first, but that makes* ABIGAIL *cling only tighter. Eventually,* ARTHUR *gives up his resistance and sobs, clinging to* ABIGAIL *just as tightly.*

SCENE 6

ARTHUR is sitting by the Murray River, deep in his sobering, aching thoughts. JODY enters, approaching him.

JODY. You've been spending a lot of time here, Mr. Stevenson. *(ARTHUR does not respond.)* Miss Abbie is worried about you. *(ARTHUR continues to stare with intense concentration at the river.)* Well, I came to say goodbye.

This finally stirs ARTHUR.

ARTHUR. Goodbye?

JODY. I've been laboring all day on that stump. Those roots dug deep, clinging and digging into the earth like a woman to her grief. You understand what I mean?

ARTHUR. Stubborn things, those stumps.

JODY. But I did get them out. They can come out, Mr. Stevenson.

ARTHUR. But what happens when you dig one out, only to find another?

JODY. I'm all done, sir. And don't worry about paying that last bit. I suppose I'm the one with the debt after all that has happened here. Especially with—Pindari.

ARTHUR. That had nothing to do with you, Jody.

JODY. I knew what Zeek was, didn't I?

ARTHUR. Jody . . .

JODY. We all carry our guilt in our tucker bags. Can't help that. I guess I just wanted to—well, thanks heaps. For everything.

ARTHUR. Where are you going?

JODY. Walkabout.

ARTHUR. Still doing the swag travel then?

JODY. No. This will be the fair dinkum walkabout. One that Pindo would be proud of.

ARTHUR. However that murderer turns out, Jody, you were a true mate to us at the end there. To Pindari, too.

JODY nods, almost unable to contain the emotion anymore, before she is able to rasp out:

JODY. Bless you, sir.

JODY hitches her traveling gear up onto her back and exits. A didgeridoo starts playing as Dreamtime begins to change the scene. ARTHUR closes his eyes, as if this too painful to bear.

ARTHUR. No. This was for me and Pindari. I don't want any more of it.

Enter PINDARI.

PINDARI. How are we going to talk then, eh?

ARTHUR stands, at full attention upon hearing PINDARI. Upon seeing PINDARI, ARTHUR rushes to him, but PINDARI holds up his hand to gently fend him off.

ARTHUR. Pindari!

PINDARI. Can't touch me, brother.

ARTHUR. Pindari, I don't understand. How is this possible?

PINDARI. My spirit is stronger than that body there. You're surprised, eh?

ARTHUR. Very surprised.

PINDARI. It shouldn't have been a surprise. You knew the spirit in me. You saw it many times.

ARTHUR. I suppose you're right. Faithless me.

PINDARI. I rose up. I conquered. Now it's your turn. It's time to see.

ARTHUR. See what?

PINDARI. That thing you didn't see before. That you refused to see.

ARTHUR. No, Pindari, please . . .

The lights and mood change to Dreamtime. A didgeridoo plays. A number of DREAM SPIRITS, *rise into the scene and dance, as in the previous scenes. The* RAINBOW SERPEANT SPIRIT *emerges as the focal* DREAM SPIRIT. *The* YABBRA *emerges from the* DREAM SPIRITS, *as previously. The* RAINBOW SER-PENT *pursues the* YABBRA *and starts to beat the* YABBRA *mercilessly. One of the* DREAM SPIRITS *speaks in its British cockney:*

YABBRA. Please, Gov'nor! Help me, sir!

ARTHUR. No...

YABBRA. 'E's going to kill me! I'm going to die 'ere, if you don't help me! I can see you, you can see me—'e doesn't see you yet, though, sir, you can surprise him!

ARTHUR. I can't help you...

YABBRA. Please! Please!

ARTHUR. Pindari...

YABBRA. You can help me...

As before, another DREAM SPIRIT *emerges from the group, a female, and stands beside* ARTHUR *urging him. She talks in a British accent.*

FEMALE DREAM SPIRIT. Help him, Arthur. Arthur, have some pity, you can help him.

ARTHUR. I can't do it...

FEMALE DREAM SPIRIT. Help him!

ARTHUR. Why are you showing me this again? I already know what happens! And then I let it happen to you! Again and again!

PINDARI. The story isn't over yet. Your part of the story is not finished!

ARTHUR. I failed, Pindari!

PINDARI. How could you fail a test that you haven't taken yet?

ARTHUR. What?

PINDARI. Watch! *(Emerging from the* DREAM SPIRITS *is* NYIMBUNJI, *a Weeum, a kind of holy man. He dances, as if supplicating a deity.)* Nyimbunji, a Weeum, which means in your language, Clever Man, or a man of powers and high initiation. This holy man, he saw the Rainbow Snake commit such an outrage upon a holy creature as the Yabbra bird, and so he called upon the great Dirawong! *(DIRA-WONG, a god-like goanna—a large, Australian lizard, similar to a komodo dragon. The* DIRAWONG *protects the* YABBRA *and faces off with the* RAINBOW SNAKE. *The action between the two characters occurs as* PINDARI *explains it.)* The Dirawong! A great goanna lizard in the Dreamtime. Only he was mighty enough to defeat the Rainbow Snake! Dirawong gave us the law, the stories, and the songlines, he taught us the medicine and the paintings and the dreamings. He gave us community and culture . . .

ARTHUR. Pindari, this story can't help me anymore. I don't think it ever could.

PINDARI. I am not finished.

ARTHUR. Yes, you are!

PINDARI. Look into the reflection, you stupid idiot!

ARTHUR. Insult me all you want. I'm an idiot, I'm afraid, I'm a coward! And I'll just tell you that it's all true. I have failed everyone. That man in England is dead. You're dead.

PINDARI. Miss Abbie is not dead.

ARTHUR. Miss Abbie? Of course Abigail is not dead. She is safe at the— house. *(Fear suddenly strike* ARTHUR.*)* She is safe, isn't she?

PINDARI. The Bunyip stalks the river.

ARTHUR. No, oh no. Do something for her! Can't you do something?

PINDARI. I am dead, my friend. The storyteller's lips are in another world. I am now separate from the story.

ARTHUR. I'm—I'm freezing up again . . .

PINDARI. Then freeze, if you must. Let her die. Let it all die. You think this story is not for you?

ARTHUR. You think a story can fix this?

PINDARI. You think you're above it, beyond it?

ARTHUR. I think they're nothing more than whispered, desperate cathechisms!

PINDARI. You will find soon enough how real my stories are, Arthur. For by then you become the man with the shadow for a soul. That will become your story.

ARTHUR. I was jealous. You were the man I wanted to be.

PINDARI. Then be that man, if you want it so much. I'm not there to take that role anymore.

ARTHUR. I can't!

PINDARI crouches down and looks at ARTHUR. There is a moment of connection, of stillness.

PINDARI. Love doesn't think of its own safety.

ARTHUR struggles only momentarily before he finally breaks free from the internal struggle.

ARTHUR. Abigail!

ARTHUR leaps up and exits. Suddenly the Dreamtime changes, spilling over into the real world, the DREAM SPIRITS overlapping with the more realistic happenings at the house, which is now lit. ABIGAIL is on the porch, sweeping. She stops, looks at the tree, and smiles, approaching it.

ABIGAIL. Have any songs for me tonight?

Enter ZEEK. Neither ZEEK nor ABBIE make any indication that they see PINDARI.

ZEEK. Talking to trees, that something the abo taught you?

ABIGAIL freezes upon hearing ZEEK's voice. As she slowly turns around, ZEEK cock's his gun upon her.

PINDARI. The Rainbow Snake thought that he had free reign over the Yabbra. He thought he was heaps powerful, heaps mighty!

ZEEK. Yeah, how about you don't move any further than that, all right, little sheila?

ABIGAIL. You better watch it, Mr. Stevenson's inside.

ZEEK. Nice try. I saw his car by the river. Not that the bludger would be much use to you now. Dodgy behavior last time I was here, wouldn't you say? Couldn't even muster the bravery to raise his gun. Not like you and Jody. I was pretty impressed by you, especially, Miss Abbie. Wouldn't have expected those kind of stones from a soft looking sheila like you.

ABIGAIL pulls out JODY's knife, raising it against ZEEK.

ABIGAIL. Jody gave me her knife. Back off.

ZEEK. You think you can get to me with that thing before I shoot you? Not bloody likely. Now throw it over there or I'll shoot you dead right now. *(ABIGAIL reluctantly does so.)* Where is Jody?

ABIGAIL. You've come for Jody then?

ZEEK. I've come for all of you. I've left too many loose ends, if you know what I mean. You all know my face. You, Mr. Stevenson—especially Jody. She knows my haunts, my paths. Where is she?

ABIGAIL. She's gone, Zeek.

ZEEK. Don't lie to me!

ZEEK fires the gun above ABIGAIL's head.

ABIGAIL. I'm not lying!

ZEEK. I think it's about time to make our way inside, don't you?

ABIGAIL. Help! Please!

ZEEK fires his gun over ABIGAIL's head again, this time farther down towards her. She is becoming completely unglued, but then strives to regain some composure.

ZEEK. Next time the bullet will find its way between your eyes. You understand? *(ABIGAIL nods.)* No one's around anyway—I looked for the neighbors. Everyone's gone.

ABIGAIL. Well, get it over with then.

ZEEK. Too late for that now. I wanted no trouble, you know. Just to live out the rest of my life wandering for my sins. But I guess you were right—the trouble found me.

ABIGAIL. The man you killed . . .

ZEEK. Just a dirty abo. We both had too much grog and some words passed between us which escalated. We got rough and he—lied. Tried to make me angry. Said I was just like him and that he had proof. That he was my cousin, that he was looking for his family. I told him otherwise, told him where he could put his pack of lies. I wasn't a dirty bung. I knew what was happening, even before he pulled out the knife. I have a dark gift, Miss Abbie, a bright curse. I saw it all happen before he could do it, I saw a vision of him lunging at me. I saw the threat, but knew I could dodge it, the abo being as pissed as he was. But I used that vision and I decided to raise the stakes. Before he pulled out his knife, I pulled out a gun. The gun won. I threw out my life with just a little pub fight.

ABIGAIL. And how is this going to help anything, Zeek? How is this going to fix it?

ZEEK. Fix it? There's no fixing it! I thought I was a good man once, you know. I thought I had integrity and compassion. And I thought, if I tried hard enough, ran fast enough, I may just be able to re-claim it. But there can never be any fixing it!

ABIGAIL. It's not too late to do something good. You can let me go.

ZEEK. Maybe once, even recently—but I'm gone now, Miss Abbie. Whatever I was, whoever I was, it's been ravaged by dark water—and then by black fire! And if I'm going to burn, hell, I'm going to spread some of the flames!

ABIGAIL. If you're going to kill me, then kill me!

ZEEK. What? Without having a little fun first? Not bloody likely.

PINDARI. The Rainbow Snake was wrong. He was not the ruler of the world. The Dirawong healed and rose up and found the Rainbow Snake!

Suddenly ARTHUR enters, charging towards ZEEK.

ARTHUR. Zeek!

The gun goes off, as ARTHUR tackles ZEEK.

PINDARI. The Dirawong, that great Goanna, battled the Rainbow Snake!

The gun is knocked away. ABIGAIL goes for it, but ZEEK pushes ARTHUR off and reaches the gun first. However, ARTHUR is back on his feet and barreling towards ZEEK. ZEEK fires the gun and ARTHUR is knocked back on the ground.

ABIGAIL. Arthur!

ZEEK. Well, looks like the dill had some backbone after all.

ZEEK goes to inspect the body, jostling it with his toe, when ARTHUR is suddenly alert again, kicking ZEEK.

PINDARI. In this fight the Dirawong was injured—even the mighty Dirawong could bleed when the Rainbow Snake's poisonous strike bit Dirawong on the head. It was very sorry business.

Gaining his composure, ZEEK trains the gun at ARTHUR and is about to fire. Seeing the opportunity, ABIGAIL retrieves the knife and tries to stab ZEEK in the back. ZEEK is able to twirl and grab her before she is able to stab him and wrestles the knife from ABIGAIL and knocks her to the ground. In the struggle, however, he has dropped the gun.

ZEEK. That's it, you're dead—right now!

ZEEK goes for ABIGAIL. ARTHUR swiftly and instinctively goes for the gun and, without the least bit of hesitation, he shoots ZEEK. ZEEK falls dead on ABIGAIL. ABIGAIL quickly pushes ZEEK's dead body off of her and stands, backing away from him. Both ARTHUR *and* ABIGAIL *stare at the body and then, both at their emotional brinks, stare at each other in surreal silence for several moments, the only thing heard being their heavy breathing.*

ABIGAIL. Arthur—I thought he killed you.

ARTHUR. He would have—if you hadn't tackled him.

ABIGAIL. And I would have been dead, too, if you hadn't . . .

She stops short and they stare at each other. ARTHUR *and* ABIGAIL *rush to each other, cling to each other, weeping, as every strained grief and fear that they have kept locked within himself comes pouring out like a waterfall.*

ARTHUR. I didn't lose you . . .

ABIGAIL. This tree is still standing. Shhhh . . .

ARTHUR *suddenly cringes in pain, clutching his shoulder.*

PINDARI. The Rainbow Snake ran to the Burraga, what the white people call the Tasman Sea, and made himself into an Island so Dirawong wouldn't recognise him. Dirawong reached the coast and laid down, facing the sea, waiting for Rainbow Snake to come back. The mark of red on top of the land shows the wound where Rainbow Snake bit Dirawong in the Dream Time

ABIGAIL. We need a doctor.

ABIGAIL *helps* ARTHUR *inside.*

PINDARI. And there the Dirrawong is, remembering, contemplating his wound, but ever vigilant in his defense against the Rainbow Snake.

PINDARI *and the* DREAM SPIRITS *fade and disappear.*

SCENE 8

That evening. ABIGAIL *comes out onto the porch, gazing into the sky. The wind picks up and we hear, perhaps even see, the wind blow through the tree, making the branches sway and the leaves rustle.* ABIGAIL *approaches the tree once again, wrapping her arms tightly around herself, enjoying the tree's quiet, soothing speech.* ARTHUR *comes out of the house and comes to* ABIGAIL, *with a bandaged shoulder in a sling.*

ABIGAIL. You're supposed to be asleep.

ARTHUR. You heard the Doctor. I'm going to be fine. The bullet made a clean exit.

ABIGAIL. Does it hurt?

ARTHUR. Like nothing else I've ever experienced. Hopefully what Doctor Freemantle gave me will start working soon. Either way, I'm not going to be sleeping any time soon. Are you all right?

ABIGAIL. I think so—yes, I'm all right.

ARTHUR. Are you—are you going to be able to come back here?

ABIGAIL. Yes. It may be surreal for a while, but—I think this is the only place that will be able to grant me any sort of peace after what we just went through.

ARTHUR. Peace. Will I ever get any peace?

ABIGAIL. What's wrong?

ARTHUR. I just killed a man. Whoever expects to do that? I tortured myself for not interfering once, but then when I do . . .

ABIGAIL. Arthur, you saved my life.

ARTHUR. At the cost of another.

ABIGAIL. Do you regret it?

ARTHUR. *(Looks at* ABIGAIL *squarely.)* No. Never. *(Looks away.)* But I can't jostle that image out my head. Me pulling the trigger and then seeing Zeek's body fall, like a cracked, burning tree. *(The Eucalyptus Tree's distant music begins to be heard again. ARTHUR looks up as the beautiful music washes over them.)* Really, who makes that music?

ABIGAIL takes ARTHUR by the hand and takes him over to the tree. She places his hands upon it.

ABIGAIL. Listen.

ARTHUR. Pains like this don't heal easily, Abigail.

ABIGAIL. Maybe not. But listen.

They listen for a moment, the breeze through the eucalyptus leaves intermingling with the music. ARTHUR tries to drink it in, but breaks away.

ARTHUR. I can't get rid of him! His dead eyes staring up at me as his blood pools beneath his . . .

ABIGAIL. There's a tension.

ARTHUR. Pardon?

ABIGAIL. A tension. Neither extreme is allowed without a resistance from the other side.

ARTHUR. I need more than pretty maxims or easy philosophy, Abigail.

ABIGAIL. Arthur, please. Come back here.

ARTHUR. There's a story that I remember my Father telling me when I was very young, before I moved to England and things changed. Would you like to hear it?

ABIGAIL. Very much.

ARTHUR. In a day when there used to be only sunshine, a shadow came into the land. Not knowing what a shadow was, the people happily welcomed it into their society. But there was an old man among them who recognized the shadow, who was the only one old enough to remember its last visit. The Old Man was undecided whether to let it remain to teach the people, or to fight for the comfort they had achieved . . .

The music continues to wash softly over them, the wind continues to blow through the eucalyptus branches and the lights fade quietly to black.

THE END

Anna Hargadon as Abigail Baker, David Lasseter as Arthur Stevenson. Photo by Bryn Dalton Randall.

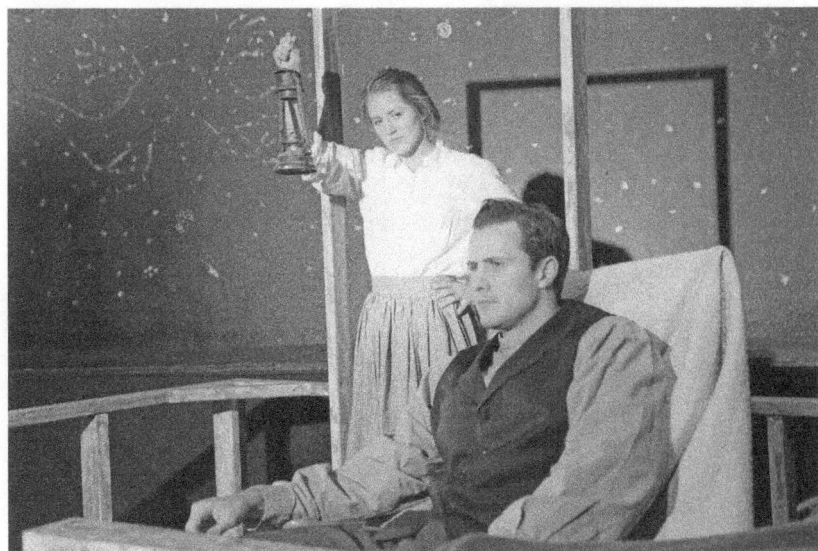

Anna Hargadon as Abigail Baker, David Lasseter as Arthur Stevenson. Photo by Bryn Dalton Randall.

Anna Hargadon as Abigail Baker, David Lasseter as Arthur Stevenson. Photo by Bryn Dalton Randall.

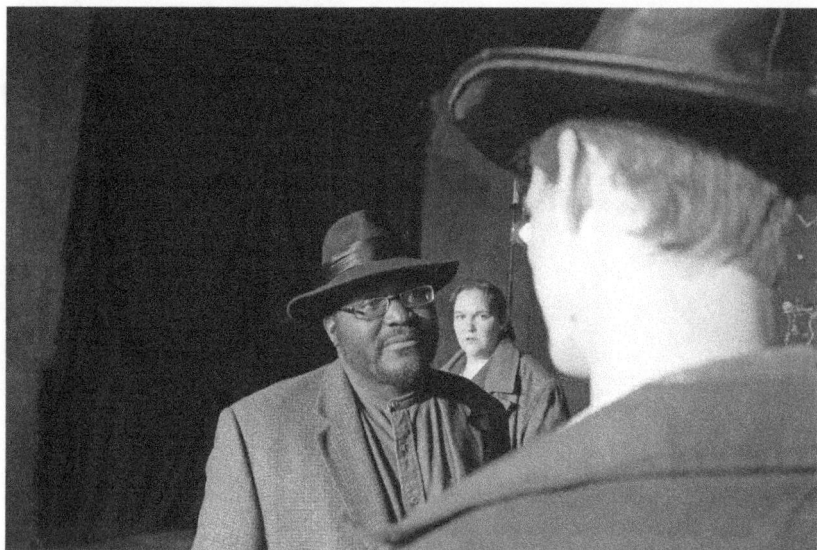

Robert Burch as Pindari, Bryn Dalton Randall as Jody, Stephen Geis as Zeek. Photo by Mahonri Stewart.

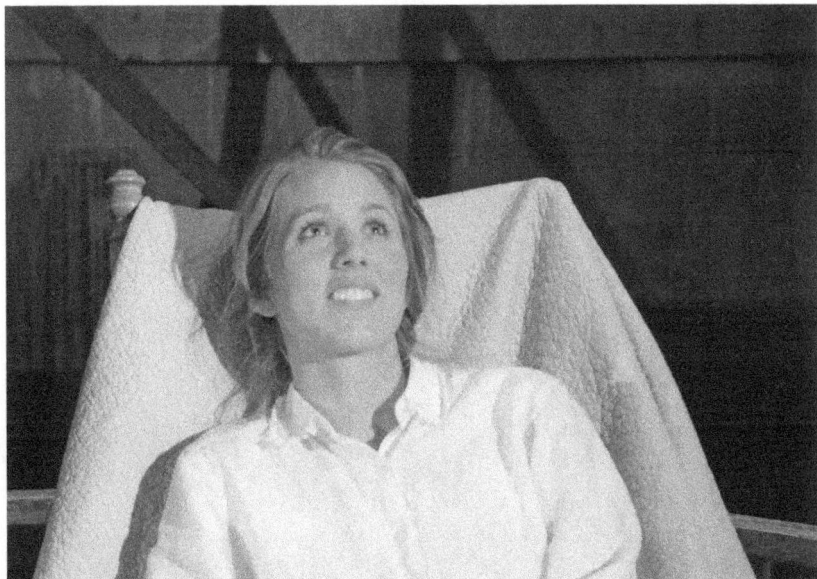

Anna Hargadon as Abigail Baker. Photo by Bryn Dalton Randall.

Bryn Dalton Randall as Jody and Stephen Geis as Zeek. Photo by Mahonri Stewart.

David Lasseter as Arthur Stevenson and Anna Hargadon as Abigail Baker. Photo by Bryn Dalton Randall.

Stephen Geis as Zeek. Photo by Bryn Dalton Randall.

Robert Burch as Pindari and David Lasseter as Arthur Stevenson. Photo by Bryn Dalton Randall.

Anna Hargadon as Abigail Baker. Photo by Bryn Dalton Randall.

Bryn Dalton Randall, Neal Hooper, and Anna Hargadon as Dream Spirits. Photo by Mahonri Stewart.

Bryn Dalton Randall and Robert Burch as Dream Spirits. Photo by Mahonri Stewart.

Neal C. Hooper as the Bunyip. Photo by Bryn Dalton Randall.

Robert Burch as Pindari; Neal C. Hooper, Bryn Dalton Randall, and Anna Hargadon as Dream Spirits. Photo by Mahonri Stewart.

Robert Burch as Pindari, Bryn Dalton Randall as Jody, and Stephen Geis as Zeek. Photo by Mahonri Stewart.

Neal C. Hooper as Dirawong and Brynn Dalton Randall as the Rainbow Snake. Photo by Mahonri Stewart.

Stephen Geis as Zeek, Anna Hargadon as Abigail Baker. Photo by Bryn Dalton Randall.

Neal C. Hooper as the Trooper, Stephen Geis as Zeek, and Bryn Dalton Randall as Jody. Photo by Mahonri Stewart.

Stephen Geis as Zeek, Robert Burch as Pindari, Neal C. Hooper as the Trooper, Bryn Dalton Randall as Jody, Anna Hargadon as Abigail Baker, and David Lasseter as Arthur Stevenson. Photo by Mahonri Stewart.

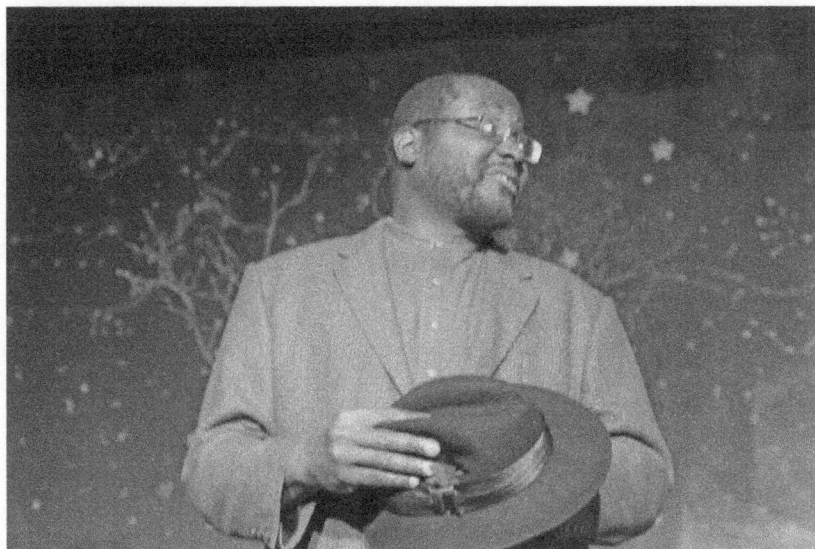

Robert Burch as Pindari. Photo by Bryn Dalton Randall.

Anna Hargadon as Abigail Bake, David Lasseter as Arthur Stevenson. Photo by Bryn Dalton Randall.

David Lasseter as Arthur Stevenson, Anna Hargadon as Abigail Baker. Photo by Bryn Dalton Randall.

Rings of the Tree

A Multi-Media Play

Production History

Rings of the Tree first premiered, in its traditional, non-multimedia version, at Utah Valley University's Blackbox Theatre in Orem, UT on September 6, 2007. It had the following cast and crew:

CAST

Diana Applesong: Jamie Denison
Truman Nibley: Jordan Cummings
Colin: Mahonri Stewart
Echo: Sarah Preston
Jacquelyn Lyons: Penny Pendleton
Roman Lyons: Daniel Whiting
Felicity Pope: Bryn Dalton Randall
Lane Knight: Bryce Bishop
Manchester Lyons: Matthew P. Davis

CREW

Executive Producer: D. Terry Petrie
Producer: Mahonri Stewart
Director: Sarah Stewart Waugh
Stage Manager: Tiffany Shaw Taylor
Assistant Stage Manager: Karolynne Crook
Costume Designer: Anne Ogden Stewart
Costume Construction: Anne Stewart, Karla Summers, Kristi Summers,
Anna-Marie Johnson, Mandy Lyons, Carol Ogden, Betty Layton
Fight Choreography: Amos Omer
Set Design: Daniel Whiting and Sarah Stewart
Original Music: Nathaniel Drew
Publicity: Mahonri Stewart and James Arrington

Zion Theatre Company and Imminent Catharsis Media then premiered *Rings of the Tree's* current, multimedia form[1] at the Off Broadway Theatre in Salt Lake City, UT on February 3, 2012, with the following cast and crew:

CAST

Diana Applesong: Jaclyn Hales
Truman Nibley: Danor Gerald
Colin: Lawrence Fernandez
Echo: Heather Jones
Jacquelyn Lyons: Shona Kay
Roman Lyons: Tanner Harmon
Felicity Pope: Anna Daines Rennaker
Lane Knight: Shea Potter
Manchester Lyons: Blaine Quarnstrom
Film Extras: Jyllian Petrie, Anna-Marie Johnson,
Jason Sullivan, Adam Argyle, Brian Grobb, Anne Betts,
Chase Ramsey, Jacob Porter, Celia Grant

CREW

Director: Jyllian Petrie
Multimedia Directors: K. Danor Gerald, Jyllian Petrie
Executive Producers: Mahonri Stewart, K. Danor Gerald
Producer: Nathaniel Drew
Stage Manager: Anne Marie Betts
Cinematographers: Charles Unice; Danor Gerald; Brian Paul;
Jason Nacey; Jason Falasco; Denver Riddle; Tyson Maughan;
Jyllian Petrie; Bryan Juber
Costumer: Anna-Marie Johnson
Sets/Props: Jason Sullivan

---

1. This multimedia/stage version, which was performed in 2012, is based more on Mahonri Stewart's screenplay version of the story, rather than the original stage play in 2007. It is essentially the same story, but there are key differences between the two versions.

Lighting Design: Joe Fox/Mike James
Makeup Design: Jessica Harmon
1st Assistant Director (Film Portions): Allie Barr
Production Manager: Penny Pendleton
Original Song "Rings of a Tree": Kristen Jensen and Nathaniel Drew
Original Music Composition/Mixer:
Nathaniel Drew/Lawrence Fernandez
Fight Choreographer: Adam Argyle
Poster Design: Trevor Robertson
Horse Wrangler: Tony Hutcheon
Stunt Double: Tony Hutcheon

The screenplay version of *Rings of the Tree*, upon which the multimedia version is based, won the LDS Film Festival Award for Best Screenplay in 2011.

Dedicated to my sister Sarah Stewart Waugh.
Sarah was Rings of the Tree's *original director and*
the one who tapped my shoulder and
introduced me to the lovely Woman of period drama and romance.

Also dedicated to my brother Mark Stewart.
Mark, like a Timelord,
briefly whisked me into the world of fantasy and wonder.
I haven't lost the taste of it since.

Rings of the Tree

Act One

SCENE 1

Screens dot the stage, which throughout the production show various images, locales, etc. They light up showing various outdoor images of a large, Victorian estate. We see on the screens COLIN *on horseback approaching the house.* COLIN *enters. He is not a bad looking man, perhaps even handsome, and he carries a kind of over confidence in everything he does. He is also keenly intelligent and always exudes a strong presence. He is wearing the high fashions of the Victorian era. Coming out to meet him are three servants,* JACQUELYN, MANCHESTER, *and* ROMAN LYONS. MANCHESTER *is* JACQUELYN'S *and* ROMAN'S *father, thus considerably older than both of them,* JACQUELYN *and* ROMAN *being in their early to mid-20's. They calmly walk towards* COLIN.

ROMAN. I'll take your horse to the stable, sir.

ROMAN exits. MANCHESTER approaches COLIN, while JAC-QUELYN follows.

MANCHESTER. Very good to see you again, Mister Colin.

COLIN. Has Miss Diana been alerted to my arrival?

MANCHESTER. I told her myself just moments ago.

COLIN. And she did not come out to greet me?

MANCHESTER. Jacquelyn will show you the way, sir. Won't you, Jacquelyn?

JACQUELYN. Yes, Father.

JACQUELYN escorts COLIN and the screens change to show them traveling down the halls of the Applesong Mansion.

COLIN. I appear as I ought to?

JACQUELYN. Quite so, sir.

COLIN. I know how your mistress is particular.

JACQUELYN. You know her well, sir. You have been her longest associate.

COLIN. Associate? After all this time, I would hope that I have earned the title of "friend."

JACQUELYN. Friend then.

COLIN. You're unhappy here.

JACQUELYN. Pardon me?

COLIN. I know that she's been very fair to you.

JACQUELYN. You are so certain of that, sir?

COLIN. You can make no progress in this house. No movement. While my life, it's been nothing but movement. I find that a little philosophy distracts the mind.

JACQUELYN. I have a little too much time to think as it is, sir. I would prefer a little more action.

COLIN. I can see that. I can relate to that. I can't dwell too long upon any one thing, or I could be dwelling upon it forever.

DIANA enters or appears on a ladder, having just grabbed a book from one of the screens full of the images of books, as if it were a bookshelf. DIANA is an absolutely stunning woman of a timeless kind of beauty, wearing the clothing of Victorian high fashion. She has the bearing and carriage of a queen or a goddess, and is not easily intimidated, nor frightened. But there is a kind of sadness that sits in her eyes at most times. DIANA looks at the spine of the book she has just reached.

DIANA. Hm. I actually have not read this one. Curious.

JACQUELYN enters with COLIN. COLIN calls up to DIANA.

COLIN. Diana!

DIANA. Colin. It has been some time. Thank you, Jacquelyn. *(JACQUE-LYN exits.)* Is this a social call?

DIANA begins to climb down, with book in hand.

COLIN. You know my need for variation. Thought that England was the place for me at the moment. I had such a frightful time in Russia.

DIANA. You are always welcome.

COLIN. Am I?

DIANA. To the point, Colin, to the point.

COLIN. The point, the point! I said this was a social call.

DIANA. Then socialize.

COLIN. Did I do something to upset you?

DIANA. I—I am sorry, Colin. I did not mean to be rude.

COLIN. Well, you know that I see you as flawless, even in the face of your flaws.

DIANA. Doting, always doting.

COLIN. Does that bother you?

DIANA. Would it change your behavior if it did?

COLIN. Well, I am pretty stuck in my ways.

DIANA. Stuck. Yes, we're both stuck, aren't we?

At this, DIANA stands and walks to a window. COLIN walks over to her.

COLIN. So severe. Too severe.

DIANA pulls away.

DIANA. And you are too bright.

COLIN. Thus we go together like day and night.

DIANA. It will take more than dash and daring, Colin.

COLIN. What will it take then?

DIANA. Colin...

COLIN. I am serious.

DIANA. I am done.

COLIN. I am different. You know that.

DIANA retreats to an ornately carved chess board. This frustrates COLIN. DIANA fingers the queen piece.

DIANA. Shall we play a game? Chess?

COLIN. Diana...

DIANA. You said I was severe. A game will lighten me considerably, I think.

COLIN. Something out of doors then. Croquet?

DIANA. Croquet.

They move to another point on the stage, and the screens change to create classic British gardens, where they begin playing croquet. JACQUELYN reenters, watching DIANA and COLIN playing. MANCHESTER enters, approaching her.

JACQUELYN. Miss Applesong and Colin went to play croquet in the Garden.

MANCHESTER. Mister Colin to you.

JACQUELYN. Oh, Father must we play act even in private?

MANCHESTER. We always maintain our...

JACQUELYN. Always? Must our family always?

MANCHESTER. Always.

JACQUELYN turns to leave.

MANCHESTER. Where are you going?

JACQUELYN. Out. Today is supposed to be my day off.

MANCHESTER. What are you going to do?

JACQUELYN. Miss Applesong may do what she likes, but I will not be fenced in.

MANCHESTER. Who knows what you find to do out there for so long.

JACQUELYN. The world is an awfully large place, Father, and I will willingly waste my time in it.

JACQUELYN exits, brushing off ROMAN, as he approaches from the opposite direction. ROMAN approaches his father.

MANCHESTER. I've been grateful to you, Roman. At least I have one child who shares my ideals. I worry so much. Your mother was like her.

ROMAN. Mother hadn't the stomach to do what we must do.

MANCHESTER. Speak respectfully of your mother.

ROMAN. Wherever she is, we're better off without her.

MANCHESTER. I never was and never will be better off without her.

MANCHESTER exits then ROMAN exits. DIANA and COLIN are still playing croquet as they continue their discussion.

DIANA. It is flattering, Colin, truly it is, but every time you ask you already know my answer.

COLIN. I more than anybody know the lonely life you lead here.

DIANA. Oh, don't bring up such sentiment with me, Colin. You know that such emotions were burned out of me long ago. They are not convenient for those like us.

COLIN. Marry me, Diana. I am the only one else who understands your plight.

DIANA. And thus I also thought you understood my decision. Please, respect it.

COLIN. Your concerns, your fears, they do not apply to me.

DIANA. Colin, I know that it may all seem that the stars are aligned in a favorable match for us—but I can't. Not now.

COLIN. Not *now*? Is there a glimmer of hope for me yet then?

DIANA. If you can hope beyond hope, perhaps.

COLIN. I knew I could crack you someday.

DIANA. Do not misunderstand me, Colin . . .

COLIN. Of course. Hope beyond hope.

> COLIN *hits the colored ball through the loops, and hits the stake.* COLIN *and* DIANA *exit.*

SCENE 2

One the screens we see time passing within the garden and ECHO *enters, sitting at a garden table.* ECHO *is a beautiful woman who appears quite young. She is exceptionally well dressed in the highest of Victorian fashions.* ECHO *exudes confidence and a lust for life in all its glory.* ROMAN *enters, bringing tea.*

ROMAN. Your father was here yesterday.

ECHO. So I heard.

ROMAN. More tea?

ECHO. Thank you. (*ROMAN pours the tea. He puts in two sugars and cream.*) You know how I like it.

ROMAN. I know you well, Miss Echo.

ECHO. Always at hand when I'm around.

ROMAN. A distinct pleasure I reserve for myself, Miss Echo.

ECHO. I once thought it was because you didn't trust me. That you were keeping a close eye on me.

ROMAN. I hope you disabused yourself of that notion.

ECHO. I did. I have a good memory.

ROMAN. And thus you remember my declaration of love for you.

ECHO puts aside her tea and walks through the estate's gardens. ROMAN follows her, trying to catch up.

ECHO. You were twelve years old at the time. You could hardly expect me to take you seriously.

ROMAN. On the contrary, my lady. You could have depended upon that declaration for the rest of your natural life.

ECHO. There is nothing natural about my life, Roman.

ROMAN. Miss Echo—Darling Echo . . .

ECHO turns and confronts ROMAN.

ECHO. I do not approve of this house of illusions, Roman, so I will not create any smoke and mirrors for you either.

ROMAN. You do not need to . . .

ECHO. I am out of your reach.

ROMAN. No—but—I love you.

ECHO. You could never fathom me enough to love me.

ROMAN. Please, hear me out . . .

ECHO. Mr. Lyons, I did not come here to have this conversation. I have come here to see Diana, and thus I would appreciate it if you did your job and fetched her for me.

ROMAN bows severely and, without another word, turns and exits to fetch Diana. As the sun begins to set, DIANA walks through her gardens to find ECHO sitting at the base of a magnificent, old tree which has appeared on one of the screens. ECHO is sitting, watching the sunset. DIANA sits besides ECHO, her coolness contrasting ECHO's heat.

DIANA. Thank you for waiting.

ECHO. Patience is a luxury that we both can afford. I love this old tree. *(DIANA doesn't even look at the tree, but continues staring forward.)* But you long for the sunset. *(Pause.)* Diana, I'll get right to the point of my visit. I want you to finally promise me to never see my father again. I have warned you and I will warn you again . . .

DIANA. You once told me that I hide myself within my walls, Echo. Yet you hide something behind those eyes. I am not a chess piece, be it your pawn or your father's queen.

ECHO. You misunderstand me. I wish to be your ally.

DIANA. I have no allies.

ECHO. You may think you are goddess in this Olympus of yours . . .

DIANA. And what does that make you, a demi-goddess? A nymph? An illegitimate heir of Zeus?

ECHO. You need friends.

DIANA. You all die, you all shrivel in the heat of the sun. There is no crutch which I can lean upon in this world, they are all broken. Even you, Echo.

ECHO. Really, Diana . . .

DIANA. Next time you choose to visit me, Echo, play some games with me, engage in frivolous conversation. But do not think you will be able to use my secret, intimate thoughts and feelings in any of your schemes.

> As DIANA *retreats from her,* ECHO *stands looking after her.* ECHO *then turns to the tree. As a gentle breeze picks up and rustles the leaves within the tree,* ECHO *closes her eyes, enjoying the wind with a smile.*

> *The lights black out on* ECHO *while* DIANA *dashes through the halls, coming to a room with the projections of a large fireplace. She goes to the fireplace and moves a secret panel, behind which is a lock. She pulls out a key, which is hanging around her neck and unlocks the door. There is an ornately carved box within it, which* DIANA *quickly takes out. She opens it and relief finally pushes out her worried expressions. We do not*

see what is in the box, but it is obvious that whatever she was looking for was still in the box.

DIANA is about to put the box back, when MANCHESTER approaches DIANA from behind. DIANA cries out in surprise upon hearing him, but turns to discover MANCHESTER.

MANCHESTER. Are you afraid that she's after it?

DIANA. I don't see how she would know that I have it. But—it's just the kind of thing that she would want.

MANCHESTER. Do you truly think Miss Echo is so dangerous?

DIANA. I do not know what to think of her. (*DIANA places the box back into its place.*) In hiding it, I'm protecting her. I'm protecting everyone.

DIANA locks the container and shuts the panel. The lights and images turn off to blackness.

SCENE 3

In the blackness there is a sound in the distance that is difficult to identify at first, very different from the sounds we have heard so far. A modern car suddenly appears on the screens, speeding past and disappearing down the road.

The car leaves the forested area and approaches the Applesong Mansion, the only house within sight. Four individuals enter: TRUMAN NIBLEY. TRUMAN is a handsome man, probably in his late twenties or early thirties. TRUMAN has a confidence and an intelligence that exudes from him. He is neither loud, nor flashy, but watchful and observant. LANE KNIGHT. LANE is a relaxed, fun loving personality, although not always perhaps the brightest bulb in the bunch. What he lacks in sophistication, he more than makes up for in good nature. FELICITY POPE. FELICITY is exceptionally modern, fashionable, and socially aware. She is also intelligent, not in the bookish sense, but in a way that shows street smarts and a quick wit. And finally, to our surprise, we see . . . JACQUELYN. Yet, instead of the Victorian servant's outfit we are accustomed to seeing her in, JACQUELYN is now dressed in modern clothing. Her taste in modern outfits show a sense of the rebellious, with all such necessary accoutrements. The three others look to JACQUELYN. JACQUELYN leads her three companions through the house, holding a candelabra for light. She places the candelabra and lights some kerosene lamps, etc. to bring more light into the room.

FELICITY. This is ace, Jackie! No electricity at all?

JACQUELYN. No electricity at all, except for the servant's quarters. Bit gobsmacked, are you?

LANE. I still think she's feeding us codswallop.

JACQUELYN. Believe what you want, Lane, but in this house, there isn't a single bit of electricity, wireless or otherwise—not a single modern convenience. Charles Dickens could be transported here himself and never know it was the 21st century.

FELICITY. Wicked.

LANE. Oi. This place is giving me the heebee-jeebies.

FELICITY. Come on, Lane, you think it's haunted?

FELICITY spooks LANE from behind, which makes LANE jump.

LANE. Shove off.

JACQUELYN. Haunted—that's not too far off.

LANE. We're trespassing, ain't we?

JACQUELYN. Of course not, Lane. I live here, don't I? I invited you.

LANE. Then why are we here at three o'clock in the bloody morning, Jackie? Crikey, that's a bit subversive, in't?

FELICITY. The better question is what kind of nutter lives in a place like this? Some eccentric billionaire?

LANE. An old lady with a load of cats? A mad scientist?

FELICITY. A vampire?

LANE. All right, I'm already creeped out, aren't I? Shut it about the vampires.

JACQUELYN. Remember the deal. Not too many questions.

FELICITY. You're killing us with curiosity, Jackie.

JACQUELYN. You lot wouldn't believe me, if I told you.

FELICITY. Why not give us a chance?

> TRUMAN *has been taking it all in quietly, walking about the room, observing and investigating everything. The others pick up on this.* JACQUELYN *approaches* TRUMAN, *with a specific and special interest in him. She analyzes his reaction.*

JACQUELYN . You've been quiet, Truman.

FELICITY. Nothing new there.

JACQUELYN. What are your thoughts?

TRUMAN. When we went through those huge gates, past those massive walls, I didn't know what was on the other side. People have been wondering about what's behind these walls for so many years. And here I am, seeing the mystery. Nobody was right, nobody knew what this place was.

FELICITY. Nobody except for you, Jackie.

JACQUELYN. And now you all know as well.

TRUMAN. I felt as if I had stepped into some kind of portal or something. All of those kilometers of forest—a buffer to this house. This house.

LANE. Listen to him, it's like it's his birthday.

TRUMAN. I feel like a time traveler, that we went through some sort of worm hole—like Alice's rabbit hole. I expect to run into the Cheshire Cat or the Queen of Hearts any moment.

FELICITY. I'm expecting more of the likes of the Mad Hatter.

JACQUELYN. Ah, don't expect anybody more than Tweedle Dum and Dee. They're about as much as you lot could comprehend. Except maybe Truman, of course. Truman could meet the Jabberwocky and the creature would have to defer to him.

LANE. Please, just don't let it be a vampire. I didn't like the comments about the vampire.

FELICITY. Why, Jackie? Why does the owner do this?

JACQUELYN. Not too many questions, or we leave right now.

To their uncomfortable surprise, a figure enters the room, with a candle or kerosene lamp of his own. It is MANCHESTER, *in his Victorian clothing.*

MANCHESTER. Your guests will be leaving right now, regardless, Jacquelyn.

JACQUELYN. Father!

FELICITY *and* LANE *almost bolt in surprise upon seeing* MANCHESTER, *but* TRUMAN *puts a calm, steadying hand upon each of them. They remain as* MANCHESTER *hovers around all of them.*

MANCHESTER. I have been wandering the streets, searching for you. You were supposed to come home this morning.

JACQUELYN. I am an adult, Father, you don't need to . . .

MANCHESTER. You dare—you dare bring outsiders here! After all that the Mistress has done for us. This is a most base betrayal of her trust!

JACQUELYN. Trust? She doesn't trust anyone, Father, not even you. Thus the walls, thus the woods, thus the secrets.

MANCHESTER. You shame me, you shame all of us! Do you want to be thrown out of here?

DIANA emerges from the shadows, in her full Victorian splendor, to the surprise of the new arrivals.

DIANA. I think that's exactly what she wants.

DIANA circles them, inspecting them. When DIANA comes to TRUMAN, she takes a special interest in him. TRUMAN's reaction is similar, as the two of them feel an inexplicable connection to each other.

TRUMAN. If we've done something wrong, we're sorry.

DIANA. You should not be the one apologizing, sir.

TRUMAN. Please, don't blame Jackie. She has lived such a secretive life—we kept goading her to let us in on whatever she did. We pressured her. I take full . . .

DIANA. You are very quick to take on someone else's burden. What is your name, stranger?

TRUMAN. Truman. My name is Truman Nibley.

DIANA. Truman.

DIANA comes closer to TRUMAN, continuing her analysis. TRUMAN never breaks his gaze with her, bravely standing for his friends. JACQUELYN is growing increasingly uncomfortable by this situation, not particularly liking the silent connection that has been building up between TRUMAN and DIANA.

JACQUELYN. Miss Diana, I . . .

DIANA. Are you a laborer, Mr. Nibley? Or perhaps a captain of industry?

TRUMAN. Pardon?

JACQUELYN. She wants to know if you have a job.

TRUMAN. Yes. I work as a manager for a department store.

DIANA. What if I told you, I could pay you five times your current wage?

This catches TRUMAN *off guard. He looks to his friends and then back at* DIANA *incredulously.*

TRUMAN. Five times? You—you want to hire me?

DIANA. I am being quite serious. I could either have you arrested for trespassing—or I could offer all of you a job.

They are all shocked.

MANCHESTER. Now, Miss Diana, certainly you wouldn't . . .

DIANA *comes over to* LANE *and* FELICITY, *inspecting their clothing, with more than a little disgust.*

DIANA. Of course you would have to get out of those garish clothes and into something more proper—I do not fathom what they have done to fashion out there.

FELICITY. Miss, er, Miss . . .

DIANA. Applesong. I am Diana Applesong.

FELICITY. I'm not sure we understand what you're suggesting here. Are you truly—?

DIANA. Once I know that you can be trusted, you could visit the outside world every weekend, but you could not mention anything that goes on here. And you are most certainly not to mention any of the outside world's doings to me. All of your food, your lodging and other expenses will be provided here, and you will have full use of the grounds, the stables and the house, when you are not working.

LANE. Did she say five time our current wage? Good value! I'm in!

TRUMAN. What's the catch?

DIANA. Catch?

TRUMAN. You don't know us.

DIANA. But now you know me. And that alone is more than unsettling to me.

TRUMAN. You want to silence us?

DIANA. If you accept, you do not mention what happens here to the outside world. I have a strong sense of—privacy. And I've always been willing to pay handsomely for that privacy. I am being perfectly plain with you.

JACQUELYN. And what about me?

DIANA. What about you, my dear?

JACQUELYN. You won't need me anymore, with so many new servants.

DIANA. Do I not?

JACQUELYN. Let me go.

DIANA. You have always been free to go.

JACQUELYN. You don't need me.

DIANA. I do need you.

JACQUELYN turns away, and swiftly exits.

MANCHESTER. But, Miss Applesong . . .

DIANA. I do not have to justify my decisions to you, Manchester.

MANCHESTER. Yes. Of course. You are in full dress, Miss Applesong. Were you not in bed?

DIANA. There are often thoughts that keep me up at night. Manchester, find our guests some rooms. It is late, we will sort this all out in the morning.

Exit DIANA.

LANE. What. The. Bloody. Hell.

Black out.

SCENE 4

DIANA is sitting before an easel, painting the morning landscape, which painting appears on one of the screens. Gradually she hears a sound in the distance which she can't distinguish. She peers into the distance and is shocked to see a distant airplane on one of the screens.

DIANA. My word . . . *(DIANA stares at the foreign object for a moment.)* No—no. *(DIANA forces herself to look away and bring herself back to her painting. But, in a moment of indecision, DIANA paints the airplane into the skyline of the picture.)* No!

DIANA smears the image of the airplane, and throws down her brush, turning away from the painting. TRUMAN enters the scene and approaches DIANA.)

TRUMAN. Miss Applesong . . .

DIANA. Mr. Nibley, I gave you explicit instructions to get into different clothing!

TRUMAN. I—I am sorry, Miss Applesong.

DIANA. You are never to come to me in such apparel! Do you understand?

TRUMAN. Yes, of course. Immediately.

TRUMAN turns to leave, but DIANA stops him.

DIANA. I—I am sorry, Mr. Nibley. Please, come here.

TRUMAN turns back to her and comes to her. He notices the painting)

TRUMAN. You are a very talented woman, Miss Applesong.

DIANA. I have had a good deal of time to myself, Mr. Nibley. One is able to cultivate many talents that way.

TRUMAN. I see.

DIANA. You have had a lot to think about.

TRUMAN. Yes.

DIANA. And?

TRUMAN. Can we take a walk?

DIANA. Certainly.

TRUMAN and DIANA start walking through the forest or the estate's gardens, which appear on the screens. They are silent at first. TRUMAN then barrels into the conversation.

TRUMAN. When a woman cloisters herself in her own private corner of the world, it means that she is hiding something. Usually not very nice things, not very pleasant things.

DIANA. Well, once you think a thing through, you are direct, Mr. Nibley.

TRUMAN. Then, please, respond with some direct answers.

DIANA. It's more complicated than that—but, yes, you are right. My life isn't very pleasant at all.

TRUMAN. And then, with the wave of your hand, tossing money into our lap, you try buying our silence. Our silence about what?

DIANA. That is none of your concern.

TRUMAN. If you want me to be a part of this household, it certainly is!

DIANA. I did not say that I wanted you to be a part of this household. Not like that. Not like . . .

TRUMAN. Not like an equal, you mean? Not trusted, not a confidante? Just, "Yes, Mum. Thank you, Mum. Whatever you say, Mum."

This creates an uncomfortable silence, as DIANA mulls this over.

DIANA. What a different world you must live in.

TRUMAN. I will not—I repeat, I will not allow myself to become part of something corrupt. If you're some sort of crime lord, or drug dealer, or spy . . .

DIANA. Pardon me?

TRUMAN. I am a man of morals, Miss Applesong. I will not compromise those principles no matter how much money you give me.

DIANA. Mister Nibley, you completely have the wrong idea about me.

TRUMAN. Do I? I hope so.

DIANA. Although I am glad to hear that you are smart enough and—good enough to think of these things. But let me assure you, in protecting myself as I do here, yet I try to harm no one in this world.

TRUMAN. Protect yourself? Are there—are there people who want to hurt you?

DIANA. Not in the sense you are thinking. The world out there is turbulent. A sea of troubles, Mister Nibley. It will swallow you, bruise you, cut you, suck out your breath, draw out your blood . . .

TRUMAN. Miss Applesong . . .

DIANA. This house, Mister Nibley, can be a protection to us. A fortress.

TRUMAN. Do you need help?

DIANA. Well, as you can see, it's a large estate. It takes quite the toll on Manchester and his two children . . .

TRUMAN. Do *you* need help?

DIANA. I—I am a very strong woman. Impervious.

TRUMAN. What has hurt you so much?

> DIANA *stops walking and looks at* TRUMAN, *analyzing him.* TRUMAN *picks up on this immediately and, in a genuine, unrehearsed moment, takes her hand.* TRUMAN *does not let go and* DIANA *does not resist the touch.*

DIANA. Mr. Nibley, I . . .

TRUMAN. I know you don't really know me, Miss Applesong, but—you seem like you're in some sort of trouble. I would like to help.

DIANA. The problem is, Mister Nibley, that I am always the one most capable of helping others.

TRUMAN. But you can't help others while you are locked away here.

DIANA. Exactly.

TRUMAN. I don't know what has happened to you. Maybe you're right—perhaps I can't understand what has happened to you.

DIANA. I do not think you can.

TRUMAN. But you have to understand that I will strive to be worthy of whatever trust you choose to bestow upon me. I'll give you some time to think.

> *TRUMAN gently lets go of her hand, bows—adapting himself to this new world—and exits. DIANA looks after him and then exits in the opposite direction.*

SCENE 5

> *ROMAN and COLIN walk into a room within Diana's mansion. ROMAN checks the door behind them, to see if they're alone, and then quietly closes it. He turns to COLIN and nods.*

COLIN. This better not be another fruitless treasure hunt, Roman.

ROMAN. No, sir—I don't think so.

COLIN. You don't think so?

ROMAN. You can't expect perfection.

COLIN. I would settle for competent.

ROMAN. Records, sir. Not from my father—he's rather careful about that sort of thing. His paper shredder in the servants quarters is well used. But I found some old diaries—from Diana's father.

COLIN. And?

ROMAN. There was still more of it. It was preserved.

COLIN. I knew it.

> *To their surprise, they hear whistling.*

COLIN. Since when did your father whistle?

ROMAN. He doesn't.

To the shock of both of men, LANE enters, dressed in Victorian servants' attire. Unlike the dress of the other men, LANE's clothing has lace at neck and the hands. When LANE enters, there is a stunned silence all around. This was the last thing any of them were expecting.

LANE. Erm, hello.

ROMAN. What in blazes?!

In a sudden, swift movement, ROMAN pulls out a gun and points it at LANE.

LANE. Oi!

ROMAN. Who are you?

LANE. Don't shoot!

ROMAN. Who are you?!

LANE. My name's Lane! Lane Knight!

COLIN lunges toward LANE and, in a trained, swift, and unflinching manner, he grabs LANE's arm, twists it behind his back, and pins him to a wall.

COLIN. *(To ROMAN:)* Put the gun away, you idiot. I'll take care of this. *(To LANE:)* How did you get in here, Mr. Knight?

LANE. It's not what you think! We—we're supposed to be here!

COLIN. We?

Enter TRUMAN, in Victorian clothing. TRUMAN upon seeing his friend in danger, rushes to COLIN and pulls him off and then they scuffle and fight. LANE grabs ROMAN and, as they also fight, LANE takes the gun. We hear someone running towards the room, and MANCHESTER bursts in, horrified by the sight.

MANCHESTER. What is happening here? Mister Nibley, get off Mister Colin! Mister Knight, let go of my son!

LANE. Your son? Well, sir, your son just went all aggro and pulled this bloomin' gun on me!

LANE and TRUMAN let go of COLIN and ROMAN. There is a moment, as they all catch their breath, where they dust off and assess each other. MANCHESTER comes over to LANE and takes the pistol.

MANCHESTER. Roman, why do you have this?

ROMAN. To protect Miss Diana.

MANCHESTER. You know as well as I do that Miss Diana does not need this kind of protection!

Enter JACQUELYN and FELICITY in period clothing.

JACQUELYN. What's all of the commotion?

TRUMAN. It's all under control now. It was a misunderstanding.

COLIN. Manchester, what are these people doing here?!

MANCHESTER. They are guests of Miss Diana. In fact, they are prospective employees.

COLIN. What? After all of this time, she just recklessly . . . ?

MANCHESTER. I understand your concerns, sir. If you and Roman can follow me, I will give you all the details.

MANCHESTER exits the room, with ROMAN following, but before he exits, COLIN grabs TRUMAN by the arm and whispers into his ear:

COLIN. Good work, boy, you caught me by surprise there. Be careful, though. If you ever choose to pick a fight with me again, I'm afraid you have a few handicaps that give me the upper hand.

COLIN lets TRUMAN go. The two of them exchange angry glances, and then COLIN gives a dark smile. TRUMAN turns away, trying to cool off. Exit COLIN.

LANE. Not so much as a "sorry, mate."

FELICITY. Well, boys, that's a way to make a first impression.

Exit FELICITY, LANE, *and* TRUMAN. *The house fades away from the screens, and then is replaced by the gardens, including the beautiful, old tree from previous scenes. Appearing with the gardens is* DIANA. *Enter* COLIN.

DIANA. I am assuming you have met the new help.

COLIN. What do you think you are doing?

DIANA. I am still trying to figure that out myself.

COLIN. You are playing a dangerous game.

DIANA. And who exactly is my opponent in this game?

COLIN. When are you going to trust me?

DIANA. When you earn that trust!

COLIN. *(Pause.)* And these new additions? You trust them, do you?

DIANA. No.

COLIN. Then who? Who do you trust, Diana?

DIANA. Trust is a myth. We are all myths, stories we tell each other to give reassurance and some semblance of comfort against the terrible winds of tragedy that we all know are coming.

COLIN. For once, have some optimism . . .

DIANA. Optimism! What do you or I have to look forward to, Colin?

COLIN. Everything! We have an endless future of possibilities.

DIANA. No. Everything we touch will turn to ash.

Exit DIANA. *Then, in frustration, exit* COLIN.

SCENE 6

We are now in the servant's quarters. The servant's quarters aren't like the rest of the Applesong estate; they are afforded every modern convenience and thus are a distinct contrast to DIANA's *home.* LANE, TRUMAN, *and* JACQUELYN *are in the Common's Room, which appears on the screens, entertainment center complete with a large screen, high definition television, athletic equipment, pool table, video games, etc.* JACQUELYN *is showing* TRUMAN *the channels on the big "screen" television.* LANE *eyes the jacuzzi.*

LANE. Will you take a look at this thing! Miss Applesong may be living in the stone age in this part of the house, but she certainly lets her servants live it up!

FELICITY enters and eyes Lane humorously.

FELICITY. You look like a prat.

LANE. That's not my fault. Why do we have to wear these bloomin' monkey suits?

TRUMAN. Very nice.

LANE. And why does Truman look so much better than I do?

JACQUELYN. Truman always looks better than you do.

LANE tugs at his collar.

LANE. This itches. My collar's tight.

FELICITY. Whinge, whinge, whinge . . .

LANE. And why am I wearing lace?! Truman's doesn't have any lace!

Lane plops on a bean bag. FELICITY *rounds up and forms the balls on the pool table on one of the screens. She grabs a stick and breaks the formation.*

FELICITY. Never thought I would be a servant. I was going to go corporate, you know. Be a liberated woman and all that rot. Now I'm going to be—wait. Don't tell me I'm going to be changing chamber pots! Tell me that they have indoor plumbing!

LANE. *(Tugging at the lace)* I'm wearing lace. Blimey, I can't believe I'm wearing lace!

JACQUELYN notices TRUMAN sitting in a corner. She walks and sits next to him. She takes his hand, which he withdraws.

JACQUELYN. Are you all right?

TRUMAN. We're losing our freedom, aren't we? If we take this job, our lives will revolve around this place. And who knows what kind of life that will be?

JACQUELYN. Believe me, it's not usually that dramatic.

TRUMAN. That's the first time that I've ever been in the same room with a live gun. I was all set to join up, especially after . . .

JACQUELYN. After what?

TRUMAN. Especially after talking to Miss Applesong. But—we really don't know what we're getting into.

FELICITY. Yes, but isn't it worth whatever it is? We're set. Is that a loss of freedom or did we just escape the vicious system out there.

JACQUELYN. Diana's been good to my family.

TRUMAN. So if it is so good, Jackie, why do you want to leave?

JACQUELYN. Maybe I'm just a bit of a drama queen.

TRUMAN. Be straight with us, Jackie. If you can just walk out the door anytime and never come back, why don't you?

JACQUELYN. *(Pause)* I'm sorry, mates. I should have never brought you here. Father just texted me. He wants us back at the house. There's something important going on.

They all "travel" to the house, as the screens change to the main building. In the room DIANA, COLIN, ROMAN, and MAN-CHESTER are already situated.

MANCHESTER. We have everyone now, Mum.

DIANA. I heard there were dramatic happenings this morning, Truman.

TRUMAN. Our most sincere apologies, Miss Applesong.

DIANA. It is probably best to establish a few things. Colin and his daughter Echo are the only two others who know of my life here. They are welcome at any time and are to be treated as guests, as long as they adhere to same rules and conventions peculiar to the household. *(To COLIN:)* And that doesn't include attacking the hired help.

COLIN. My sincerest apologies. Hopefully, we can put all of that unpleasantness behind us.

DIANA. You are to serve Mister Colin and Miss Echo as you serve me.

TRUMAN. I haven't made up my mind to serve anyone yet.

DIANA. I—I am sorry, Truman. I thought after our—discussion last night . . .

TRUMAN. We are still undecided.

FELICITY. Not all of us are undecided. If it is still all right, Lane and I have made our own decisions.

DIANA. Then you two are staying?

FELICITY. Yes, Mum.

LANE. Biting my arm off, Miss Applesong. *(DIANA looks confused by the statement.)* Uh, roaring to go—hunky dory—really excited to be here, Mum!

DIANA. I see. *(It is evident that DIANA is less concerned about FELICITY and LANE, as she focuses on TRUMAN again. She comes to him and tries to engage his eyes, which TRUMAN averts.)* Your friends see the wisdom in accepting my offer, Truman. Why do you delay?

COLIN. Frankly, Diana, I see no point in trying to persuade any of them to stay.

LANE. Who's he to speak against us? He doesn't know us from Adam.

COLIN. To the contrary, I do. Do you even realize whose house you have come under, Mister Knight? Do you realize the power of those who stand before you?

FELICITY. Now aren't we high and mighty?

COLIN. High, yes. Mighty, yes.

FELICITY. Just because Miss Applesong wants to live hundreds of years ago, mate, it doesn't mean you ought to. We're all equals here.

COLIN. Miss Pope, I am certain that you feel such, and I commend your sense of self worth—but there is much more going on here than you understand.

DIANA. I wish to keep them here, Colin.

COLIN. Do you think they would be able to truly bear up under the truth of their situation here? Do you think they could understand?

TRUMAN. Understand what?

DIANA looks at TRUMAN. She is about to confide something, before COLIN interrupts.

COLIN. Don't set yourself up for another heart break, Diana.

FELICITY. Miss, I don't understand what this bloke is talking about, but you'll find us bright and capable. You can rely on us.

COLIN. She cannot rely on you! You don't understand, she can't rely on anyone! Only I can help her. I am the only one in the world who knows what her life means.

For the first time in this scene JACQUELYN approaches DIANA. Wordlessly she takes DIANA's hands, and looks her in the eyes. A silent understanding happens between the two of them, and DIANA simply nods.

DIANA. Thank you, Jacquelyn. (*Pause. She then turns to MANCHES-TER*) Manchester, can you fetch Roman's pistol to your daughter?

LANE. Not the gun again!

MANCHESTER obeys and hands JACQUELYN the gun, which to this point he had kept in his own safe keeping.

COLIN. Surely, Diana, you don't mean to . . .

LANE. Why are we getting out the gun again?!

DIANA. Do not worry, Mister Knight, none of you are in danger.

FELICITY. I must say, Miss Applesong, this is all becoming—alarming.

JACQUELYN inspects the gun and makes sure everything is in order.

DIANA. It will be clear soon. Are you ready, Jacquelyn?

JACQUELYN nods.

LANE. I'm still wondering why we have a bloomin' pistol in the room!

DIANA makes a signal, at which JACQUELYN raises the gun on COLIN. COLIN looks legitimately shocked.

COLIN. Wait!

TRUMAN. Jackie, no!

TRUMAN tries to stop JACQUELYN, but is unable to get to her before she fires the gun at COLIN. COLIN is shot, slams into a wall, and then slumps to the ground.

DIANA. Now shoot me, Jacquelyn.

FELICITY. What?!

JACQUELYN now fires at DIANA and she, too, is knocked to the ground by the force of the bullet. There is a stunned silence.

TRUMAN. Jackie, what have you done?

COLIN slowly rises from where he fell. While TRUMAN, LANE, and FELICITY are flabbergasted, MANCHERSTER and ROMAN don't seem particularly surprised. JACQUELYN smirks at COLIN.

COLIN. I'll wager you enjoyed that.

JACQUELYN. You better believe it.

COLIN notices the bullet hole in his jacket.

COLIN. Blazes, girl, do you know how much this jacket cost? A wretched hole right in the breast.

Again, to everyone's shock, DIANA rises as well.

DIANA. Thank you, Jacquelyn.

DIANA stoops down and picks what remains of the bullet, which looks as if it slammed against something it could not penetrate—which is exactly the case. There is a stunned silence as the three newcomers let what just occurred sink in.

LANE. Somebody better tell me what just went on there.

TRUMAN. Haven't you figured it out yet, Lane? It's brilliant.

FELICITY. What's brilliant?

TRUMAN. They can't die. Miss Applesong and Mister Colin are immortals.

Blackout.

SCENE 7

DIANA is retreating from COLIN, the gardens appearing on the screens.

COLIN. So what possible good do you see coming from that shambolic fiasco?

DIANA. I am not accountable to you, Colin.

COLIN. After that episode, you certainly are! Or did you not think that it was not only your cover you were blowing off there?

DIANA finally stops and faces COLIN.

DIANA. How was I supposed to know that Jacquelyn would shoot you, too?

COLIN. So what is it about these people—these children—what is it about them that caused you to suddenly confide in them after two hundred years of secrecy?

DIANA. Call it a—gut feeling.

COLIN. A gut feeling? A gut feeling! Have you gone absolutely gormless?

Enter TRUMAN, running after them.

TRUMAN. Miss Applesong—Miss Applesong!

TRUMAN catches up to them, breathing heavily from the run.

TRUMAN. That—oh—whew—that was brilliant! Cracking brilliant!

COLIN. Easily pleased, are we, Mr. Nibley?

TRUMAN. Easily pleased? You may be accustomed to that sort of thing, but for me—well, this rearranges my whole view on the world.

COLIN. Mr. Nibley, you've just caught a glimpse of something you will never be able to understand. Enjoy puzzling about it for the rest of your life.

TRUMAN. And you're not just pulling our leg? They weren't blanks or a trick gun or some rot like that?

COLIN. I could try shooting you with it, if you're not convinced.

TRUMAN. No, no, that won't be necessary. This is—this is monumental. History making.

DIANA. It is certainly not history making, Mr. Nibley. For there will be no record of it. No one must know.

TRUMAN. Yes, yes, of course. Why, you would be—I don't know, a spectacle, a twisted kind of celebrity. Scientists, governments—they would all want to get a gander at you. An ounce of your blood would go for millions of pounds.

DIANA. Then you see our dilemma.

TRUMAN. I certainly see it. I can vouch for all of us, I think. This secret will never leave this house.

COLIN. It better not, Mr. Nibley, for if it is let out, then not even the hounds of hell will be more fearsome to you than my retribution.

DIANA. Colin . . .

COLIN. I am serious. Diana, this thing you have done better not come back and bite us.

TRUMAN. He has a point, Miss Applesong. There is no real reason for you trust us. If we could get the world to believe us, we could utterly ruin the sanctuary you have built here and, well—I am just as puzzled as Mr. Colin is that you took this leap into the dark. (*DIANA looks at* TRUMAN *with an odd mixture of affection and fear.*) Miss Applesong?

DIANA. I am sorry, Truman. Certain things are just dawning on me.

TRUMAN. I am not sure if I understand.

DIANA. After so many years, I consider myself a good judge of character. All of you passed my scrutiny. Especially you, Mr. Nibley.

TRUMAN. I hope to be able to live up to that trust.

DIANA. Now I didn't say trust . . .

TRUMAN. In either case, I am at your service, now and always.

DIANA. Not always, Mr. Nibley. Only a handful of people among the entire world even have a grasp as to what that word means. But if you can leave Colin and I alone for a moment, I am sure that there is much he wants to discuss with me.

TRUMAN. Yes, Miss.

Exit TRUMAN.

COLIN. What is it, Diana? What is it about them that has brought out this trust so quickly?

DIANA. I already said it is not trust . . .

COLIN. Trust! What else can you call this reckless abandon? It is a trust that not even I, after hundreds of years of friendship, have ever been able to fully gain.

DIANA. You keep secrets from me, Colin.

COLIN. Ridiculous.

DIANA. I recognize a secret. For I know what it's like to keep a secret.

COLIN. I know you. Who else knows you like I do?

DIANA. And yet after such a long time, I feel like I don't know you, Colin.

COLIN. Of course you know me.

DIANA. Oh, yes, I know the flippancies, the subtleties, the blatancies. I know the flirtations, the false emotions. The cunning, the planning, the manipulation . . .

COLIN. Now you are being cruel and unfair—

DIANA. Yes, I know your personality. But I was surprised to realize recently how little I know *about* you.

COLIN. You know everything there is to know about me. You are my dearest friend.

DIANA. How old are you?

COLIN. What?

DIANA. How old are you?

COLIN. You know how old I am.

On the screens, we start to see glimpses of COLIN's *and* DIANA's *past history with each other, including when she was a child, while he looks exactly as he does now.*

DIANA. No, I don't. I asked soon after I discovered we shared the same condition, but you changed the subject. I never asked you again after that.

COLIN. Three hundred years old.

DIANA. When I was a child, you told me stories about ancient Rome.

COLIN. They were just stories. I made them up. That's natural when telling stories to a child.

DIANA. How old are you?

COLIN. I am telling you the truth.

DIANA. After living for thousands of years, a man can accumulate a whole world's history of secrets.

COLIN. I haven't lived for thousands of years! I swear to you, this coming October I will be three hundred and nine years old. *(At this COLIN comes close to DIANA, intimately touching her face, putting his hand around her waist, bringing his body closer and closer to DIANA's, which is also highlighted by the screens. This surprises DIANA, but she doesn't move.)* And do you know why I kept my age from you all that time ago?

DIANA. Why?

COLIN. I thought you might think you were too young for me. For I loved you even then.

DIANA *retreats from this personal position of vulnerability, and creates some distance between her and COLIN. The images of their touches on the screen stop and revert back to the garden.*

DIANA. I think it is time for you to leave.

COLIN. You say that I kept a secret from you, Diana? Well, there it is. There is my deep, dark secret.

DIANA. Leave.

COLIN. Diana, did you hear what I said?

DIANA. You are not capable of love.

COLIN. I have lived with this love longer than any man that walks the earth has been alive. Nations have risen and fallen, yet my love has remained constant. And yet again and again, you lock me out.

DIANA. I lock you out for your protection, as much as mine.

COLIN. I am not as fragile as all that. Neither of us is what one would call fragile.

DIANA. I tell myself that lie as well. But I am finally starting to disbelieve it.

DIANA exits. Then COLIN exits.

SCENE 8

ECHO pulls FELICITY into the house, nearly bowling over LANE, who looks at them bewildered, shrugs, and then exits. ECHO grips FELICITY by the hands as if she were some preteen BFF. ECHO has dropped some of the period formality and acts enthusiastically modern with this new member of the inner circle.

ECHO. This is smashing!

FELICITY. What is?

ECHO. Well, you of course! To see Diana actually let other people onto her secret! It's marvelous!

FELICITY. Yeah, it's pretty cool. But, Miss Echo, I've heard a bit about you these last few weeks and I've been wondering—Colin is your Dad, yeah?

ECHO. Yeah.

FELICITY. Then—then are you like them, yeah?

ECHO. Immortal? No, not exactly. My Mum wasn't like my Dad. She was mortal. So you could say I'm a bit of a half breed. Half mortal, half immortal. I'll live for a bleedin' long time, but I'll eventually die.

FELICITY. If you don't mind me asking . . .

ECHO. I don't mind you asking.

FELICITY. How long will you live?

ECHO. From what Dad has told me, about five hundred years seems to be the average.

FELICITY. And how old are you now?

ECHO. I was born in 1895.

FELICITY. Wicked.

ECHO. Yeah. Wicked.

FELICITY. Staying young like that—you must've had some fun times.

Images of FELICITY's *exciting life through the years appear on the screens.*

ECHO. The twenties took the biscuit. I still get out my flapper dresses every once in a while when I go dancing.

ECHO *hikes up her skirts and starts dancing the Charleston.*

FELICITY. That's blinding brilliant!

ECHO. People get a kick out of them, asking me where I got such authentic looking costumes. I just tell them that I'm a time traveler.

FELICITY. You've lived through so much. Do you—do you ever get tired of it? Tired of life?

ECHO. Hell no! I aim to live it up. I'm out there in the world, enjoying every last drop of it until I fall dead dancing a few hundred years from now.

FELICITY. And Mr. Colin?

The images on the screens fade away.

ECHO. My father worked hard to get his immortality, so I suppose he has to live with his own consequences.

FELICITY. What do you mean? Wasn't he born with it?

ECHO. Oh, that was just was a passing saying. Don't pay attention to it.

FELICITY. No, what did you mean?

ECHO. I said ignore it.

FELICITY. *(Pause.)* All right. I—I'll get Miss Applesong for you.

DIANA enters the room.

DIANA. No need, Miss Felicity, I am right here. Would you excuse us?

FELICITY. Yes, Mum.

FELICITY exits. ECHO, in a whirl of energy, laughs and grabs DIANA by the hands, twirling her.

ECHO. I'm so proud of you!

DIANA. Echo!

ECHO. I wouldn't have guessed in a hundred years! I thought I had you sorted, but you're still full of surprises, you stuffy old thing! (*Breaking from the twirl, they both flop onto one of the couches, ECHO laughing. After catching her breath, to her own surprise, DIANA starts laughing as well. ECHO punches her lightly on the shoulder.*) There you go!

DIANA. There I go!

ECHO. Progress!

DIANA. Yes, I suppose. Progress!

ECHO. You must let me take you shopping.

DIANA. Pardon me?

ECHO. I know all the best shops, and I know you've been hoarding all that money! We'll have a ball!

DIANA stands, the mirth of the moment suddenly gone.

DIANA. I think you have misunderstood, Echo. I have only added to the staff.

ECHO stands, becoming serious as well, addressing DIANA in earnest.

ECHO. Diana, you have a chance to start fresh here. This could be a kind of gateway into a whole new life.

DIANA. I have led too many lives already.

ECHO. Diana, I know you don't always trust me. Do you think I don't see that? But I worry about you, I think about you constantly.

DIANA. There is no need. I am best left forgotten.

ECHO. No! There's marvelous things out there, Diana, marvelous joys. Metal vehicles that fly so fast in the air . . .

DIANA. No . . .

ECHO. Devices that can take your portrait in a matter of seconds . . .

DIANA. I do not want to hear it . . .

ECHO. Boxes that people can instantaneously write to each other through from thousands of miles apart!

DIANA. Stop!

ECHO. There is so much you are missing. So much miraculous life that you are missing!

> ECHO *grips* DIANA *by the hands. They lock eyes and for a moment, just a moment, it looks like that* ECHO *may have gotten through to her. But almost as soon as that hope fired up in* DIANA*'s eyes, it is just as quickly extinguished.*

DIANA. I am so tired, Echo.

> TRUMAN *enters the room with* COLIN *following.* ECHO *and* COLIN *exchange uneasy glances.*

ECHO. Father.

COLIN. Daughter.

> TRUMAN *and* DIANA *are riveted on each other, hardly noticing* COLIN *and* ECHO *anymore.*

TRUMAN. Mister Colin insisted on seeing you immediately, Mum.

DIANA. Oh, don't call me "Mum," Truman. Coming from you, it makes me sound old.

TRUMAN. Miss Applesong then?

DIANA. Diana.

TRUMAN. *(With a genuine smile.)* Diana.

COLIN. My oh my. It takes me hundreds of years to reach that kind of intimacy and Mr. Nibley reaches it in little over two months.

The two break from their conversation, putting on a sense of formality.

DIANA. You may leave now, Truman.

TRUMAN. Yes, Diana.

TRUMAN darts COLIN a triumphant look before he exits. DIANA looks after him, wistfully. COLIN clears his throat. DIANA looks back, startled.

COLIN. Is this why I am neglected? Is *he* why I am neglected?

DIANA. He has become a—friend.

COLIN. I thought you didn't want friends. I thought you didn't want companionship. I thought you didn't want emotion. Isn't that what this farce is all about?!

DIANA. Colin, I am not sure you are seeing the issues clearly . . .

COLIN. After these centuries of devotion, of loyalty, of love that I have given to you, I am rebuffed again and again! Then this young whelp of a boy comes and steals you from me!

DIANA. He hasn't stolen me. You misunderstand. I couldn't . . .

ECHO. Why couldn't you, Diana? When you were looking after that young man—I haven't seen that kind of light in your eyes for over a hundred years.

DIANA. You know my answer to that, Echo.

ECHO. Oh, yes, yes! You'll lose him, you'll lose him! He will eventually die! Wo, Wo, unto Diana! She might actually feel pain!

DIANA. Do not mock me.

ECHO. You don't think I've known loss, Diana? You don't think I've seen loved ones wilt and die in my hand like crushed lilacs?

COLIN. Don't interfere, Echo!

ECHO. But I will live my life, however long God wills that life to be! I will dance and sing and celebrate it to the grave!

DIANA. But you will eventually reach that grave, Echo. That's the difference between you and me. I will never reach the other side. I will go on forever, losing and losing and never regaining.

ECHO. Then don't focus so much on the old lives—live now! Re-create yourself, give yourself a new birth!

COLIN. No, that is not what she wants, Echo. Not even you understand. *(Back to DIANA)* But I understand, Diana. I know the life you live. Please. Please, I am begging you. For the first time in this eternal parade of years see me for what I really am.

DIANA. And what is that?

COLIN. Your salvation.

DIANA. *(Pause.)* I have very much enjoyed this visit. You are always welcome. But now it is time for both of you to leave. Manchester will see you out.

> *DIANA exits. There is uncomfortable moment between ECHO and COLIN. ECHO finally breaks the silence after they are sure that DIANA can't hear them.*

ECHO. It looks as if you're not going to get your way with her, Father.

COLIN. And what was it you were trying to do in there?

ECHO. Playing my part, of course. If I start being too eager for your cause, then she'll connect us too closely.

COLIN. Well, I think you're playing your part a little too convincingly.

ECHO. You're being an ass, Father. She's obviously not taking the bait. You must make for yourself a new queen. And that all depends on . . .

COLIN. I wanted her.

ECHO. And it appears you can't have her. So focus on the job. You emailed me that Roman had found something.

COLIN. Yes, he has. Her father's diaries. We were certainly right.

ECHO. It's there then?

COLIN. You can become immortal, Echo. Isn't that what you wanted? You can join our Pantheon. Oh, by the way, Roman is under the impression that in exchange for his help, that he will also partake and in doing so he will become the kind of lover that is worthy of you.

ECHO. Oh, Father, don't tell me you have been indulging his sick fancies. The boy's a beast.

COLIN. He's proven useful. Next time that you see him, play along. Chat him up a bit. *(Pause.)* I haven't given up on her yet.

ECHO. When we find what we're looking for, you can create someone who is much more willing.

COLIN. I do not lie to her when I say that I love her, Echo.

> ECHO *looks over at her father. In a rare moment of affection between the two of them,* ECHO *reaches out and holds her father's hand. He doesn't let go, but rather grips it tightly. Blackout.*

SCENE 9

> DIANA *is onstage, playing the piano forte, organ, or harpsichord. The instrument appears on one of the screens as* DIANA *interacts with it. After all these centuries, she has become quite an expert. The first piece she plays is quite somber. After a moment, she stops.*

DIANA. Oh dear. I am dreadfully depressing.

> DIANA *starts another piece, this one more classically upbeat. However, as* DIANA *plays, the fast nature of the piece brings out more frustration and anger from her than anything else. She plays furiously until she crashes down on the keys and*

screams. She sits there, crying passionately until TRUMAN enters.

TRUMAN. Diana, Manchester wanted to know whether you would prefer rice or potatoes or . . . *(Seeing her distress:)* Diana, are you all right?

DIANA stands and retreats a bit, trying to mask her tears.

DIANA. Quite fine, thank you.

TRUMAN. Right then.

TRUMAN turns to exit, but then reconsiders. He turns back.

TRUMAN. Diana, if you need a friend . . . I can be a friend.

DIANA. A friend. It's a commodity I haven't been able to afford for many, many years.

TRUMAN. It's a standing offer, if you should ever need it.

TRUMAN, again, turns to leave. DIANA stops him.

DIANA. Truman . . .

TRUMAN. Yes, Diana?

DIANA. I—why are you here? Is it the money?

TRUMAN. If I thought I would be miserable here, no amount of money would have made me stay here. And if I felt my place was truly here, no lack of money could drive me away.

DIANA. Then what convinced you? Why would you choose to come into this prison?

TRUMAN. I wanted to help you.

DIANA. Help me? A speeding train couldn't crush me, a famine couldn't starve me, the most potent poison couldn't stop my breath, a dagger made of diamonds couldn't pierce me . . .

TRUMAN. You—you did all those things to yourself?

DIANA, who has been looking away from TRUMAN this whole time, now turns towards him. She hesitates. She then sits, and

*pats the cushion next to her, inviting Truman to join her. He
does so. She looks at him gravely, searchingly, and then finally
decides to fully open up to him.*

DIANA. I have lived too long already. *(Glimpses from the stories that
DIANA is telling about her life appear on the screens as she tells it.)*
Truman, I was born in 1705. My parents doted on me—they loved
me. But they were not like me. I was able to marry a fine man. His
name was Frederick and I loved him dearly. We had twelve children.

TRUMAN. Twelve children!

DIANA. I am very fond of children. I loved each of them fiercely. Oh,
and we had children into our sixties. The few doctors we entrusted
with the secret were baffled.

TRUMAN. Uh—I know this may be an indelicate question coming
from the eighteenth and nineteenth centuries, as you do . . .

DIANA. You may ask it.

TRUMAN. Women, they only have a certain amount of eggs . . .

DIANA. Mine, like the rest of my body, regenerate.

TRUMAN. Amazing! Well—I mean—I hope I'm not being too prying . . .

DIANA. You are not. Once I realized that—as I'm sure you can imagine,
it had its advantages and disadvantages.

TRUMAN. But don't you have any children that are like Echo? If Colin
fathers such half immortals, then shouldn't you . . . ?

DIANA. Theoretically. But even with Colin it is rare. I was never lucky
enough to have such children who could—tarry with me a little
longer.

TRUMAN. But—but didn't anyone notice?

DIANA. Let us just say that we became very good at being secretive.
When we went out into public, he often introduced me as his daughter—then after many more years, his granddaughter. But he was my
husband. The man I loved and continued to love and still love to
this day.

TRUMAN. Diana—I—I can't even fathom your loss.

DIANA. Do you know how many death beds I have been to?

TRUMAN. Too many.

DIANA. After the death of my second husband Victor and all our children through him, I created this place and have remained in the year 1860 ever since, not daring to let anyone onto the grounds except Colin and Echo and the descendants of my servants. Until you three, that is.

TRUMAN. Why did you let us in?

DIANA. I am not sure if I completely know the answer to that myself.

TRUMAN. Diana. I—I'm not a great man. I haven't done anything to distinguish myself. I don't know what I can offer to a two hundred year old immortal that could be of any use to her, except that I believe I have a good heart and that I can be a good friend. If that's of any use to you . . .

DIANA. It is of infinite use to me.

TRUMAN. Then let age spot my skin, and let hair go white, and yet I will be your servant still. And your friend.

DIANA. Truman—I feel so . . . (DIANA *stands and comes closer and closer to* TRUMAN, *appearing as if she may embrace him. However, at the last moment she turns away.*) I can't do this—not again.

DIANA *dashes out of the room, desperately trying to restrain her emotion.*

TRUMAN. Diana!

DIANA *moves out of the "house," which disappears from the screens and arrives outside at the tree, when* TRUMAN *has caught up with her. He is struggling for air, as* DIANA *is faster and fitter than he is, being immortal.*

DIANA. You will die!

TRUMAN. Yes, I will. I can't stop that.

DIANA. My life is like the rings of this tree, Truman! Expanding and expanding and never terminating!

TRUMAN

DIANA! Please, let us help you. Let me help you!

DIANA. Colin can help me. He understands, I will send for him right now.

> *TRUMAN comes very close to DIANA. She does not pull away.*

TRUMAN. If I were I made of stone or steel, perhaps then I could be immortal, too.

DIANA. And if I were made of flesh, then perhaps I could die happy with you. But that is not how it is.

> *TRUMAN slowly comes closer to DIANA. She walks away leaning against the tree. TRUMAN gently turns her to face him. She finally meets his gaze again. Hesitantly, carefully, TRUMAN goes in to try and kiss her. It appears that DIANA may turn away. However, at the last moment, she accepts the gentle kiss.*

TRUMAN. My standing offer.

> *DIANA hesitates, but then kisses TRUMAN back, hesitantly. Then again. Then they continue to kiss passionately. Blackout.*

Act Two

SCENE 1

ROMAN is hovering behind MANCHESTER in the servants quarters, as MANCHESTER is getting ready for the day: putting on his period clothing, tying his cravat, etc.

ROMAN. Father, do you trust me?

MANCHESTER. Of course I do.

ROMAN. I don't believe you do.

MANCHESTER. You've always been my most reliable child. I wish that Jacquelyn would follow your example. What is wrong, Roman?

ROMAN. I know you still keep things from me.

MANCHESTER. Now, Roman, you know that we have a great responsibility to keep Miss Diana and her privacy safe.

ROMAN. That has always been my top priority. How often do I have to prove that to you?

MANCHESTER looks at ROMAN searchingly.

MANCHESTER. You're right. Someday I will be gone. Jacquelyn won't stick around for much longer . . . we both know that. You'll be the one to inherit these responsibilities.

ROMAN. Father?

MANCHESTER. I have something to discuss with you.

The lights black out on them and DIANA appears, sitting at the dining table, with TRUMAN, LANE, and FELICITY serving her.

DIANA. Felicity, Lane, can you leave Truman and me alone for a moment?

FELICITY. Yes, Mum.

LANE and FELICITY exit.

DIANA. Sit with me, Truman.

TRUMAN. I thought—well, I didn't think that was quite up to protocol.

DIANA. No. It isn't.

TRUMAN. And you're all right with that?

DIANA. Quite all right. There's a lot about us that's not—up to protocol. (*TRUMAN sits at the table with DIANA.*) Please, have some food. It appears Manchester outdid himself tonight.

They both eat.

TRUMAN. Well then.

DIANA. Well then.

TRUMAN. What does this mean?

DIANA. Does it have to mean something?

TRUMAN. It would appear so.

DIANA. I found that I am uncomfortable getting involved with the hired help, after all.

TRUMAN. I told you that I am staying.

DIANA. Of course you are. Just not as my servant. From here on out, you are my guest. My friend. The others will be able to pick up the workload without you.

TRUMAN. Oh.

DIANA. Why do you seem disappointed?

TRUMAN. I liked helping you.

DIANA. I—hm. I have been debating about an item, Truman. I am thinking about selling the estate. I could get a good deal of money for it.

TRUMAN. Yes, you could. But, Diana, I thought this was your fortress. Your protection.

DIANA. I am thinking about buying a new house. Something simpler. Less oppressive. I was thinking we would raise our children there.

TRUMAN chokes on his drink.

TRUMAN. Our—our children?

DIANA. You want to be a father, don't you?

TRUMAN. Well, yes, of course.

DIANA. Good. We would have had issues, if you didn't.

TRUMAN. Erm . . .

DIANA. You don't like the idea of a new home?

TRUMAN. Oh, no, that sounds splendid, but—Diana, was that a proposal?

DIANA. Of course not.

TRUMAN. All right then.

DIANA. That is your job.

TRUMAN. Oh.

    Pause.

DIANA. So?

TRUMAN. So what?

DIANA. Are you going to ask me?

TRUMAN. Well, yes. *(Pause. TRUMAN then, in shock, realizes:)* Oh, you mean now.

DIANA. You are darling when you're flustered.

TRUMAN. You caught me off guard! Well, at least give me a moment to gather my wits.

    TRUMAN gathers his composure. Gaining the proper serious-ness, he kneels besides DIANA, taking her hand.

TRUMAN. Diana, will you . . .

DIANA. Yes!

    TRUMAN stands, flustered again.

TRUMAN. Are you at least going to let me ask the bloody question?!

DIANA. Excuse me. Of course.

TRUMAN kneels again. This time he is able to ask in a deeply sincere way.

TRUMAN. Diana, I am just a man. I am common. Yet what I am is yours. Will you descend down enough to carry me up to your high place and be my wife?

DIANA brings TRUMAN to his feet.

DIANA. Truman, you have wings to fly wherever you could possibly want to be. For as long as life unites us, I am yours.

They kiss. After the kiss, DIANA seems suddenly sad and distant.

TRUMAN. What's wrong?

DIANA. Why would something be wrong?

TRUMAN. Are you happy, Diana?

DIANA. As happy as one like me can hope to be.

TRUMAN embraces DIANA tightly, which she gladly welcomes. Time passes upon the screens, changing from one season to the next and the two dance as if they are caught up in the current of time, when suddenly they are separated and DIANA disappears. COLIN enters to the bewildered TRUMAN, who is now suddenly in the servant's quarters.

COLIN. I'm surprised to find you here, Truman. I thought you had moved up in the world.

TRUMAN. I'll move into the house after the wedding.

COLIN. Quite the social climber! From a store manager, to a valued servant, to a wealthy immortal's fiancée!

TRUMAN. Well, with how things are going, we might as well be friends, shouldn't we?

COLIN. No. I don't think so.

TRUMAN. Now let's not go down that . . .

COLIN. I know you mean well, but you're going to break her heart, Truman.

TRUMAN. Look, mate, she's happy. What's the use in arguing that?

COLIN. For how long?

TRUMAN. Happiness needs to be seized when it is presented to us.

COLIN. Yes, live in the moment! Carpe Deum, Invictus, and every other self indulgent, reckless dream philosophy that tries to abandon obligation in this life!

TRUMAN. Would you prefer her to be cut off from all happiness?

COLIN. I would prefer that you weren't so selfish.

TRUMAN. I am not being selfish!

COLIN. After you have gone to the grave eating, drinking and having been very merry with Diana, she will have to pick up the shards of her heart once more and start over.

TRUMAN. I'm not going for your ruse, Colin.

COLIN. Consider Diana instead of your own feelings. Two immortals live in this world, one a man and another woman. Like Adam and Eve, God made her and I to be each other's help meets. I know that I am not an ideal man—but I will last.

TRUMAN. I may die, but that doesn't mean that my love is any less . . .

COLIN. I hope that this love you profess for Diana is real and that you will not bind her into another inevitable tragedy, another inevitable loss.

TRUMAN. You just want her for yourself.

COLIN. I want her to be happy. I think, because of circumstances, I am more equipped to give her that.

TRUMAN. She doesn't love you.

COLIN. She didn't let herself love me. But perhaps with the help that you've been in her life, perhaps she's now prepared to love again.

TRUMAN. Pardon me if I doubt your sincerity.

COLIN. Look me in the eyes.

TRUMAN. Pardon?

COLIN. Look me in the eyes.

> *COLIN stares into TRUMAN's eyes. With a softness and vulnerability he rarely shows, COLIN delivers the following:*

COLIN. Truman, I am not the ideal man, as Diana seems to think you are—but she isn't the only one who has known grief, she isn't the only one who has known—immense loss. She alone has brought me out of the dark, miasmic hell of my long life and shown me that eternity can be a blessing and not a curse. Without her, I am a demon of perdition. With her, these long corridors have finally become bright. *(Pause.)* Am I lying to you, Truman?

TRUMAN. No.

COLIN. Then I leave the rest to you and Diana. If you wish to banish me from heaven, do it soon. For if you marry her, I will not have the heart to ever come here again.

> *COLIN exits. Then TRUMAN, thoughtful, also exits.*

SCENE 2

> *ECHO is outside of a dressing room, which appears on one of the screens, looking through a rack of clothes. DIANA's voice comes through the door.*

DIANA. You go out in public like this?!

ECHO. Come now, by today's standards that is absolutely Puritanical!

DIANA. I feel so exposed . . .

ECHO. Let me see you.

> *The dressing room door opens and DIANA steps out, dressed to the nines in modern, very fashionable clothing. She looks stunning. ECHO inspects her.*

ECHO. It's a start. Now that hair.

DIANA. My hair?

ECHO. It's too late to back out now, Diana. I'm going to make you a
modern woman.

> *They exit. Modern music plays as we see a montage of DIANA
> and ECHO interacting with the modern world, which appear
> on the screens. DIANA looks around in wide eyed marvel at
> the modern people on the streets and is often shocked by the
> extreme styles and clothing exhibited. She shrieks when a car
> speeds by her while she is on the curb. ECHO calms her and
> laughs at her innocence. In a store window DIANA stares at a
> television in wonder. DIANA asks ECHO what the strange little
> devices people keep putting to their ears and texting on are.
> We see DIANA and ECHO setting up a social network page on
> ECHO's laptop, but are a bit consternated when it asks her age.
> ECHO, with some coercing of a reluctant DIANA, brings DIANA
> into a stylist's. [This scene is optional:] DIANA gets her hair cut
> at a stylist's to a short, flattering length. She argues with the
> STYLIST and ECHO about how short to make it, as the STYL-
> IST and ECHO keep wanting to make it shorter and shorter,
> while Diana insists to keep it as long as possible. Eventually
> DIANA gives the STYLIST the go ahead and, to DIANA's hor-
> ror, DIANA she sees her own hair fall to the floor in long locks.
> We are revealed DIANA with a completely new, quite modern,
> and stylish hair style, as she and ECHO walk out of the styl-
> ist's. DIANA tugs at her hair, partially mourning its sudden loss,
> while also sensing something new and exciting is happening to
> her. ECHO continues to drag DIANA in and out of more shops
> as their shopping spree rockets on. We see DIANA is several
> outfits, some of them outlandish and wild and verging on the
> indecent, which, despite ECHO's interest in them, DIANA flatly
> rejects, sometimes pulling at the clothing to cover more skin.
> We begin to see DIANA becoming more confident in her deci-
> sions, not allowing ECHO to manage her wardrobe, and blends*

the modern with a retro-Victorian style. What comes of it is quite a beautiful blend of the classic and the fashionable, as DIANA *finds clothing that uniquely exhibits and expresses her.* ECHO *looks on her final choice as the music fades:*

ECHO. Well, it's not what I would have chosen . . .

DIANA. But?

ECHO. But it suits you.

SCENE 3

TRUMAN, *still in Victorian clothing, is laying on his back looking up at the stars, which appear on the screens.* JACQUELYN, *also still in Victorian clothing, goes and lays by him in the grass, looking up as well.*

JACQUELYN. Quite a different experience than in the city, eh? Just look at that Milky Way.

TRUMAN. I wonder what Diana would say about our taking the stars out of the sky.

They see a shooting star.

JACQUELYN. Make a wish. *(Beat.)* I hope it was a good one. *(TRUMAN seems disturbed.)* What is it?

TRUMAN. I—I don't know how to . . .

FELICITY *and* LANE, *in their Victorian attire, come trouncing their way from the house, interrupting, flopping down on to the ground, and disturbing the quietness of the moment.*

LANE. Well, mate, I'm flat out!

FELICITY. If I have to change one more chamber pot tonight, I swear I'll throw the whole thing out the window!

JACQUELYN. Lovely.

FELICITY. Now, Truman, I've been meaning to talk to you. I've had enough bad relationships that I think I can give you a heads up on a few things.

LANE. Bullocks, here she goes . . .

FELICITY. Now, with Diana, remember not to give too many overt compliments. Don't constantly tell her how beautiful she is. Not too much physical affection—there's just a time when you need to keep your tentacles to yourself. Not too much talk of the future. And no declarations of love!

LANE. Oi, mate, she's out to make you as charming as a codfish!

FELICITY punches LANE in the shoulder.

FELICITY. Lane, this woman hasn't been in a relationship for over a century and a half.

LANE. They're engaged! If that doesn't give a man some license I don't know what does!

FELICITY. Diana's in a fragile, emotional state.

LANE. I figure it's like riding a bike. Once you learn how to snog somebody, you never forget.

FELICITY. Ah, leave it to you to boil it down to that!

TRUMAN gets up, frustrated and walks a good distance away. JACQUELYN gives LANE and FELICITY the evil eye.

LANE. What's wrong with him?

JACQUELYN. Let me handle this.

JACQUELYN leaves the other two baffled behind and goes to stand beside TRUMAN. After a few moments, she speaks gently:

TRUMAN. I'm not good for her.

JACQUELYN. Truman, she's very lucky to have you.

TRUMAN. If I love her, if I really love her, then I will let her go to the man who will make her really happy.

JACQUELYN. Have you been talking to Colin?

TRUMAN. He loves her. I've seen it in his eyes.

JACQUELYN. So do you. Now the question to ask at this point is who does *she* love?

TRUMAN. Jackie, it's not that easy. The person she really loved has been dead for over a hundred years.

TRUMAN. Nevertheless it's a choice she doesn't need a man making for her.

Suddenly, to both of their shock, they see headlights coming towards the mansion in the distance on the screens. LANE *and* FELICITY *run to them.*

FELICITY. Is that . . . ?

JACQUELYN. Come on. *(They hear the doors of the car close and* ECHO *and* DIANA *enter.)* Echo, Diana will have a fit if you they find that you have driven that . . .

ECHO. *(To* DIANA, *who is in the car:)* Come on out. Don't be shy.

DIANA exits the car and reveals her new, modern look. There is a moment of shock from TRUMAN, JACQUELYN, FELICITY, *and* LANE.

JACQUELYN. Diana?

ECHO. Doesn't she look fabulous?

DIANA. I know this may, well, this may seem inconsistent. *(Long pause.)* Well, is anybody going to say anything?

JACQUELYN. Diana, what does this mean?

DIANA and ECHO *exchange looks and* ECHO *nods.*

DIANA. Well, Echo and I had a long talk—it was more of an argument, really—but at the end of it, well, she convinced me—that—I am half sick of shadows. I am going to live.

Blackout.

SCENE 4

The Mansion appears on the screens. The house staff, now including MANCHESTER *(who is particularly rocked by this change) and* ROMAN, *stand around in a room as they hear raised voices arguing in the next room.* TRUMAN *winces as he hears his name mentioned a few times, while* JACQUELYN, LANE, *and* FELICITY *stand by him in support.* COLIN *storms out of the room, the only one left in Victorian clothing, with* ECHO *and* DIANA *following him.*

ECHO. Well, that's really mature, Dad! Just storm out of the room!

DIANA. Colin, please, wait . . .

COLIN stops at TRUMAN, staring at him darkly.

COLIN. So I see how much you truly care for Diana's happiness.

TRUMAN. Colin, I know this is going to be very hard for you to accept, but . . .

DIANA. Not even you can ruin my happiness now, Colin.

COLIN. I was to be your happiness. *(Beat.)* You want to marry this—this child! For that is what he is compared to you! A child!

TRUMAN. Colin, I know that—that you care for Miss Diana, but if you understood our feelings for each other and that they are much like yours, I know that you would . . .

TRUMAN places his hand on COLIN's shoulder. In an instinctual move, COLIN shocks everyone by grabbing TRUMAN by the hand and throws him. TRUMAN barely has a chance to groan in pain before COLIN is on top of TRUMAN, pummeling him.

COLIN. You are dead, boy!

DIANA reacts swiftly, as she grabs COLIN by the hand and, with surprising strength, throws COLIN against a wall.

DIANA. Don't touch him.

A fierce, fight ensues between the two immortals, with DIANA *showing a surprising array of instinctual skill and strength. After she beats him,* COLIN *tries to go for* TRUMAN *again, but* DIANA *grabs his hair, forces* COLIN *to his knees.*

COLIN. Diana, it doesn't have to be this way.

DIANA. Get out.

COLIN. Now or later, it's going to happen. Eventually, he will die and rot. And then, once again, your heart will die and rot. To us, his will be the life of a butterfly.

DIANA. I would prefer to marry a butterfly than a devil, no matter how eternal the devil is.

DIANA smashes COLIN'S *face into the floor and stands back as* COLIN *rises. Everyone stands apart from* COLIN *and* DIANA *in shock and awe, except for* JACQUELYN *who has rushed to the unconscious* TRUMAN *to make sure he's all right.* DIANA *joins her.*

JACQUELYN. I think we need to get him to a hospital . . .

ECHO. We can take my car.

They make to carry TRUMAN *outside, but* COLIN *blocks the doorway.*

COLIN. Diana—don't you see? You and I—together we have the power within us to conquer the world.

DIANA. Get out of our way, Colin.

COLIN. With our immortality, Diana, comes another dynamic—children. Echo is proof of what happens when an immortal joins with a mortal. But what happens when two immortals join together?

This catches DIANA'S *attention, as she stops briefly considers this.*

DIANA. They make immortal children.

COLIN. Yes, yes, yes! Imagine as you carry that man's fragile body in your arms—I want you to imagine your little children, your little babies—imagine if you could have your children with you forever.

DIANA. No—no.

COLIN. Diana! You would never have to attend another death bed ever again for your family members. Imagine it! Can that man-child give you that?

DIANA. Please, Colin, let us through. He needs help. You have really hurt him . . .

COLIN. And if we have enough children, no army on earth can stop them. Think of it, we are immune to blades, to guns, to bombs, to nuclear and biological weapons. I've waited patiently for centuries to find somebody like you. This is fate, this is destiny, this is God.

DIANA. Is that what this has been about this entire time? You want to build an immortal army out of my children?

COLIN. No, no, not like that! But, imagine—we would inherit the earth, Diana.

DIANA. Get out of our way.

COLIN. Diana!

DIANA. I will not let my children become your soldiers and executioners!

They all push past COLIN, *leaving him. All leave, that is, except* ROMAN, *who is still standing there.*

COLIN. You are released from my service, Roman. It's over.

ROMAN. No, sir, I don't think it is. There is one more thing that this house can yield that you can turn to your advantage.

COLIN. And what is that?

ROMAN. The seed of eternal life.

COLIN. Your father—he has shown it to you?

ROMAN. Not yet. But he has promised me to. It was to be tonight, but, well, we see how this evening has gone. We may still have to wait a bit.

COLIN. Damn. We'll move on it as soon as you know where it is. We can be patient.

SCENE 5

DIANA is at the hospital, which appears on the screens, amidst strange and foreboding lights, sights, and sounds that she has never encountered before. She is very frightened. TRUMAN is in his hospital room bruised, bandaged, and asleep. DIANA sits next to him, with a book of John Donne's poetry in hand. She sits by him, and stares at him sadly, old griefs crowding in around her. After a moment, DIANA opens up the book and begins to read John Donne's "The Blossom":

DIANA. "Little thinkest thou, poor flower,
Whom I have watched six or seven days,
And seen thy birth, and seen what every hour
Gave to thy growth, thee to this height to raise,
And now thou dost laugh and triumph on this bough,
Little think'st thou
That it will freeze anon, and that I shall
Tomorrow find thee fall'n, or not at all . . ."

TRUMAN stirs awake.

TRUMAN. Is that you again, Diana?

DIANA. Good morning, darling.

TRUMAN. You saved my life, you know.

DIANA. Your life would not have been in danger, if it was not for me.

TRUMAN. Please, let's not have one of those conversations.

DIANA. What kind of conversation would that be?

TRUMAN. The kind where the lover is consumed with guilt by the fact that he or she put the other lover in danger.

DIANA. Is that subject a faux paux in your time?

TRUMAN. No, just a cliché.

DIANA. I see. Guilt has become cliché in the modern world.

TRUMAN. No, no, it's just—let us say that if I were to die someday . . .

DIANA. That you will die.

TRUMAN. I don't want you to feel guilty for being alive.

DIANA. I don't think that moment will elicit guilt—just envy. And, once again, loneliness.

TRUMAN. Then let's not poison our lives with that loneliness now.

DIANA. I saw you die. When I saw Colin lunge at you, I thought you were dead. I just found you, and I thought that I had already lost you.

DIANA's tears fall. TRUMAN unable to comfort her. The lights black out on DIANA and TRUMAN as the focus of the scene switches: ROMAN sits at a laptop computer. On one of the screens, COLIN is shown sitting at his elaborate desk in his corporate office on the screen, with ECHO behind him. They are talking to ROMAN over Skype on COLIN's computer.

COLIN. Why the delay?

ROMAN. You can only have yourself to blame for that, Colin. After nearly killing Truman, both Diana and Father have been extra cautious.

COLIN. But they still trust you?

ROMAN. Yes. My Father says that they just need a little more time before initiating me into their little inner circle.

COLIN. Good.

ROMAN. But how do I know you'll follow through, Echo? Is this some ploy upon my affections to get what you want?

ECHO takes her father's place at the center of the camera.

ECHO. Listen, Roman. When you're immortal, when you're like us, you'll be my king, and my father will create for himself a new queen.

ROMAN. I'll be your equal?

ECHO. Not a servant anymore—a master.

COLIN. Yes, and then you'll be my son. But we're losing time. Do what you can to hurry up the process.

ROMAN. Of course. I'll be in touch.

ROMAN disconnects and the screen goes blank. ROMAN exits. TRUMAN and DIANA enter, eating candy floss—cotton candy— as the sounds of rides, happy screaming, and merriment occur. Scenes of an amusement park appear on the screens, including rides, vendors, booths, flashing lights, etc.

DIANA. Remarkable.

TRUMAN. I thought you might like it.

DIANA. Candy floss, you said?

TRUMAN. Yeah.

DIANA. What a remarkable new world.

DIANA looks around at some of the roller coasters, etc.

TRUMAN. Now it's about time you got on a ride!

DIANA. You are sure you are healed enough to go on these? A lot of them look a little rough. Not to mention frightening.

TRUMAN. I'm as robust as an ox now, Diana. You don't always have to be so protective, you know.

DIANA gives TRUMAN a quiet, melancholy look, but TRUMAN doesn't notice.

DIANA. So you say.

TRUMAN. Tell you what. Let's start off on a gentler one. It's my favorite.

DIANA and TRUMAN come to the "Turn of the Century" ride. There is a big, long, metal pole that sticks out of the ground. On top of the pole, there is a circular top from which secure swings are attached to chains that hang down. The whole ride kind of looks like a giant umbrella. Or a tree. On it is painted beautiful woman from the turn of the twentieth century, and it also has mirrors. The riders sit in the chairs and then the whole ride spins, making the riders rise from the ground and fly. DIANA looks at the ride with some trepidation.

DIANA. I am not sure about this, Truman. It looks frightening!

TRUMAN. Not when you're up there. Not when you're moving in smooth, gentle circles, feeling the wind redden your cheeks with his cool kisses and then feel the one you love grab your palms with his warm hands and stare at you as if you were an angel flying with him to the glories of heaven.

DIANA. But I am afraid of heights.

TRUMAN. *(Laughs.)* Diana, you're immortal. Why should you be afraid of heights?

DIANA. Because it would still hurt if I hit the ground. We can still feel pain.

TRUMAN. Then you can still feel exhilaration as well. Believe me, Diana, this is not something you want to miss.

DIANA. All right then. Teach me how to fly.

DIANA nods and the two of them go to through the line, onto the ride and strap themselves into one of the seats made for two. Even before the ride begins, DIANA grips TRUMAN tightly. DIANA squeals a bit as the ride begins on the screens, as if they were on it. DIANA relaxes and the two of them simply enjoy the moment. DIANA lays her head on TRUMAN's shoulder.

TRUMAN. After this I'll win you a teddy bear.

DIANA looks up in earnest surprise.

DIANA. You've domesticated bears?

TRUMAN simply laughs and brings DIANA in an even closer embrace as they continue to feel the gentle wind on their faces. Blackout.

SCENE 6

ROMAN turns on a light switch, as he, ECHO, and COLIN walk into the room in DIANA's house with the fireplace. ECHO holds a gun.

ECHO. It's still weird to have electricity in this place now.

ROMAN. Tell me about it.

COLIN. We need to hurry.

ROMAN. Why? They're on a trip! Traveling the world! I must say that it took some wrangling to get out of going with them.

ECHO. I'm sure you were resourceful.

ROMAN. I insisted that Father go with them—he hasn't gone on a trip like that since my mother left. But somebody had to guard the box. And so he entrusted me with the key and all.

ECHO. Let's get on with it then.

ROMAN looks at ECHO intensely, trying to gauge her.

ROMAN. Kiss me.

ECHO. Kiss you?

ROMAN. Yes.

ECHO. Why now?

ROMAN. Why not? It will be a reward for my resourcefulness. Will you kiss me?

ECHO is hesitant at first, but ROMAN and ECHO kiss. It is less than electric. When ROMAN separates, he looks at ECHO and COLIN, suspiciously. COLIN gives ECHO a dark glance, and ECHO looks ashamed.

ECHO. How are you feeling?

ROMAN. How are you? *(ECHO hesitates.)* You were never going to fulfill your side of the bargain, were you?

COLIN. You're being paranoid, Roman.

ROMAN. Give me one good reason to show you this. Why shouldn't I just keep it for myself?

ECHO raises the gun to ROMAN's head and cocks it.

ECHO. Good enough reason for you?

ROMAN. Echo, I just wanted you. Only you. I don't care about being immortal.

COLIN. Just show us where it is.

ROMAN goes to the panel on the fire place and pulls it back. He unlocks it with the key. He pulls out a golden box.

ECHO. It's finally happening.

COLIN. She'll regret not allying herself with me. When I make myself a new queen, she will regret it.

ROMAN opens the box, but there is nothing inside.

ECHO. It's empty.

COLIN. What sort of trick is this?

ROMAN. I—I don't know. *(COLIN takes ROMAN by the shirt and pins him to a wall.)* No, no, I don't know how this happened!

COLIN. You've betrayed us!

ECHO. No, Daddy, he hasn't. I have.

COLIN. Echo?

ECHO. You can come in now, Diana.

Enter DIANA.

DIANA. You're trespassing, Colin.

COLIN. Where is it, Diana?

DIANA. Far from you, that's what's important.

In a quick, decisive moment COLIN *wrestles the pistol away from* ECHO's *hand. He then grabs* ROMAN *in a stranglehold from behind and points the gun at* ROMAN's *head.*

DIANA (CONT'D). Colin, put the gun down!

COLIN. Where is it?

DIANA. I don't have it anymore!

COLIN. Don't lie to me!

DIANA. I swear, I don't have it!

COLIN. You were right, Diana—you have no idea what kind of man I am. Sorry it had to be this way, Roman.

Before COLIN *can fire the gun at* ROMAN, TRUMAN *bursts in.*

TRUMAN. No, stop!

DIANA. Truman, don't come in here!

COLIN. You should have listened to her, boy.

COLIN *throws* ROMAN *to the ground, and levels the gun at* TRUMAN. *He shoots the gun.* TRUMAN *is knocked back, slams into a wall, and crumples to the floor.* DIANA *rushes to his side, cradling* TRUMAN *in her arms.*

DIANA. Truman—Truman!

COLIN. Where is the fruit, Diana?

DIANA. Murderer!

COLIN *now levels the gun back at* ROMAN.

COLIN. Tell me where the fruit is, or Roman dies as well!

TRUMAN. Wait. *(TRUMAN stands and faces COLIN, unhurt.)* You want to know where the fruit is, Colin? Look no further.

COLIN. He ate it—the bugger ate it!

TRUMAN. Get out of here, Roman. *(Roman hurriedly exits.)* Now hand the weapon to Echo.

COLIN. No.

TRUMAN. Hand it to her!

COLIN *hands the gun over to* ECHO.

COLIN. The man's first hour in eternity and he starts giving orders.

COLIN *stares at* TRUMAN *ferociously, but then smiles.*

TRUMAN. Suddenly the Cheshire Cat, are we? Or do you fancy yourself some vicious Jabberwocky still?

COLIN. Oh, I'm worse than any fictional monster made up in some prick's head, boy.

TRUMAN. Are you now?

COLIN. You don't know old I am.

DIANA. I don't care about your secrets anymore.

COLIN. I am older than every nation on earth. I am older than civilization itself.

DIANA. And yet you haven't a thing to show for it.

COLIN. I am the originator of death. I am Cain.

DIANA. Cain? As in the Bible's Cain?

TRUMAN. No, no, that's not possible. He's a myth—just a myth.

COLIN. Welcome to hell, my boy, for that's what you chose when you ate that fruit.

DIANA. Colin, I don't understand.

COLIN. I didn't believe my father and mother when they told me whoever ate the fruit would be cursed. Well, Death was the curse, not immortality. I didn't kill my brother, they did! By eating that fruit, they killed us all! *(On the screens, we see the Tree of Life, which glows with an unearthly light. A bright powerful CHERUBIM is next to it, guarding it with a flaming sword. COLIN narrates the scene.)* It took me a hundred years to out trick that cherubim. *(ANCIENT COLIN, or CAIN, releases a snake which distracts the CHERUBIM. CAIN dashes to the tree and grabs two of the fruits, one in each fist. He quickly hides one of them in his garments and is able to bite into the other one of them before the CHERUBIM sees him and swiftly flies to him and brings the flaming sword down fiercely onto COLIN's back.)* As painful as that flaming sword was . . . it didn't pierce me. It didn't burn me. I was immortal. *(The scene changes on the screens as we see Cain look up at the Cherubim in triumph as the Cherubim stands back in shock. Then Cain is tearing through his primitive home, trying to find something.)* I saved that second fruit, but someone stole it from me. I searched for it, I hunted for it, but assumed that it had been lost to me forever. *(On the screens Cain sinks to his knees and cries out in distraught anger. The scene on the screens switches again as we see YOUNG DIANA as a child, tossing and turning in her bed, very sick. DIANA's FATHER looks over her sadly, tenderly, caring for her.)* Until I had heard legends of a girl who was saved from death by a fruit. *(The scene changes as we see DIANA's approach a MERCHANT. The MERCHANT protests ignorance until DIANA's FATHER brings out an excessive amount of gold. DIANA's FATHER gives the fruit to YOUNG DIANA. YOUNG DIANA eats it.)* It was his last chance to save his daughter. It was rumored that it would heal any disease, any sickness. He didn't know how true that turned out to be. *(The screens go dark and then change back to the mansion.)* Well, I would find this new, immortal woman and she would be my Eve. And if not my Eve, then my Lillith.

DIANA is rocked by this revelation. She has to sit down.

DIANA. I was dying . . .

TRUMAN comes to her, crouching or kneeling in front of her, taking her hands.

TRUMAN. He saved you.

DIANA. Why didn't he let me die?

COLIN. He damned you.

DIANA. I should have died!

COLIN. And now you will live forever in your sins. As will you, Truman, for you ate the other half. And that, to me, is the greatest victory I could have gained tonight.

COLIN once again tries to turn to go, but TRUMAN stands and faces him.

TRUMAN. What of all your talk of love? Was that a lie as well?

COLIN. It wasn't a lie.

DIANA. You don't know love. Only desire. Love knows sacrifice. Please, Colin—leave us in peace.

COLIN. I'll leave you. But never in peace. Peace will never come for the likes of us. (*COLIN walks calmly towards the door, but before he exits, he turns to DIANA one more time:*) We could have at least been some comfort for each other, Diana. Some—relief. Perhaps we could have even given God a run for his money. The memory of you will haunt me for the rest of my unnatural life.

COLIN exits. There is a powerful silence until ECHO goes to the door to see if he is truly gone. She turns to them, a smile creeping on her face.

ECHO. The devil took the bait. The blanks in the gun worked!

TRUMAN goes to ECHO, with great relief.

TRUMAN. I didn't know whether you had gotten to the gun before he did—when it went off, I didn't know whether I was going to be dead or alive.

ECHO. He believed you were immortal, Truman! He won't come here ever again!

TRUMAN. We had your forewarning to thank for all this, Echo. And, of course, Diana's brilliant plan.

ECHO. Diana, you're free now—you're free!

They both turn to DIANA and see that she is traumatized.

TRUMAN. Diana?

DIANA rushes to TRUMAN and embraces him tightly, the tears which she had been holding back now breaking out with a fury.

DIANA. Forever. Forever in my sins.

Black out.

SCENE 7

(It is still dark outside as we see DIANA and TRUMAN asleep in each other's arms underneath the tree on the screen. Enter JACQUELYN. She goes over to TRUMAN and DIANA and gently nudges them. They both wake up.

TRUMAN. Jackie . . .

JACQUELYN. We found him.

DIANA. Roman?

JACQUELYN. Yes.

DIANA. How is he?

JACQUELYN. He was going to commit suicide, but we found him in time. He and my father are—talking.

DIANA. Thank you. *(JACQUELYN rises and is about to leave before DIANA grabs her hand.)* Jacquelyn—you're fired.

Hope brightens JACQUELYN's face.

JACQUELYN. Do you mean it?

DIANA smiles warmly, embracing JACQUELYN.

DIANA. You brought youth and joy and love back into this house. You have given me a gift I cannot repay. This is the best that I can do. I release you. You are free to live the life you choose.

JACQUELYN. Diana, I stayed here out of love. I hope you know that. I knew that you needed me. As much I didn't want to, I . . .

DIANA. I know. You have my eternal gratitude. But now you are free.

JACQUELYN. Thank you, Mum. It's been an honor.

JACQUELYN gives DIANA one last, elated embrace. She then turns to TRUMAN.

JACQUELYN. Be happy.

JACQUELYN gives TRUMAN one last bitter sweet hug and then exits. The sun has not risen yet, but the sky is starting to lighten.

TRUMAN. Are you feeling any better?

DIANA. You are free, too.

TRUMAN. Diana . . .

DIANA. I am in limbo. I will not drag the man I love through a wasteland of grief.

TRUMAN. I made a standing offer.

DIANA. You didn't know what you were committing to.

TRUMAN. For the rest of my life.

DIANA. Don't waste it on me!

TRUMAN. You accepted that offer. (*After a brief moment of decision, DIANCE embraces TRUMAN tightly and kisses him.*) Let me go get the keys. We'll go and find that new cottage you wanted.

DIANA nods. TRUMAN goes off towards the mansion. DIANA sits beneath the tree, waiting for the sunrise. Yet, to her surprise, strange, distant, soft, but beautiful voices float all around her, like whispers. DIANA stands, trying to figure out where they are coming from. She turns and sees ECHO approaching her.

DIANA. What are those?

ECHO. Diana . . .

DIANA. You hear them.

ECHO. No. But I know what you hear.

Underneath the whispers, DIANA *now hears a distant singing. The words are unintelligible, unearthly, beautiful.*

DIANA. Why is this happening?

ECHO. God is merciful, Diana.

Out of a purse ECHO *pulls out an object wrapped in a red handkerchief. She gives it to* DIANA. DIANA, *mystified, unwraps it and has a quick intake of breath in surprise. In the handkerchief is a strange fruit. Accompanying the strange whispers, now appear faint outlines of spirit like beings on the screens.*

DIANA. That—that fruit is not like mine.

ECHO. No. Not at all alike. What did you do with the fruit from the Tree of Life?

DIANA. I threw it into a hot fire last night. It took hours to burn, but it did burn.

ECHO. Good.

DIANA. What is your fruit?

ECHO. I received it last night as a gift from a person named the Beloved. We have been in correspondence for many years now. There's a network of people like us now. A small network, but they're there. They know of you.

DIANA. You mean—we're not alone?

ECHO. When the Beloved gave me this to deliver to you, he said that you didn't choose this life, that of all people, it ought to be meant for you.

DIANA. Wait. Is it what I think it is? Is it from the other . . .

ECHO. The Other Tree. Yes.

DIANA. And you are giving it to me?

ECHO takes out the knife and cuts the fruit into half. She wraps up one half and puts it away into her purse. The other half she gives to DIANA.

ECHO. The other half I am saving for my father. If there is any hope that redemption can still touch him, then I want to give it to him someday. If he ever accepts a new path, I will put this into his hands.

DIANA. I don't—I don't how to thank you, how to tell you—you have delivered me from hell.

ECHO. Goodbye, Diana.

DIANA. Wait, what about Truman?

ECHO. Ask him.

TRUMAN. I—I saw Echo so I came back. I heard everything.

TRUMAN, who has been listening in, enters.

ECHO. I'll leave you two to talk about this alone.

ECHO walks away, leaving TRUMAN and DIANA alone. They stand there alone,
   the morning light getting brighter, sunrise nearly here.

TRUMAN. You want this, don't you?

DIANA. I could wait. Wait until you die. We could still live a full life together.

TRUMAN. Under any other circumstances, this could be very wrong, but—it's like taking you off eternal life support and letting your body take its natural . . .

DIANA. That's not what this is about. I love you, Truman, I . . .

TRUMAN. But you're not happy.

DIANA. No.

TRUMAN. I could never make you happy, could I? The wounds are too deep.

DIANA. You need me.

TRUMAN. Love knows sacrifice. If Colin ever finds out about it—who knows what he would do to prevent this? It's time for your peace.

DIANA begins to sob, TRUMAN embraces her. Slowly, DIANA withdraws from Truman and represses the tears.

DIANA. It is best if I do this alone.

TRUMAN. No. I'm not leaving . . .

DIANA. Please. I dearly love you, Truman, but this moment—I am about to see my children again. My husbands.

TRUMAN. I won't leave you when you need me!

DIANA. I need release. Final redemption. I no longer need mere comfort.

TRUMAN. Then who is left to comfort me?

DIANA. Go, my dear. Live. I have lived too many lives already, but you have hardly begun your first.

(DIANA kisses TRUMAN softly, tears now pouring down both their cheeks. With great difficulty TRUMAN walks away. The gentle voices and singing become louder and more beautiful and the spirit like figures on the screens becoming more and more solid. The sounds swirl around her as she gazes at the fruit.)

DIANA. "In the day thou eatest thereof, thou shalt surely die."

(The voices and singing crescendo. DIANA bites into the fruit and all the voices and singing abruptly stop. DIANA falls dead to the ground as the screens go dark. Lights fade to black out.)

THE END

Jamie Denison as Diana Applesong.

Mahonri Stewart as Colin and Sarah Beth Preston as Echo

Sarah Beth Preston as Echo and Daniel Whiting as Roman Lyons.

Matthew P. Davis as Manchester Lyons and Jamie Denison as Diana Applesong.

Jamie Denison as Diana Applesong.

Penny Pendleton as Jacquelyn Lyons and Bryn Dalton Randall as Felicity Pope.

Penny Pendleton as Jacquelyn Lyons, Jordan Cummings as Truman Nibley, Bryn Dalton Randall as Felicity Pope, and Bryce Bishop as Lane Knight.

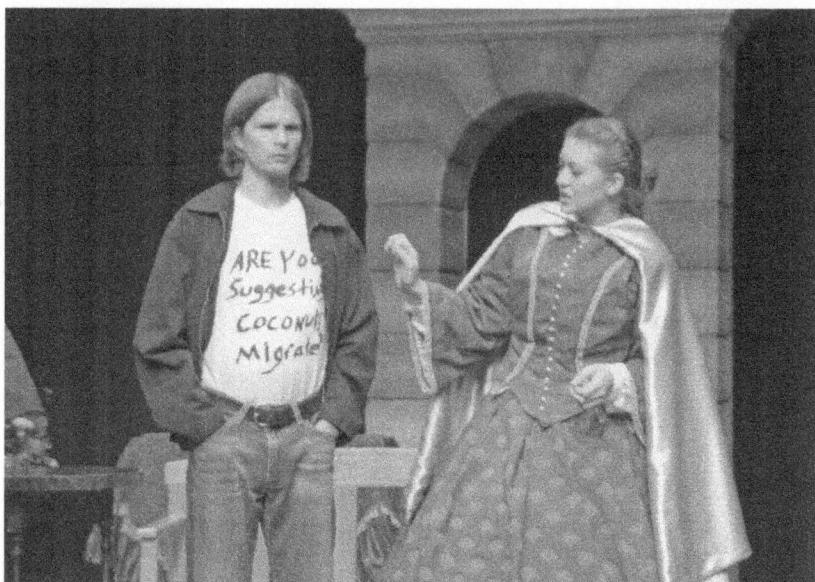

Bryce Bishop as Lane Knight and Jamie Denison as Diana Applesong.

Jordan Cummings as Truman Nibley and Jamie Denison as Diana Applesong.

Jordan Cummings as Truman Nibley and Mahonri Stewart as Colin.

Jamie Denison as Diana Applesong and Mahonri Stewart as Colin.

Jamie Denison as Diana Applesong.

Jaclyn Hales as Diana Applesong.

Danor Gerald as Truman Nibley and Lawrence Fernandez as Colin.

Jaclyn Hales as Diana Applesong and Lawrence Fernandez as Colin.

Danor Gerald as Truman Nibley.

Lawrence Fernandez as Colin.

The Opposing Wheel

A Mythical Fantasia in Two Acts

Production History

The Opposing Wheel premiered at the Castle Theatre in Provo, UT on November 7, 2014. It had the following cast and crew:

CAST
Maggie: Jyllian Petrie (Unice)
Daniel: Jason Kelly Fullmer
Ether: Jason Sullivan
Morgana: Jamie Denison
Frenzy: Rebecca Minson
Tempest: Brian Randall
Veiled Woman: Stephanie Robertson
Secret Character: Chris Clark

CREW
Director: Heather Jones
Producer/Sound/Original Music: Nathaniel Drew
Costumes: Heather Jones
Lighting: Mike James
House Manager: David Tertipes
Set: Daniel Jones
Fight Choreography: Adam Argyle
Executive Producer: Mahonri Stewart

Dedicated to

William Arthur Taysom
For Friendship,

Tricia H.H. Evanson
For Vision,

Anne Marie Stewart
For Love.

The Opposing Wheel

Act One

SCENE 1

The play for the first act takes place in the library of an old British castle. The time is the current year. The castle belongs to MAGDALENA "MAGGIE" DEVONSHIRE, *a woman in her mid-twenties to early thirties, who enters. She is dressed in a medieval dress and carries several very old books, at least hundreds of years old, if not thousands.* MAGGIE *is followed by two* SHADES, *a man and a woman. These dark spirits, or* SHADES, *are not ghosts, thus they do not wear the kind of clothing that can be historically identified. Their clothing, to them, is symbolic and represents their natures and the kind of power they each individually possess. The* SHADES *call each other* TEMPEST *(the man) and* FRENZY *(the woman).* MAGGIE *sits down and starts searching thoroughly through the ancient texts, while* TEMPEST *and* FRENZY *leisurely lounge around. For the first little while,* MAGGIE *doesn't ever look directly at* TEMPEST *or* FRENZY.

TEMPEST. *(Looking over* MAGGIE's *books.)* Bah. A dirty waste of her time.

FRENZY. Irritable tonight, Tempest?

TEMPEST. Does that surprise you?

FRENZY. It's just nice to have you in a calmer disposition for once.

TEMPEST. I'm so tired of your unrelenting flippancy.

FRENZY. The way I see it, if we can't possess a sardonic view on life, we might as well kill ourselves.

TEMPEST. Very funny.

FRENZY. "Oh, if this too, too solid flesh would melt . . ."

TEMPEST. All right, stop it.

FRENZY. "To die, to sleep! To sleep perchance to dream. Aye there's the rub, for in such sleep, what dreams may come . . ."

TEMPEST. Stop it!

FRENZY. Ah, but how can we sleep, if we were never awake? Thus if we've never slept, how can this be a dream? And if it is not a dream and we're not awake, what then are we?

TEMPEST. They're not our stories, Frenzy. I don't see why you obsess over them.

FRENZY. You have no poetry in your soul.

TEMPEST. I'm careful with my soul. It's all I have.

FRENZY. Old as eternity, and yet still so narrow. Mankind, you see, is just as much myth as fact. If you look at them simply as a fixed point, a body, an unchanging truth, then they'll fool you every time.

TEMPEST. I hope you don't mind if I don't listen to more of your anti- quated philosophy.

FRENZY. When you learn to reach into their myths and stories, then you start understanding that they are just as hidden from us as we are from them. They will be our undoing, if we don't reach an under- standing of them before they reach an understanding of us!

TEMPEST. You give them much more credit than I do.

FRENZY. That, my dear Tempest, is the reason I am in charge of this expedition.

TEMPEST. A mistake, an error of judgment on the part of our Authorities.

FRENZY. If you want to see why I am called Frenzy, then keep talking that way! Your wet storms would wilt underneath my flame!

TEMPEST. Hot air! No substance! I can blow you out in one cool breath.

MAGGIE. Will you two shut up? I'm trying to concentrate here.

TEMPEST and FRENZY both stop, shocked. They look at MAG-GIE and notice that for the first time she is looking straight at them.

TEMPEST. Does she mean us?

FRENZY. Is—is she looking at us?

MAGGIE. Looking at you? Well, I'm not sure if that's the right terminology. But I know you're there.

TEMPEST. By Beezlebub's beard, she's a Veil Ripper! Why weren't we told about this?

FRENZY. Damned bureaucracy.

MAGGIE sighs and then goes back to her books.

TEMPEST. This changes everything. I've never dealt with a Veil Ripper before. We'll need to be more careful.

FRENZY. Don't say a word.

A sound of a door opening is heard, followed by a gust of wind and rain from outside, and then the sound of the door slamming. All are startled when DANIEL, a young man in his mid-twenties, enters carrying in his arms another young man named ETHER. MAGGIE gives out a cry of surprise.

DANIEL. Sh, sh, sh! Magdalena Devonshire?

MAGGIE. Yes, but how did you . . . ? Who are . . . ?

DANIEL. Brilliant. Where may I put the body?

MAGGIE. Body? Is—is he dead?

DANIEL. Yes, currently.

MAGGIE. Pardon?

DANIEL. You're right, the table will do nicely. Hm, very nice volumes. I will have to look at those later.

DANIEL pushes the books aside and puts ETHER on the table.

FRENZY. Now this is an interesting development . . .

MAGGIE. Are you tuned to the moon?

DANIEL. Ugh, your house in infested with Shades.

MAGGIE. You can see them too?

DANIEL. No. But they do have a nasty stench, don't they? The important thing, however, is that you can see them. Enough chit chat, we have more important matters to attend to. This fellow is dead.

DANIEL starts rummaging through a back pack he carried in.

MAGGIE. Dead, he's really—oh my—you're not taking the mickey out of me, are you?

DANIEL. You can check his pulse, if you want.

MAGGIE. What happened?

DANIEL. A very nasty battle with a very nasty woman. I won't bore you with details—ah, here it is!

DANIEL takes out a wooden cup.

MAGGIE. The poor lad. Were you two close?

DANIEL. Oh no, not at all. We just met last week. But he's very important to me, so . . .

DANIEL brings out a bottle of wine or grape juice and pours some into the cup and then pours it into ETHER's mouth.

MAGGIE. What are you doing?

DANIEL. Come on, Peter Priesthood

MAGGIE. Was that his name then? Peter? Is this some kind of last rights?

DANIEL. Oh no. His name is Ether. And, no, he's not Catholic—not that his religion hardly matters at this point. But all of this can be explained later.

MAGGIE. Excuse me, but I'm in a bit of a tizzy here. I think you'd better explain now.

DANIEL. No. It can be explained later.

MAGGIE. All right. Later. *(Pause.)* Ether. Interesting name.

DANIEL. You seem rather cool and collected for a woman who has a dead body in her library.

MAGGIE. And you seem rather cool and collected for a man who just saw the body murdered.

DANIEL. Oh, but you see the difference is that I know that he's going to come back to life.

ETHER gasps and sits up violently, having just come back to life. MAGGIE gasps in shock.

FRENZY. Damn.

MAGGIE. He—he—man alive!

DANIEL. Exactly.

ETHER gasps and coughs and sputters.

ETHER. I'm back! I saw—I saw so many things—no, no, they're fading—no, wait! I can't remember anymore! It was so—so beautiful. But now it's gone.

DANIEL. It's all right, mate, you're safe now.

ETHER. No thanks to you. You nearly got me killed back there.

DANIEL. Technically, I did get you killed. Lucky for you, I clean up after myself.

ETHER. How am I alive?

DANIEL. Ah, details, details, all of you always want details. Well, you wouldn't believe me, if I told you.

ETHER. I think I'm willing to believe anything now!

DANIEL. It's a trinket I picked up. I hate that I had to use it in front of the shades. It'll be broadcast all over hell now—they're infamous tongue waggers. Isn't that right, Tempest and Frenzy?

FRENZY. Double damn!

TEMPEST. *(Simultaneous:)* How did he know our names?!

MAGGIE. *(Simultaneous:)* How did you know their names?

DANIEL. I've been well briefed.

MAGGIE. You—you just brought a man back from the dead!

DANIEL. Well, yes, but don't be too impressed. It's been done before by people much better than me and with much more style.

MAGGIE. Not in my house, it hasn't! And—and—what the hellfire and brimstone are you doing here?

DANIEL. I don't exactly know.

MAGGIE. Who are you?

DANIEL. My name is Daniel, I think.

MAGGIE. How do you know so much about me and the Shades?

DANIEL. A shiny woman in a lake told me.

MAGGIE. A shiny woman in . . . What's going on?!

DANIEL. I'm still trying to figure that one out myself.

MAGGIE. But . . .

DANIEL. I'm sorry, but at the moment things are rather urgent. We still have that matter of a murderous woman on the loose, so I need to check the perimeter of your house, if you don't mind.

MAGGIE. Mind! What does it matter if I mind?

DANIEL. Now you're getting the idea. I'll be right back—you two can, uh, get acquainted.

Exit DANIEL.

MAGGIE. Er, hello.

ETHER. Uh, hi.

Awkward pause.

MAGGIE. He's not a nutter, is he?

ETHER. Haven't quite figured that out yet. This your place?

MAGGIE. Yeah. It's a castle. We're in the East tower.

ETHER. Nice.

MAGGIE. Ta.

Awkward pause.

ETHER. And this library! How old are these books?

MAGGIE grabs the volumes suddenly and puts them back on the shelves.

MAGGIE. That really isn't any of your business.

ETHER. Oh. Sorry.

MAGGIE. As soon as your friend gets back and everything is clear, you two are going to leave.

ETHER. Uh, actually, we're not.

MAGGIE. Pardon?

ETHER. I'm sure you have a bunch of questions.

MAGGIE. A few did cross my mind.

ETHER. Well, I'll tell you what I know. I'm Ether Kimball. The other guy calls himself Daniel. But he doesn't think that's his real name.

MAGGIE. How can he not know his own name?

ETHER. See, that's the thing. He comes to me in America and tells me that the End Times are coming . . .

MAGGIE. End times? As in . . .

ETHER. . . . the Last Days. The Apocalypse. He told me that the world's going to be burned to a crisp, but that I was going to help support a man who would save a remnant of mankind . . .

MAGGIE. A remnant?

ETHER. Those were his exact words. A remnant.

MAGGIE. And what is that supposed to mean?

ETHER. I don't know. And neither does he.

MAGGIE. Well, that takes the biscuit. And how does he claim to have a baldy notion about any such thing?

ETHER. Like he said, a shiny woman in a lake told him.

MAGGIE. And you just up and left America to go with this toss pot?

ETHER. There's a lot more to him than what he first seems to be. He has a purpose. But he has many tests to pass before he fulfills that purpose.

MAGGIE. Oh, and you have such insight into his soul then?

ETHER. Yes.

MAGGIE. How?

ETHER. I dreamed the whole scenario before he told me a thing about it.

MAGGIE. You dreamed it, and then—no, wait. Pardon?

ETHER. Come now, you're the practitioner of magic, aren't you? A visionary dream shouldn't be so farfetched for you.

MAGGIE. I don't really practice magic. Not the spells and enchantments kind, at least. I—I just have certain gifts. Like you, it seems. You have prophetic dreams?

ETHER. That's why he said the woman in the lake wanted me. I often see things before they happen, almost down to the finest details. I saw fire and armies and smoke and cities laid to rubble. I saw powerful men and women use abilities I had never seen—they weren't natural. They were frightening people who were near impossible to kill. These people, these beings brought whole nations to their knees. It all got pretty depressing, but then . . .

MAGGIE. You didn't happen to get tanked up at the pub the night before, did you?

ETHER. I don't drink.

MAGGIE. Not at all?

ETHER. There were pockets of people all over the world who stood against the onslaught. A group in Jerusalem, a group in Missouri— and here in England I saw a man rise up and gather a handful of people who dared go up against the evil demigods of power that had taken root here. I was one of those people who that man gathered. And so were you.

MAGGIE. Me?

ETHER. I'm the one who directed Daniel here. I saw this house—and you, Magdelena Devonshire—in a dream.

MAGGIE. Actually, I prefer to be called Maggie.

ETHER. Okay.

MAGGIE. You saw me in a dream?

ETHER. Yeah.

MAGGIE. That's creepy.

ETHER. Yeah, it's not a line I use when I pick up girls. Do you believe me, Maggie?

MAGGIE. *(Pause.)* I have—abilities of my own. I'm not exactly one to judge. So what happened next? In your dream, I mean.

ETHER. I don't know. I didn't see anything beyond that.

MAGGIE. That's a pretty special gift.

ETHER. I've had it since I was young. Normally I had gentle dreams. Comforting ones, which burned all fear and doubt out of my heart, like a white fire of peace. But these—these aren't the same. These are darker, more urgent. These are warnings.

TEMPEST. I think that I've heard enough.

FRENZY. Tempest, don't do anything . . .

TEMPEST. They're too dangerous!

MAGGIE. *(Noting the Shades.)* Ether, we're in trouble.

ETHER. What?

> TEMPEST *starts muttering an archaic incantation under his breath. All of* TEMPEST *and* FRENZY's *spells are in Latin.*

TEMPEST. Pluvia Pinguesco Gelu Ventus Levitas Tempestas!

Outside, intense wind and rain starts to be heard. Then, soon enough, lightning and thunder.

FRENZY. You know our orders!

TEMPEST. You're too soft, Frenzy! This is what needs to be done. If there is any chance that they can stop the . . .

FRENZY. Challenge me and you'll burn. *(FRENZY tries to interfere, but TEMPEST pushes her aside. FRENZY becomes angry. She, too, starts an incantation. As she does so, a orange-red light surrounds her.)* Fervens Estus Vomica Exuro Incendia Rabies!

ETHER. Fire!

MAGGIE. It's the Shades!

ETHER. We have to get out of the castle!

MAGGIE. I can't! Anyway, it looks like a hurricane out there! We wouldn't fare much better!

FRENZY attacks TEMPEST. They tussle, and then eventually push against each other with their elements, neutralizing themselves into a stalemate for a moment.

ETHER. How do we stop them?

MAGGIE. I don't think we can. They're intangible . . .

Enter DANIEL.

DANIEL. Magdalena, where are they?

MAGGIE. It's Maggie!

DANIEL. I don't care! Where are the Shades?

MAGGIE. There!

DANIEL. *(Note: All of DANIEL's spells are in Gaelic.)* Diabhal tinneas!

After DANIEL yells out the incantation, a burst of light surrounds TEMPEST and FRENZY. They fall to the ground, severely hurt.

TEMPEST. Ow! That hurts!

DANIEL. Diabhal tinneas!

FRENZY. We're out of here!

Another burst of light. FRENZY *and* TEMPEST *scramble to their feet and exit.*

DANIEL. Diabhal tinneas!

Another burst of light.

MAGGIE. Daniel . . .

DANIEL. Diabhal tinneas!

Another burst of light.

MAGGIE. Daniel, stop . . .

DANIEL. Diabhal tinneas!

Another burst of light.

MAGGIE. Daniel! They're gone!

DANIEL. Oh. Yes.

MAGGIE. How did you do that?

DANIEL. Again, always wanting explanations . . .

MAGGIE. Why are you here?

DANIEL. Because a shiny . . .

MAGGIE. . . . woman in a lake told you. You've said that. And Mr. Visionary over here told me about the dreams. It all sounds pretty impossible.

ETHER. "Sounds" impossible. But you don't believe it's impossible.

DANIEL. More than that, with her background, she doesn't even believe it's even unlikely. Do you, Magdalena?

MAGGIE. Maggie.

DANIEL. Boring, but sure. Maggie.

ETHER. She believes us. She has every reason to.

MAGGIE. *(Scrutinizing* DANIEL *and* ETHER.*)* I think I want you to go.

DANIEL. That's not likely.

MAGGIE. As you saw—well, I guess you didn't see, but as you experienced, I have enough on my plate with Screwtape and Wormwood.

ETHER. That's not really their names, are they?

MAGGIE. Don't be daft.

DANIEL. Among other things, we're here to help with your particular infestation of devils.

MAGGIE. Oh, tosh. I can handle them.

DANIEL. Yes, we saw how you handled them.

MAGGIE. Look, without my help, you wouldn't have been able to take them on either. You didn't even know where to shoot.

DANIEL. Which is why we need you.

MAGGIE. I don't know you.

DANIEL. But we know you.

MAGGIE. You don't know me!

> MAGGIE *is about to turn and exit when Ether takes her hand to stop her. She turns, about to barrel some insults into him, but stops short when she looks into his eyes. The two feel something magic happen between them.*

ETHER. Please, don't be angry.

MAGGIE. I'm not angry. At least not anymore.

ETHER. Good.

MAGGIE. But I am a little afraid.

ETHER. Me too.

MAGGIE. It's been a long time since anyone's been here. I should be ecstatic, but . . .

ETHER. Maggie, I know what you're feeling . . .

MAGGIE. Look, Ether, you at least seem sweet, but I do like my privacy. The peace and quiet of being alone here, without any conflicts, without any of the world's arguments. It's all I've known.

ETHER. Yes, I saw that in my dream, too. I saw you here in this castle which your family inherited, pouring over your books, night after night, all alone. Searching for something . . .

MAGGIE. You know . . .

ETHER. Ever since your parents died five years ago, it's been just you. Looking for something they told you about, which has haunted you, cursed you . . .

MAGGIE. You saw . . . ?

ETHER. You have no friends, no family. Just these books. When was the last time you went outside, Maggie?

MAGGIE. Please, stop . . .

ETHER. But every once in a while, you look out your window and see the people in the village below—there but not there. In this in between place. Like in that old poem:

"And moving thro' a mirror clear
That hangs before her all the year . . ."

MAGGIE. ". . . Shadows of the world appear."

There is a small silence as ETHER *and* MAGGIE *regard each other.*

DANIEL. So as you can see, Maggie, we do know you.

With that, the spell of attraction is broken.

MAGGIE. Just because you've seen me, doesn't mean you know me. *(Pause.)* It's very late. You'll need a place to rest. Follow me.

DANIEL. You will help us then?

MAGGIE. We'll talk in the morning.

DANIEL. But you have to understand that . . .

ETHER. She said that we'll talk in the morning.

Exit DANIEL, MAGGIE, *and* ETHER.

SCENE 2

The lights raise to reveal ETHER *asleep at a desk, piles of books surrounding him, some opened and obviously searched carefully and thoroughly. A* VEILED WOMAN *enters through a secret door and stands above* ETHER. *She puts back the hood of her cloak to reveal that she wears a veil, which is sufficiently dark to hide her face. She wears an elegant medieval dress.*

VEILED WOMAN. "Words that defy explanation,
Truth that cuts through most tempered steel,
Its cocoon is your protection,
Its strength makes all of England kneel."
(Pause.) Is this not what you seek, Pilgrim?

ETHER. *(Talking in his sleep.)* I don't know what I seek.

VEILED WOMAN. What do you see in those visions of yours?

ETHER. A boat full of women—but wait there is also a man, a dead man. They bring him to . . .

VEILED WOMAN. To where? Do you understand what you see?

A sound is heard. The VEILED WOMAN *puts back on her hood and opens a secret door, into which she exits and it closes behind her. Enter* MAGGIE. *Upon seeing* ETHER, *she hardens. She comes to him and shakes him.* ETHER *mumbles and pushes back slightly, still asleep.* MAGGIE *shakes him harder.* ETHER *pushes back harder.* MAGGIE *then pushes* ETHER *off the chair.* ETHER *tumbles to the floor and then wakes up, startled.*

ETHER. Agh! Maggie—what am I doing here?

MAGGIE. Took the words right out of my mouth.

ETHER. Where is she?

MAGGIE. Who?

ETHER. The woman.

MAGGIE. You were sleeping.

ETHER. Oh. It was so vivid.

MAGGIE. Oh, I'm sure it was. A pretty blonde perhaps?

ETHER. No, it wasn't like that. And I couldn't see her face.

MAGGIE. I'm not sure if I want to psychoanalyze that one. But that is beyond the point. You were sleeping. In my library. Which means you were looking through my books.

ETHER. Maggie, I know how this looks . . .

MAGGIE. These books are priceless, irreplaceable . . .

ETHER. Maggie . . .

MAGGIE. Why were you looking through my books?!

ETHER. I was trying to help you!

MAGGIE. Help me? Help me do what?

ETHER. "Entombed within the ancient tower,
    The lost, sacred words lie dormant,
    Arms fold over the sheath'ed power,
    Opening them ends the internment,
    Springs to bright life the ancient stories,
    Holy blade rising to the sky,
    Read the words engraved for glories,
    His eyes open, his voice will fly."

MAGGIE. How do you know the riddle?

ETHER. I told you. I dream.

MAGGIE. No. You can't dream all of it—not every word, no one dreams like that! This is a trick.

ETHER. It's not a trick.

MAGGIE. Who sent you?

ETHER. We were sent by a shiny woman . . .

MAGGIE. . . . in a lake. Did you see this woman?

ETHER. No.

MAGGIE. Then perhaps there is no woman.

ETHER. I know what I saw. Merlin knows what he saw. Maggie, Providence has brought us to you, to help you.

MAGGIE. I didn't ask for help.

ETHER. I think you did. On those nights you used to cry in fits after so much wasted time, such maze-like efforts.

MAGGIE. I can do this.

ETHER. You think it's a book.

MAGGIE. Pardon me?

ETHER. You think the answer to the riddle is a book. After all the tower is a library. The riddle talks of "sacred words" and arms folded over—like the covers of a book. "Ancient stories" and "eyes will open"—it makes sense, a book.

MAGGIE. Ether, please, let's not talk about this. It's my family's secret, our quest . . .

ETHER. Reading and re-reading every volume. Hoping beyond hope that you misinterpreted something that will suddenly leap out at you. You have filled whole volumes of your own with your theories and guesswork, but they have led to dead ends every time. All day and deep into the night and then early in the morning you do this, until you are exhausted and caught in the web of your own making.

MAGGIE. How can you know all of this?

ETHER. And you have found hidden information, haven't you, Maggie? Magic and necromancy and old occult secrets are only a few of the revelations you have uncovered in those aging pages. But those aren't what interest you. You just pass by those, looking for something that will make you free.

MAGGIE. You know too much.

ETHER. Maybe. I think so.

MAGGIE. I want you to leave.

ETHER. I'm not leaving. I'm here for you.

MAGGIE. I want you to leave!

ETHER. It's not a book. What you're looking for, it's not a book.

There is a pause, as MAGGIE *looks over* ETHER, *stunned.*

MAGGIE. Of course it's a book.

ETHER. You misinterpreted the riddle.

MAGGIE. It's a book. I have gone over that riddle a million times, as did my parents before me, and their parents before them, as did every ancestor before them, even before my own family's recorded history. We all agree. It's a book.

ETHER. It's not a book.

MAGGIE. It is so.

ETHER. Then why you haven't you found anything?

MAGGIE. What do you know about it? You just got here. My family has searched for this for generations.

ETHER. And that's why they haven't succeeded, because they've been looking for the wrong thing. That's why you so desperately need a new set of eyes.

Enter DANIEL.

DANIEL. Good morning, you two!

MAGGIE. I want both of you out of here.

DANIEL. That again, is it?

ETHER. Why won't you accept our help?

MAGGIE. This is mine. The burden is mine. The glory is mine. The loneliness is mine.

ETHER. It doesn't have to be that way . . .

MAGGIE. It is that way!

ETHER. Maggie, you can't do it alone. And I don't think that you really want to do it alone.

MAGGIE. It doesn't matter what I want.

ETHER. Please, be sensible.

MAGGIE. *(Laughs.)* Sensible! Look, if I make a mistake, then I make a mistake. But if you two come in here and make a shambolic mess of things, the consequences could be dire. I don't want to see you—either of you—hurt. You don't know the world you've stepped into.

ETHER. I'm willing to take those consequences on my own head, thank you very much. You don't need to worry your conscience about that.

MAGGIE. Ether, truly, you seem nice. Really nice. Pleasant. My life isn't nice. It isn't pleasant. I've already seen you dead on a table once, let's not go through that again.

DANIEL. Oh, if that's all that's worrying you, Ether's not going to die again.

MAGGIE. You can't make that promise. No one can.

DANIEL. Actually, that's not true.

Pause.

MAGGIE AND DANIEL. What?

DANIEL. He drank from the cup.

MAGGIE. So now he's alive. We know that.

DANIEL. Ether, I'm sorry. I'm so very sorry. It's more than that. It not only brought you back to life—it made you immortal.

MAGGIE. You made him . . . ?

ETHER. That's not possible.

DANIEL. It's not only possible, it's what happened.

ETHER. But didn't you consider what I would . . . ?

DANIEL. I knew what you would want. But I also knew that we needed you. I'm sorry, I'm so sorry.

ETHER is stunned for a moment, but then a wave of anger crosses him and he punches DANIEL. DANIEL falls stunned to the ground, and ETHER exits clearly upset. MAGGIE looks flabbergasted. She helps DANIEL up to his feet.

MAGGIE. That was a rather violent reaction from a man who just learned he would have a clean bill of health for the rest of eternity.

DANIEL. Don't be naive, Maggie. I denied him the very thing he wanted most.

MAGGIE. What was that?

DANIEL. Eternal life.

MAGGIE. Isn't that what you just gave him?

DANIEL. No. You must understand, Ether is a very devout Mormon— in his mind, what I did to him was close the door to heaven.

MAGGIE considers this for a moment. Then she looks up at him, understanding.

MAGGIE. So in his mind, you just put a curse on him.

DANIEL. Yes, I'm afraid so.

MAGGIE. And you knew he wouldn't want that?

DANIEL. Yes.

MAGGIE slaps DANIEL.

MAGGIE. You know you deserved that.

DANIEL. You know a thing or two about curses, too, don't you, Maggie?

MAGGIE exits. Exit DANIEL.

SCENE 3

Enter TEMPEST *and* FRENZY, *cautious.*

FRENZY. They're not here.

TEMPEST. That's a relief. So what are we supposed to do now? A veil ripper, a prophet and a warlock! Not to mention that cup . . .

FRENZY. We're still elementals, Frenzy. That still gives us an edge . . .

TEMPEST. Not against a line up like that.

FRENZY. If we only knew what they were looking for.

> *Enter* MORGANA *from a hiding spot.* MORGANA *is a majestic woman dressed in medieval, Celtic clothing, ceremonial in appearance, as if she were part of some sort of sect or mystical order. She also carries a shield, upon which is the design of a knight that is stepping on the heads of a queen and a king. She also wears a scabbard which, curiously, contains no sword within it.*

MORGANA. I believe that's where I can help you. (FRENZY *and* TEMPEST, *shocked again, turn towards* MORGANA *and their elements start swirling around them.*) Don't be rash. I can help you. (FRENZY *considers this, but* TEMPEST *tries to attack* MORGAN. MORGAN *casts her spell before* TEMPEST *can finish his. All of Morgan's spells are in Gaelic.*) Diabhal bhí sé i bhfostú! (*A shaft of light strikes and stays upon* TEMPEST, *pinning him to the floor. He tries to resist and break out.*) Do you want to fight me, too, She-Shade? (FRENZY *considers this and then disperses her elements.*) What's your name? (FRENZY *doesn't answer.*) Oh, come on, I'm not here to hurt you. (FRENZY *still doesn't answer.*) Well, if you won't give your name, I won't give mine.

> TEMPEST *has finally given up trying to break out of the shaft of light.*

TEMPEST. All right, I give up!

MORGANA. Saor Diabhal!

The shaft of light is released. TEMPEST breathes more easily and can once again move without restraint.

TEMPEST. You're the one who killed that prophet, aren't you?

MORGANA. Well, he's not exactly dead, is he?

TEMPEST. Now only if we knew who that wizard was . . .

FRENZY smacks TEMPEST in the back of the head.

MORGANA. You don't know?

TEMPEST. Well, no.

FRENZY smacks TEMPEST in the back of the head.

MORGANA. Haven't your leaders told you anything?

TEMPEST is about to speak again, but FRENZY smacks him in the back of the head. TEMPEST decides not to speak anymore.

MORGANA. So they left you in the dark. *(Gives out a short laugh.)* Damned bureaucracy. *(The voices of DANIEL, MAGGIE, and ETHER are heard approaching.)* Hide. Wait, you can't. Between the veil ripper and the warlock, you're completely exposed. *(Pause.)* I can cover the smell for the warlock. If you hide just outside, the veil ripper won't detect you.

Exit FRENZY and TEMPEST. MORGANA recites a quick incantation and then hides. Enter DANIEL, MAGGIE, and ETHER.

MAGGIE. So tell me again—what did she tell you in your dream?

ETHER. "Words that defy explanation,
 Truth that cuts through most tempered steel,
 Its cocoon is your protection,
 Its strength makes all of England kneel."

DANIEL. And you think it's connected to your other riddle?

MAGGIE. "Entombed within the ancient tower,
 The lost, sacred words lie dormant,
 Arms fold over the sheath'ed power,
 Opening them ends the internment,

286

Springs to bright life the ancient stories,
Holy blade rising to the sky,
Read the words engraved for glories,
His eyes open, his voice will fly."

DANIEL. "Tempered steel. " "Sheath'ed power." "Holy blade rising to the sky." Both riddles are talking about a sword.

MAGGIE. That's what I'm thinking, too. And both riddles talk about words, which is why my family thought of books. But they're engraved words. Which means there's something written on the blade . . .

DANIEL. "It's cocoon is your protection." "Sheathed power." There's something special about the scabbard . . .

ETHER. But can it really be a sword? I mean the riddle, it talks about a person. "His eyes open, his voice will fly."

DANIEL. Perhaps it's personifying the sword.

MAGGIE. No, I think they're separate. "Arms fold over sheath'ed power." I kept thinking that the arms were covers of a book, and that the power was written in the book . . .

DANIEL. The riddle does talk about ancient stories. Maybe you weren't wrong . . .

MAGGIE. No, no, I think Ether's right. It's not a book. At least not directly. The riddles are being much more literal than I assumed. I kept looking for symbolism, metaphor and allegory—but what if it's being literal. What if the arms belong to a real person? What if the sword is a real sword? What if—oh, I'm an idiot.

MAGGIE goes directly to the book shelves and starts searching.

DANIEL. I thought we decided it wasn't a book . . .

MAGGIE brings down a very old volume of L'Morte de Arthur *by Thomas Mallory and places it down on a table, searching through it frantically.*

MAGGIE. If I'm right, then it is and it isn't. Here we go . . . *(Reading from the text:)* "Damosel, what sword is that, that yonder the arm holdeth above the water? I would it were mine for I have no sword. King, said the damosel, that sword is mine, and if ye will give me a gift when I ask it of you, ye shall have it." How did I not see it before . . . I know these stories . . . how did I not see it?!

ETHER. Who would have thought to be literal with fairy tales?

MAGGIE. I've read all of this. The sword was supposed to be able to cut through anything. On it were engraved words—on both sides. On one side it said "take me up," on the other side, "cast me away." And then it's supposed to have been accompanied by a magical scabbard. It protected whoever wore it in battle, but the scabbard was lost. Morgan le Fay took it and threw it in a lake. It was never found again. No, wait, these are fairy tales—fairy tales!

ETHER. Are they?

MAGGIE. Of course they are! Magical swords and scabbards, ancient enchantresses . . .

ETHER. . . . prophetic Americans, immortality granting cups, a woman who sees evil spirits . . .

MAGGIE. But that's different—these stories aren't real.

ETHER. We are now stumbling upon another reality.

MAGGIE. This is too much!

ETHER. Open your eyes!

DANIEL. Wait. "Entombed within the ancient tower . . . " It's not in your books, Maggie. It's behind them. It's in the tower.

MAGGIE. Then . . .

DANIEL. There must be some sort of mechanism or trap door or . . .

ETHER. Perhaps the library was built to hide the entrance . . .

MAGGIE. . . . but this can't be . . .

DANIEL. . . . it could be walled up, I suppose, in that case, we may need a sledgehammer or something . . .

ETHER. . . . perhaps it's in this very room!

MAGGIE. . . . can the curse be finally over?

DANIEL. Excalibur could be ours!

They all pause.

ETHER. This is monumental.

MORGANA emerges from her hiding spot.

MORGANA. So close, so far. *(Indicating DANIEL.)* I expected more out of you, especially. You're going by Daniel these days, aren't you?

They all react, DANIEL about to recite a spell.

MORGANA. Calm down, calm down!

MAGGIE. Who are you?

MORGANA. One who knows you, Magdalena Shallot-Devonshire.

ETHER. That's the witch who killed me!

MORGANA. *(With a knowing smile.)* I didn't do a very thorough of a job of it, apparently. And it looks like I won't get another stab at it either. The girl, however—Iompar speisialta bean sí!

ETHER. Get away from her!

ETHER throws himself in front of the spell which throws him back, knocking him unconscious.

DANIEL. Maggie, get behind me!

MAGGIE. Ether!

DANIEL. Don't worry about him! He's immortal, he's in a much better condition than you would have been. Just get behind me!

DANIEL tries to recite a spell, which MORGANA interrupts with a spell of her own.

MORGANA. I know all your tricks, Daniel, you're the one who taught them to me.

DANIEL. Taught you? I don't know you!

MORGANA. You, see, Daniel, I don't know if you're telling me the truth, or just flirting. Tempest! Frenzy!

TEMPEST and FRENZY enter, attacking DANIEL with their elements. MORGANA then recites a spell, which delivers the knockout blow. DANIEL slumps to the floor, unconscious. MAGGIE now faces MORGANA, TEMPEST, and FRENZY alone.

MAGGIE. Is he . . . ?

MORGANA. No, Daniel needs to be left alive. You, however, my dear, are causing me much deeper complications. I don't quite know what to do with you.

FRENZY. She must be left alive.

FRENZY and TEMPEST flare their elements.

MORGANA. Nice to see you found your voice again. As to the girl, that's for me to decide. She's mine.

MORGANA makes a magical stance, ready to cast a spell if needs be.

FRENZY. You might be able to handle the two of us, but I doubt you'd have such luck with Beezlebub or Mephistopheles.

MORGANA considers this.

MORGANA. I might take my chances.

FRENZY. If you make enough of a ruckus, Lucifer himself has been known to descend upon persistent trouble makers.

MORGANA pauses and then stands down.

MORGANA. *(Pause.)* The girl lives. Which is the conclusion I would have come to anyway. *(FRENZY and TEMPEST flare down their powers.)* Can we chat now? *(FRENZY and TEMPEST don't reply.)* The silent treatment again, is it?

MAGGIE. What are you going to do with me?

MORGANA. I haven't figured that out yet.

MAGGIE. What do you want?

MORGANA. Ah, my sweet Magdelena, you're frightened. Here, I'm not going to kill you, we've already established that.

MAGGIE. Not that you didn't consider it.

MORGANA. I don't take life as lightly as you think, Maggie. Life is a gift from the Lord and the Lady.

MAGGIE. So says the spider to the fly.

MORGANA. (Considering MAGGIE for a moment.) Well, we might as well be familiar with one another. You can call me Morgana. Tell me, dear one, about the curse upon your family.

MAGGIE. How do you know about that?

MORGANA. Just humor me. In fact, let's make a deal. For everything you tell me about yourself, I'll tell you something about myself. That sounds like a nice game, doesn't it? Question for question.

MAGGIE. How do I know you'll tell me the truth?

MORGANA. She-Shade, do you know the Gaelic truth binding spell?

FRENZY. Gaelic's a bit crude for us, but yes.

MORGANA. Magdelena, this spell will make it so that we have to tell each other the truth. It works both ways. But it's the kind of spell that has to be voluntary. Will you allow yourself to be bound by it with me?

MAGGIE considers this. She eyes the devils.

MAGGIE. It will only be between you and me?

MORGANA. That's how it works. A clever spell, relying upon the Law of Fair Play.

MAGGIE. All right. But the shades will have to leave after they cast the spell.

TEMPEST shakes his head. FRENZY puts her hand on TEMPEST's shoulder. TEMPEST swats away her hand, staring hard at her. TEMPEST *flares up.* FRENZY *puts up her hand. It appears that* TEMPEST *may challenge her, but he flares down.*

FRENZY. We agree to the conditions.

MORGANA. Then cast the spell and get out of here.

FRENZY. *(Note: this is the one spell in the play where the Shades cast in Gaelic, rather than Latin)* Cothrom fírinne.

FRENZY and TEMPEST *exit.*

MAGGIE. I hope they're not listening in somehow.

MORGANA. You don't trust them.

MAGGIE. They're devils.

MORGANA. I've found that most devils have a good deal more honor than most humans I know.

MAGGIE. Do you really care about honor?

MORGANA. Yes. Which, by the way, is your first question. With this spell you only get seven questions, so I'd use the rest of yours a little more sparingly.

MAGGIE. Oh. Thank you.

MORGANA. Like I said. Honor.

MAGGIE. All right then. Question for question. I've asked mine first, now it's your turn.

MORGANA. How much do you know about the curse put upon you?

MAGGIE. Only what exists in my family's history. At some point in the Middle Ages, an enchantress put a curse upon us that required us to stay within this castle until we found the key that would unlock our destiny. If I ever tried to wander out of this castle, I would die. So I have not been beyond our little courtyard my entire life.

MORGANA. "Unlock your destiny." Do you know what that destiny is?

MAGGIE. I don't. That's two questions for you. My turn. Why did you kill Ether?

MORGANA. Because I was following Daniel. After he recruited Ether, I discovered that they were trying to get to you and I couldn't have that.

MAGGIE. But why would that . . .

MORGANA. Wait. My turn. Ether's a mystery to me. What do you know about him?

MAGGIE. Only what he's told me. He's a Mormon from America who is now immortal and dreams about the future, which has allowed him to know an uncomfortable amount of things about me. I also know that I am intensely attracted to him and can't breathe whenever he walks into a room.

MAGGIE yelps, brings her hand to her mouth and blushes.

MORGANA. *(With a smile.)*Sometimes with this spell embarrassing things slip out.

MAGGIE. Why did you care that Daniel and Ether were coming for me?

MORGANA. Because you alone can do what I most fear. My next question: do you trust these men?

MAGGIE. No. Neither of them. Especially Daniel.

MORGANA. Good. Then perhaps you and I can be allies after all.

MAGGIE. I don't want to be allies with you. You're a murderer.

MORGANA. I'm not a murderer.

MAGGIE. That's not what I've heard. How are you not a murderer?

MORGANA. Is that your question?

MAGGIE. That depends if that's yours.

MORGANA. Ah. Good save by making that last one a statement, by the way.

MAGGIE. I think I'm finally getting the hang of it. And that was my question, by the way, which answers your last question.

MORGANA. I can tell that we'll both need to be more careful.

MAGGIE. But you still haven't answered my last question.

MORGANA. I do not kill unless I'm protecting myself, or I am protecting the Right. But in saying that I mean I am not afraid of taking a life, if I feel that person will jeopardize the future as it should be.

MAGGIE. That's pretty severe.

MORGANA. I rise to the severity around me. My next question: Would you be willing to join my cause if I showed you why you shouldn't trust these men?

MAGGIE. Yes. I don't like that answer, but it's the one I have to say. What is it that I can do that you fear most?

MORGANA. You can free my enemy. Could I trust you to be constant to me, if you joined me?

MAGGIE. That depends on whether you deserve constancy.

MORGANA. All right. That's a fair enough answer.

MAGGIE. Is your enemy and what I'm looking for connected?

MORGANA. Yes. Are you afraid to die?

This last question baffles MAGGIE. *She takes a moment to answer.*

MAGGIE. I'm afraid to die with an unfulfilled existence. Are you the one who cast the spell on my family?

MORGANA. Yes.

MAGGIE. Who are you?! What am I looking for?!

MORGANA. Sorry, questions and answers is over.

MAGGIE. You! You are the one who did this to me, to my family, for a hundred generations! But how is that possible? You look as young as I do.

MORGANA. Magdelena, listen to me, I know the emotions that this must stir up . . .

MAGGIE. Emotions! I wish you had more emotion, I wish you had a real heart so that you knew that what you did was . . .

MORGANA. . . . utterly wrong. Monstrous. Unforgiveable. I live with that every day of my life.

MAGGIE. And you expect to earn my trust with me knowing that?

MORGANA. Actually, I had hoped you wouldn't have been smart enough to ask that question. But I still harbor the hope that you will not work against me, if I explain things. Magdalena, I'm about to show you a good deal of trust. I hope it's not a mistake. I've always been—fond of your family.

MAGGIE. I doubt that.

MORGANA. Do not pay attention to the past, Magdalena, but to the future that I'll speak of. Then I believe you'll understand me. Look, I'll show you something to make up for everything. I'll put my future in your hands, as you and your family were forced to put yours into mine. That will at least help right this wrong, all right? Miotaseo-laíocht éirigh réaltacht!

> As MORGANA *speaks the incantation, rising out of the floor, or from the books shelves, a table appears upon which lays a regal man, either dressed in stunning, medieval armor or medieval clothing. Under the man's crossed arms lays a marvelous sword. The noise of the rising table awakes* ETHER, *but he currently goes unnoticed.*

MAGGIE. Oh my . . .

MORGANA. Magdalena, this is who and what you seek. The part of the riddle about the sword you guessed right. That blade is the ancient Excalibur, given by the Lady of the Lake. The man you see is Arthur Pendragon, the Once and Future King. I am Arthur's half-sister, Morgan Le Fay. The legends, though at times distorted, are true.

MAGGIE. If he was here all of the time—if you could access him—then why did you need us? Why did you curse my family?

MORGANA. The laws of the universe require equality—balance. For me to manipulate a situation to my favor, to gain access to certain spells, I must sacrifice something in return.

MAGGIE. Sacrifice? Like what?

MORGANA. Some of the sacrifices are subtle—sometimes you just simply feel weak afterwards. Sometimes the sacrifices are more substantial. In this case, to be able to hide up Arthur, I had to make sure that there was the possibility of someone finding him.

MAGGIE. If you've kept him hidden all this time, then why show him to me now?

MORGANA. Honestly, because you were on the verge of finding him yourself. So I thought that it was far more likely that you won't break the curse, even with him before you, once you discovered the reason for his captivity.

MAGGIE. I don't think you understand me very well then.

MORGANA. I think I do. You're a woman. Once I tell the kind of ruler Arthur really was, then you will not want to wake him up. You'll give up anything, even your freedom, to make sure that he does not gain control of the world once again.

MAGGIE. All right, I'm listening.

MORGANA. Arthur Pendragon was no friend to women, nor pagans. His authoritarian rule had a two pronged purpose. First, the advancement of Christianity. Second, the subjugation of women through the system of chivalry.

MAGGIE. Chivalry? But wasn't the whole point to protect and honor women?

MORGANA. Oh, those men in armor gave lip service to women, surely. They sang songs, they performed heroic deeds, they praised us to the moon—but once they bedded us, or married us, or silenced us with their kindness, things certainly changed then. Exalted and put away in our beautiful towers, crippled and voiceless, with no door to escape.

MAGGIE. But that was a different time. Surely, seeing this new place, this new time, new rules of conduct . . .

MORGANA. Don't be naive. It is harder to change a man's mind than to turn back the tide. Not even his wife, not even poor Guenevere was spared from his exacting code. For her supposed indiscretions, they were going to burn her at the stake—that is until, Lancelot saved her, of course. But Lancelot was no better, always simply wanting to claim her, never truly desiring to honor her.

MAGGIE. All of that's true as well then?

MORGANA. All of the romantic stories, all of the swoon inducing rhetoric—take that all away and Arthur and his knights were no more than cheap bullies. Well, despite our expert abilities, we could not make ourselves men, nor would we accept their Christ and offend our older gods, thus they found their many ways to punish people like me—people like you.

MAGGIE. But what does any of that matter now? It is the 21st century. He'd be just a man now. In a world of democracies and republics, why on earth would you be so afraid of him?

MORGANA. There's deep magic attached to that man, Maggie. Arthur was a greater and more skilled man than any Alexander or Caesar or Napoleon. If Mordred hadn't stepped in and stopped Arthur, he would not have been simply content with England. He would have reached out to take the whole known world. I may have abhorred his flaws, but I never underestimated his abilities.

ETHER. *(Rising.)* Maggie, don't listen to her!

MORGANA. You have no part in this conversation!

ETHER. Oh, I think that I do! You're very persuasive, ma'am, but your story is as one sided as a pancake.

MORGANA. *(Confused.)* Pancakes have two sides.

ETHER. Maggie, if I may remind you this is the woman that . . .

MAGGIE. She's right, Ether. You have no part in this conversation.

ETHER. What?

MAGGIE. I know you're trying to watch out for me, but trust me to make my own decision on this one. The issues at hand deeply involve her and I. You have no claim on it.

MORGANA. Very wise, Magdelena. I suppose that means I have your support.

MAGGIE. My support? You have cursed my innocent family so that you could settle your own private disputes.

MORGANA. It was a hard decision to make, but you have to understand the alternative . . .

MAGGIE. As you said, like the women of your age I was "put away in a beautiful tower, crippled and voiceless, with no door to escape." In what way has your own behavior differed than this man's who you hate so much?

MORGANA. How dare you compare me to that tyrant? Where are my kingdoms? Where are my knights swearing blind obedience? Where is my excess of power to control the destinies of millions of people? In what possible ways could I be compared to him?

MAGGIE. I was your kingdom. I was your stewardship. You had an excess of power over my life. And what did you do with that influence? You had your foot on my throat, ready to crush it.

MORGANA. This man is not worthy!

MAGGIE. Maybe you're right. Perhaps this man is no friend to women. But then it is also true that you are no friend of mine.

MORGANA. I can be your ally! If you join me, you can trust me!

MAGGIE. I'm not stupid. I won't have any alliances.

MORGANA. You cannot stand alone in this life!

MAGGIE. You taught me to stand alone!

> *MAGGIE dashes to ARTHUR.*

MORGANA. No!

MORGAN goes to stop MAGGIE, but ETHER restrains MORGANA.

ETHER. I've got her, Maggie!

MORGANA. Get your filthy hands off of me! Magdalena, think of what you're doing!

MAGGIE. All I've done my whole life is think. I'm bored of it.

MORGANA. No!

MAGGIE takes Excalibur from ARTHUR's dormant body and lifts it to the sky.

MAGGIE. "Entombed within the ancient tower,
  The lost, sacred words lie dormant,
  Arms fold over the sheath'ed power,
  Opening them ends the internment,
  Springs to bright life the ancient stories,
  Holy blade rising to the sky,
  Read the words engraved for glories,
  His eyes open, his voice will fly!"

MORGANA. No...

ARTHUR's eyes open. He sits up, then stands, weakly at first. Yet then a new energy seems to course through him and a strength and power is evident just by looking at him.

ARTHUR. I am made free. *(Noting MAGGIE)* Fair damsel, are you the one who has done this?

MAGGIE. Yes.

ARTHUR. Then I owe you my life and freedom. You may ask any gift of me that is within my power to give, and it shall be yours.

MAGGIE. Then, sir, I—I ask for the scabbard of Excalibur.

ARTHUR. The scabbard. *(Pause.)* That is wise, my lady, but, alas, I cannot give it. My cursed half-sister Morgan Le Fay threw it in a lake, and it has not been recovered since.

MAGGIE. I think you will find yourself mistaken in that, sire. You'll find the scabbard on her.

MAGGIE motions ARTHUR's attention for the first time to MORGANA.

ARTHUR. Why, it is true! The scabbard! The Christ has smiled upon me after all my troubles to have seen it once again! But why does this man hold this woman captive? It surely does not bring him any worship to do so and shows a villainous disposition.

ETHER. Do you not recognize this woman, your, uh, majesty?

ARTHUR. By my honor, no.

ETHER. She claims to be your half-sister, Morgana. She tried to stop us from freeing you.

ARTHUR. Then I have misjudged you, sir, if what you say is true, and I owe you a debt of gratitude as well. But Morgana, you say? This damsel is no kinswoman of mine. I know my half-sister well and I would recognize her in any guise.

MORGANA. Arthur, for all of your ability, you can still only see what's in front of you.

ARTHUR. Woman, you are mad to think that you are Morgan Le Fay.

MORGANA. No, Arthur, I have been wise. I have cheated death. For thousands of years my daughters and then their daughters and then their daughters have taken upon my spirit and let me inhabit them. They are the Maidens of Avalon.

ARTHUR. What foul magic is this?

MORGANA. It's truly me, Arthur. I am the one whose father was killed so that our mother could fornicate with your father! I am the one whose husband and son honored you more than they ever did me and betrayed me with their disloyalties. And it was my dear lover, my beloved Accolon, who you butchered. I am the one who you have eternally wronged and I will remember every story so that you and your kind will never forget them!

ARTHUR. False woman, it is you! Your taunting tongue will forever expose you for who you are, Morgana! You dare say that I wronged you? You, who constantly tried to slay my person and to meddle with my wife? You, who helped destroy the very foundations of Camelot? And you talk of Accolon, that traitor who conspired with you against me? I would be justified in cutting off your head right now, for your maidenhood has long been lost by your sins and you are no lady to be protected by the laws of chivalry! Your death is warranted, witch!

MAGGIE. Arthur, please, no!

ARTHUR. You defend this woman?

MAGGIE. I have no love for her, that is sure. She cursed my family and has devastated my chances for happiness.

ARTHUR. Then the more guilty, she!

MAGGIE. Please, have mercy. Spare her.

ARTHUR *considers this.*

ARTHUR. If she has wronged you, then why do you defend her?

MAGGIE. Is it not the Christian thing to do, sire?

ARTHUR. By my honor, you are a wise maiden and true. I will grant both of your requests: Morgana may have her life for now, and you may have the scabbard of Excalibur.

ARTHUR *TAKES THE SCABBARD FROM MORGANA AND HANDS IT TO MAGGIE.*

MORGANA. Hypocrites.

ARTHUR. As for you, if you come against me again, Morgan Le Fay, your life is forfeit. May you ponder upon the mercies granted upon you this day by this fair maiden. You may release her, good sir.

ETHER *lets go of* MORGANA, *but she stands still, staring hard at* ARTHUR.

MORGANA. You may feel powerful in your supposed mercy, but it means nothing. If you had killed me, another of my daughters would have filled this body's place. Exterminate one of them, and another shall rise from their ashes. You cannot be rid of me, Arthur. I have made sure of that. The Maidens of Avalon will always be set against you.

ARTHUR. Through your flagrant heresies, you have damned your soul to hell.

Enter TEMPEST *and* FRENZY.

TEMPEST. By Mephistopheles' mullet! What happened here?

ARTHUR. Wicked woman, you have brought the minions of Satan with you! I sense them even now.

ETHER. Oh, don't tell me they're back!

TEMPEST. Is he another veil ripper?!

FRENZY. Oh no. No, no, no, I'm afraid it's much worse than that.

TEMPEST. Well, I don't care who he is, or what you say, Frenzy, this one's a goner!

FRENZY. Tempest, don't!

TEMPEST. Not this time, Frenzy! Not this time!

ARTHUR. Where are you, devils? I can't see you, but Merlin certainly taught me how to smell you! Prove your worship and reveal yourself, you cowards!

TEMPEST charges towards ARTHUR, *his elements flaring.*

TEMPEST. Pluvia Pinguesco Gelu Ventus Levitas Tempestas!

MAGGIE. Arthur, sire, he's coming right for you!

Thrusting where MAGGIE *indicated,* ARTHUR *stabs* TEMPEST *with* EXCALIBUR. *Those who can see what has happened, watch in shock and awe.*

FRENZY. Tempest!

TEMPEST. How . . . ?

ETHER. I can see him . . .

ARTHUR. We all can, because of Excalibur. Merlin was right. It can get rid of your kind.

TEMPEST. What—what have you done, human?

ARTHUR. Demon, I am Arthur Pendragon, son of Uther Pendragon. I am the King of Camelot, the Lord of England. I am God's chosen, the Once and Future King. Remember the name of him who sent you to that which you earned through your misdeeds. I am banishing you from earth, to inherit your eternal home. You are being damned.

TEMPEST. You can't.

ARTHUR. Excalibur can.

ARTHUR twists the blade and pulls it out. TEMPEST screams demonically and vanishes in a flash of smoke.

FRENZY. Oh, hell.

FRENZY exits in a dash, as does MORGANA.

ETHER. Wow.

MAGGIE. I'm free—I'm really free.

MAGGIE collapses in gratitude and relief. ETHER rushes to her.

ETHER. Maggie, are you all right?

MAGGIE. I—I don't know how I am.

DANIEL stirs.

ARTHUR. Who is that man over there? Is he injured?

ETHER. Oh—Daniel!

They all rush to DANIEL, but upon seeing his face, ARTHUR steps back in shock.

MAGGIE. I had forgotten all about him!

DANIEL. *(Getting up.)* Oh, that's nice. I only just saved your life. I did save your life, didn't I? Or are we all dead? *(Seeing ETHER.)* Oh good, you're here, Ether. Still alive. *(Seeing* ARTHUR.*)* But who's the role playing dude?

ARTHUR. It cannot be—you were caught in the enchanted cave. Did the witch finally let you out?

DANIEL. Pardon?

ARTHUR. What sort of spell allowed you to become so young?

DANIEL. I don't think I'm following.

ARTHUR. Don't you recognize me?

DANIEL. Should I?

ARTHUR. It's me! It's Arthur!

DANIEL. And who do you think I am?

ARTHUR. Why, don't be daft! You're my counselor, my most valued friend.

DANIEL. What?

ARTHUR. You're Merlin!

DANIEL. What? What?!

Blackout.

END ACT ONE

Act Two

SCENE 1

The VEILED WOMAN *from the beginning of* ACT ONE, SCENE II *is singing a sad, mournful song with a Medieval or Celtic tune. Mid-way through the song,* MAGGIE *enters and listens undetected.*

VEILED WOMAN. My love sails on furthest seas
Yet remains here close with me.
My honor battles far afield
Yet my passion holds my hand.
One is a ghost who needs not me
And one is always close to see.
One is kind but always distant
One is wild but always near.
My soul has left me on my own
My body I have always known.
My soul has left me on my own
My body I have always known.

MAGGIE. Who are you?

VEILED WOMAN. Oh! I—I thought you all had gone outside for the ceremony.

MAGGIE. We had, but it's about to rain, so we've brought it inside.

VEILED WOMAN. Then they are coming!

The VEILED WOMAN *goes to retreat, but* MAGGIE *stops her by grabbing her wrist.*

MAGGIE. You're solid. I—I thought you were a ghost.

VEILED WOMAN. I am.

MAGGIE. Or a devil.

VEILED WOMAN. I am.

MAGGIE. Why are you in my castle?

VEILED WOMAN. Please, let me go.

MAGGIE. I need to know who you are.

VEILED WOMAN. I mean you no harm. Please, let me go.

MAGGIE. Not until you answer my questions.

VEILED WOMAN. He can't see me. Please, do not tell him that you saw me.

MAGGIE. Who?

VEILED WOMAN. Please, have mercy . . .

MAGGIE. How long have you been here?

VEILED WOMAN. I have always been here. *(ETHER, DANIEL, and ARTHUR are heard.)* Let me go!

> *The* VEILED WOMAN *wrenches herself free and exits. Enter* ETHER, DANIEL, *and* ARTHUR. ETHER *is dressed like a medieval knight, complete with a sword and a shield.*

ETHER. Maggie, why, look at me!

MAGGIE. Hm?

ETHER. As if I stepped right out of a story book!

MAGGIE. I still think it was a stupid request.

ARTHUR. Dear lady, do not begrudge Ether's righteous gift from me. He could have had anything that I could grant and he chose an honorable course. It will bring him much worship to be a knight of the round table.

MAGGIE. Well, at least a Mormon knight is a fitting kind of fate. From what I understand of the Mormon culture, you have your own kind of code of chivalry and vows, don't you?

ETHER. And the highest covenants and vows are taken by both genders, so don't take that tone with me.

MAGGIE. Sensitive much?

ETHER. Having been locked up here, how is that you know so much about the world, Maggie? I doubt any of those ancient texts tell much about my Church, unless you have some Nephite plates hanging around here.

MAGGIE. I do have the internet, Ether. When J.K. Rowling used to visit us before my parents died, she hooked it up for us.

ETHER. Really?

MAGGIE. When we're through with all of this nonsense, maybe I'll even add you on Facebook.

ETHER. But that's still . . .

MAGGIE. . . . not much of an existence, I know. It was the shadowed mirror from which I saw the world. But now that's over. I'm free.

DANIEL. I still think that Maggie should be accorded the same honor being bestowed upon Ether.

MAGGIE. We've already been through this, Daniel—er, Merlin.

DANIEL. Still call me Daniel. It's weird enough coming from *Game of Thrones* over there.

MAGGIE. Either way, I still wouldn't take the position, even if he offered it.

ARTHUR. Which I would never do.

MAGGIE. So since I am determined to remain independent and he is determined to only have male knights, we'll all just have to make do.

ETHER. Uh, can we go on with this? I'm kind of nervous.

ARTHUR. Fear not, good sir, for your heart is worthy. Now kneel before me. (*ETHER kneels and ARTHUR pulls out his sword and raises it.*) "God make you a good man and fail not of beauty. The Round Table was founded in patience, humility, and meekness. Thou art never to do outrageousity, nor murder, and always to flee treason, by no means to be cruel, and always to do ladies, damsels, and gentle women succor . . . Thou shouldst be for all ladies and fight for their quarrels, and ever be courteous and never refuse mercy to him that asketh mercy, for a knight that is courteous and kind and gentle has favor in every place. Thou shouldst never hold a lady or gentle woman against her will. Thou must keep thy word to all and not be feeble of good believeth and faith. Right must be defended against might and distress must be protected . . . Thou shouldst not fail in these things: charity, abstinence and truth. No knight shall win worship but if he be of worship himself and of good living and that loveth God and dreadeth God then else he getteth no worship here be ever so hardly. Do not anything that will in any way dishonour the fair name of Christian knighthood for only by stainless and honourable lives and not by prowess and courage shall the final goal be reached. Therefore be a good knight and so I pray to God so ye may be, and if ye be of prowess and of worthiness then ye shall be a Knight of the Round Table."

ETHER. Uhm, Amen.

ARTHUR. I dub you Sir Ether, of Provo. (*ARTHUR brings his sword down upon* ETHER's *shoulder and then crosses it over* ETHER's *head to the other, knighting him.*) Rise, Sir Ether, Knight of the Round Table.

ETHER. Thank you, Sire.

ARTHUR. Now, if you will pardon me, I have much to discuss with Merlin.

DANIEL. Daniel.

ARTHUR. Merlin.

DANIEL. Daniel.

ARTHUR. Merlin. I am sure you will see the sense of this soon, my friend.

DANIEL. I'm not your friend. I hardly know you.

ARTHUR. Whatever bewitchment this is, I am sure with your arts we will be able to discover it. Good day, Lady Magdalena. Good day, Sir Ether.

Exit ARTHUR.

DANIEL. This is going to be a long day.

Exit DANIEL.

MAGGIE. I hope you know that you made a fool of yourself.

DANIEL. I know you disagree with all of it, Maggie, but I wish you could at least try to be happy for me.

MAGGIE. All right. Goodie for you. Enjoy your little frat club.

DANIEL. Didn't you hear the oath?

MAGGIE. Oh, you thought it was nice, did you?

DANIEL. It was beautiful.

MAGGIE. I thought it was dismal.

DANIEL. Dismal? You think honor and humility and mercy are dismal?

MAGGIE. Those are just buzz words to hide a pernicious system of oppression.

ETHER. You're sounding a good deal like Morgana.

MAGGIE. Well, I didn't disagree with everything she said. I didn't disagree with most of it, in fact.

ETHER. And so you'd prefer that we were more like her?

MAGGIE. *(Pause.)* No. But I don't want us to be like Arthur, either.

ETHER. He's glorious!

MAGGIE. Oh, so you think he's a saint then?

ETHER. No. A true king.

MAGGIE. I thought you Americans didn't like Kings.

ETHER. Well, he's—something else then. But glorious!

MAGGIE. You're impossible.

MAGGIE goes to exit, but ETHER gently stops her.

ETHER. Maggie, wait. Look, I know he's not perfect. No leader is, they're bound to have their flaws, their prejudices, their misconceptions. And, for what it's worth, I personally would have felt it an honor to have you knighted next to me . . .

MAGGIE. You didn't say as much.

ETHER. It wasn't my place to. And, anyway, you said you didn't want it.

MAGGIE. I don't.

ETHER. I see.

MAGGIE. Look, I know it sounds noble, and like you're being something, doing something, but can't you see through all that? It's not about protecting the weak. It's about keeping them weak!

ETHER. Maggie, men and women need each other! They depend upon one another! Even Arthur recognized his debt to you.

MAGGIE. But gave me none of the honor.

ETHER. Oh and what do you thinking possessing Excalibur's scabbard is?

MAGGIE. Since when was a scabbard anything special compared to a blade?

ETHER. Don't patronize me, Maggie. I know exactly why you chose the scabbard instead of Excalibur. I reckon that I'm as familiar with the myths as you are. In fact, let's go straight to the passage, shall we?

ETHER goes to where MAGGIE left L'Morte de Arthur and starts flipping through the pages.

MAGGIE. You don't have to show off . . .

ETHER. Just trying to be accurate. Here we go: "Then Sir Arthur looked on the sword, and liked it passing well. Whether you liketh better, said Merlin, the sword or the scabbard? Me liketh better the sword, said Arthur. Ye are more unwise, said Merlin, for the scabbard is worth ten of the swords, for whiles ye have the scabbard upon you, ye shall never lose no blood, be ye ever so sore wounded; therefore, keep well the scabbard always with you."

MAGGIE. You know *L'Morte de Arthur*, so what? All it proves is Arthur loves his phallic symbols.

ETHER. And what happened when he cast away his scabbard?

MAGGIE. He never cast it away. Morgana stole it.

ETHER. I wasn't talking about that scabbard. I was talking about Guenevere.

MAGGIE. Oh.

ETHER. When Arthur cast away Guenevere, that's when he lost his kingdom. Maggie, in one sense you are completely, utterly right. Whatever their role is, women are underestimated and undervalued.

MAGGIE. Whatever their role? Come on . . .

ETHER. Look, Maggie, whatever Arthur feels about you, whatever the world's societies or religions or governments feel about you, let me make it clear how I feel about you.

MAGGIE. All right.

ETHER. Magdalena, I have seen you confront demons and liberate kings. I have seen you outwit and outmaneuver a centuries years old enchantress. You are the most capable and mighty person I have ever met.

MAGGIE. Ether—that means a lot to me.

ETHER. And you've come to mean everything to me.

MAGGIE. What are you saying?

ETHER. You know, I so often see you full of so much rage or sorrow, crying out all the injustices heaped upon you, mourning all the losses you've endured, but I don't think I've ever seen you look quite like you do at this moment.

MAGGIE. Like what?

ETHER. Happy.

MAGGIE. You know, Ether, sometimes I think you're grand . . .

ETHER. Thank you.

MAGGIE. . . . and sometimes I just want to learn a spell to shoot your head off.

ETHER. I thought you didn't actually practice magic.

MAGGIE. You know, Daniel and Morgana practice their spells and collect their relics, but they're always trying to pull from these magics and powers that surround them. They forget that the magic is right here, inside all of us.

ETHER. The gift that God placed within us.

MAGGIE. Yes, at this moment with you I can believe that.

Tense pause, then MAGGIE *kisses* ETHER. *After they separate, there is another tense pause.*

MAGGIE. I'm going for a walk.

MAGGIE turns to leave.

ETHER. What?

MAGGIE. I've been cooped up in a castle all my life. Now that I'm free, I think it's natural to want to take a walk.

ETHER. But—but—now?

MAGGIE. *(With a sly smile.)* You could come with me, if you want. I'm sure we could find something to do in the fields and forests around the castle.

ETHER. The fields and—oh! A walk sounds wonderful!

MAGGIE. I thought you would approve.

ETHER. But you remember that I'm . . .

MAGGIE. Don't worry, we'll keep it chaste—enough.

Exit MAGGIE and ETHER.

SCENE 2

Enter DANIEL and ARTHUR.

DANIEL. It's impossible.

ARTHUR. Thus says the man who performs magic.

DANIEL. Magic is not magic as people understand the term. Magic is a knowledge, a science. A more complex understanding of the laws of the universe and how to manipulate them.

ARTHUR. You have told me that before. Which just convinces me further that you are truly the man that I call . . .

DANIEL. What you're telling me is not manipulating the laws of the Universe, it's breaking them!

ARTHUR. The Law of Relativity.

DANIEL. How do *you* know about the Law of Relativity?

ARTHUR. You taught me. Time is not what we think it is, you said. Space is not we think it is, you said. It can be manipulated, it can be traveled through, like a man swims through water. You will become that eternal swimmer. And then you will come back to me. You will teach me. And you already know this. Tell me about your childhood.

DANIEL. First you're Einstein, then you're Freud?

ARTHUR. Tell me about your childhood.

DANIEL. I can't.

ARTHUR. And why is that?

DANIEL. Because I can't remember it.

ARTHUR. My good Merlin, my dear friend, you will one day remember it. For you told me of your childhood. You told me of the fire and the tempests. The machines of war raging against each other in the sky, under the sea, and on the moon. The weapons that melt steel and flesh. Whole nations on fire, whole continents uninhabitable, the world in anarchy. In your youth you knew a world of blood and heat and steam.

DANIEL. Well, that's not possible. As bad as history has been, it hasn't been that bad.

ARTHUR. That's because your past is no past at all. It is not part of history, it is part of prophecy.

DANIEL. And how is that supposed to make sense?

ARTHUR. It does make sense to those who know the right language! It is why you taught me the order of things, how to create a righteous, unified society. You said that I could save a remnant of mankind from that fate. But I failed you, Merlin. Camelot failed. All your harsh criticisms of my behavior were well founded after all.

DANIEL. I don't know you well enough to criticize you.

ARTHUR. That didn't stop you then.

DANIEL. You're King Arthur—you're famous and glorious and the heralded hero through the ages . . .

ARTHUR. I am ignorant. After all the fighting, all the preparation, all the safe guarding of our principles and our lands . . . I saw it ravaged before my eyes. And it was all my fault. I welcomed death, Merlin. I should not have been brought back.

DANIEL. What do you mean?

ARTHUR. I thought I was Destiny's Child! Ah! More like Destiny's Fool! All the prophecy and pomp around the sword in the stone and the circumstances around my birth . . .

DANIEL. You were to be a savior.

ARTHUR. Do not use that word in connection with me again! It soils the holy character of it. The Son of God was as pure as an unspoiled lamb! But what of me? I was not the savior of my people, I was the destroyer.

DANIEL. From what I understand of the stories, I believe that role belonged to others.

ARTHUR. Then you don't understand the stories well enough.

DANIEL. That could certainly be true.

ARTHUR. Merlin, you don't understand your nature yet. Adam's fallen race are the wheels of time going forward, ever forward, never able to stop our movement, never able to fix our path. Our sins and stains blot our existence, never to be purified. We shred our happiness, wrack our hopes, abandon our chances, and then are never able to go back to repair the damage. You, however, are an opposing wheel. You, my friend, are able to remit our sins, and absolve our guilt. Swimming through time to spread Christ's Grace.

DANIEL. Stop talking in riddles!

ARTHUR. Oh, you're the one who taught me the art. Merlin, you were my teacher, now must you be taught?

DANIEL. Everyone must be taught.

ARTHUR. Then hear this lesson. Merlin, this is not your time. Neither is it mine. You come from the end of the world. You saw the End as it transpired, and you came back to teach me how to prevent it.

DANIEL. I don't believe in that religious mumbo jumbo. It is the rhetoric of tyrants and the crutch of fools.

ARTHUR. How can you say that? You have tasted of the deep magic.

DANIEL. And seen that there is no mystery to it.

ARTHUR. Then that is a revelation of God, not a refutation.

DANIEL. Rubbish. Complete, absolute . . .

ARTHUR. You will not be a heretic in my day, Merlin. You were more priest than wizard, despite what people said about you. You, more than any other man, taught me that we must rely on God, for his miracles can be just as great today as they were when Moses battled against Pharaoh's magicians with the staff that God had given him. You were our Moses!

DANIEL. Now I know I'm not the man you think I am. I've never considered myself to be religious.

ARTHUR. Your spells in those days had the power of the Holy Spirit behind them, rather than the power of the devils that I feel you struggle within you now. Is it them that you draw power from here?

DANIEL. Devils?

ARTHUR. Yes, you believe in devils well enough. You know of them, you have experienced them! But I have known Christ, Merlin, and I tell you now that through him you can deliver mightier miracles than any of the shadow shows you've played at here. (*There is a sound.* DANIEL *and* ARTHUR *remain still for a moment.*) Someone's here.

ARTHUR *draws Excalibur.*

DANIEL. Come out and show yourself, coward. Show yourself!

MERLIN *recites an incantation and the secret door used in Act One, Scene 2 opens and reveals the* VEILED WOMAN.

ARTHUR. Morgana!

VEILED WOMAN. No! No, I am not Morgana!

DANIEL. Who are you?

VEILED WOMAN. Merlin—when I first heard your voice, I dared not believe it. But here—now—and so young. We have held onto our vibrancy, but how did you turn back your age?

DANIEL. You know me?

VEILED WOMAN. I—I must go!

ARTHUR. Woman, stay! I think I know you.

VEILED WOMAN. You never knew me.

ARTHUR. Stay—I command you to stay!

VEILED WOMAN. Sire, I have remained here for all these years to protect you, not to obey you.

ARTHUR. Then I will force you to obey me!

VEILED WOMAN. "Thou shouldst never hold a lady or gentle woman against her will."

ARTHUR. Who are you?

VEILED WOMAN. I was yours. Now I am my own.

Exit the VEILED WOMAN, *back into secret door, which closes.*
ARTHUR *looks after her, stunned.*

DANIEL. Should I go after her, Arthur? Arthur? (*ARTHUR stumbles and breaks down weeping.*) Who was that?

ARTHUR. My greatest love and my greatest enemy.

DANIEL. Guenevere. My, we almost have a complete chess set now!

ARTHUR. You were right about me, Merlin. Every tongue lashing, every indignant lecture—I deserved every word.

DANIEL. Arthur, you're not looking at this with the right perspective...

ARTHUR. No wonder Morgana hated me.

DANIEL. Now stop that.

ARTHUR. I must be alone.

DANIEL. Arthur...

ARTHUR. I must be alone!

Exit ARTHUR.

DANIEL. Arthur!

Enter MORGANA.

MORGANA. Please, don't call him back. I've been waiting for ever so long to get you alone. (*DANIEL twirls and, upon seeing* MORGANA, *starts an incantation, which* MORGANA *immediately interrupts with one of her own, which pins* DANIEL *to the ground.*) Balbh draíodóir! You're really slow on the draw these days, Merlin. (*DANIEL, tries to speak, but can't.*) Look, I'll release the gag spell on you, if you promise to behave. I just want to talk. (*DANIEL nods.*) All right, but if you're not courteous, right back you go. Saor draíodóir!

DANIEL. That hurt.

MORGANA. (*With a smile.*) I know.

DANIEL. Well, you wanted to talk. Talk.

MORGANA. You don't have to be sour.

DANIEL. Well, last time we met, you gave me a rather large headache. Why do you want to be so chatty now?

MORGANA. Well, the damage is done. The ogre's awake. I can't change that.

DANIEL. And that's it? You give up?

MORGANA. Oh, no. Not by a long shot. We'll still have plenty of chances to tango, sexy.

DANIEL. You really do give mixed signals.

MORGANA. Part of my allure.

DANIEL. What is it that you want?

MORGANA. Some answers.

DANIEL. Then you've come to the wrong source.

MORGANA. Well then, if this were an ideal world, I would want Arthur's head on a platter, instead of walled up in this place. If I couldn't have his head, then I would settle for his heart.

DANIEL. His heart, it would seem, is already taken.

MORGANA. Yes, she always was his weakness, which we saw in the end. Oh, but you didn't see it, did you? At least not this you, this shadow, a mere portion of who you will become. It's very sad, I know that as well as anyone. Those closest to Arthur—Guenevere, Lancelot, myself—we all failed him in the end.

DANIEL. And you relish that?

MORGANA. No. Not in the least.

DANIEL. Respect for your enemy?

MORGANA. No, not the slightest shred of respect. But love. You can't help loving a man like him once you've seen his heart. Very cliché, but very true. Most clichés are. Is that what you saw in him, Merlin, his heart?

DANIEL. My name is Daniel.

MORGANA. Your name is Denial.

DANIEL. I am not Merlin!

MORGANA. Perhaps not yet then. Yet the day will come, or in my case, has been . . . the day has been when you will toll fear into my heart and your talents shall make you a legend. But today is not that day.

DANIEL. Are you gloating?

MORGANA. I was never able to match you in my day. But now, well yes, it's a little exhilarating.

DANIEL. Definitely gloating.

MORGANA. Merlin, dear Merlin! Don't you understand? I adore you. You were always such fun, even though you outclassed me every time. I loved the challenge, though. But, you see, you bet on the wrong horse. Like you are now, Arthur was but an echo of what he was meant to be. Great man that he is, he did not turn into the savior you wanted him to be.

DANIEL. I don't expect him to be anything.

MORGANA. Then he has fulfilled that expectation to the letter. A fallen hero, a tragic king, a failure.

DANIEL. You're gloating again.

MORGANA. Maybe a little bit.

DANIEL. Morgana, I don't care about the past. My commission is about the future.

MORGANA. If the Lady in the Lake thinks that sending a debunked, Christian king; a trapped pagan; a starry eyed, Mormon dreamer; and an amateur wizard against the future onslaught is going to make the slightest bit of difference, then she is much more deluded than even I originally thought.

DANIEL. Perhaps, but that doesn't mean I'll be any less true to her command.

MORGANA. See, there you are, that's what I love about you! Always fighting on, even when you know you're going to fail. The spirit of Camelot!

DANIEL. You needn't be so flippant.

MORGANA. I'm not being flippant, Merlin—I mean Daniel. Well, I love bantering with you, but I'm not here for that. I wanted to warn you.

DANIEL. Warn me? About what?

MORGANA. That Arthur's going to break your heart. I am the one who let you out of the cave which the Damsel of the Lake put you in by enchantment. When you emerged from that cave and saw Camelot in ashes, I saw your eyes shatter and your spirit heave. It broke my own heart to see it. And it will be that cursed man's fault.

DANIEL. You expect too much out of men, Morgana.

MORGANA. I don't expect anything from them, that's my point! The ideals of unity and cooperation and honor you taught, they were lost upon him.

DANIEL. Arthur is a good man.

MORGANA. Neither his mind, nor his soul are large enough to do anything but create a pale imitation of the Utopia you had in mind.

DANIEL. And I suppose you think you could have done better?

MORGANA. Not then. But now I can. I—I have an order of women at Avalon who have proven that. They are willing to give up their very lives for the greater good.

DANIEL. Oh, how original. You have your own feminine knights of the round table then!

MORGANA. Arthur never had knights so true and loyal as the women in my order. And, Daniel, I want to offer you what Arthur never offered us. Become part of our order.

DANIEL. You want me to become a pagan nun? Sorry, I don't wear skirts.

MORGANA. No. I want you to become our ally. I want you to help us save the world.

DANIEL. From what?

MORGANA. The Lady In The Lake was right about one thing. A great evil is coming. You and Magdalena and even Ether can be a part of our preparations against it.

DANIEL. And Arthur?

MORGANA. He will never have a place beside me.

DANIEL. I see.

MORGANA. Don't make any rash decisions. Just think about it. All right?

DANIEL. *(Pause.)*All right.

MORGANA. Splendid. I'll see you around then, sexy.

DANIEL. Morgana . . .

MORGANA. Yes?

DANIEL. You tried to kill me.

MORGANA. No, I didn't. I tried to stop you.

DANIEL. But you did accomplish killing Ether.

MORGANA. And you happen to have the grail, of which I had been previously informed. I knew you would use it on him—in fact, I planned on it.

DANIEL. Why would you want me to make him immortal?

MORGANA. None of this has been about what *I* wanted, Daniel. There's a larger end game to all of this than you understand. But that's years off yet. Just know that it all worked out as it needed to.

DANIEL. All right.

MORGAN. Remember, analyze the entire board before committing yourself to a move. No rash decisions.

DANIEL. No rash decisions.

Exit MORGAN. DANIEL *considers all of this for a moment, and then exits.*

SCENE 3

Enter MAGGIE *and* ETHER. MAGGIE *has changed from her modern clothing to a Spring-time medieval dress, with flowers strewn through her hair. At the moment they are both very buoyant and happy.*

MAGGIE. Oh, Ether! I didn't know that the wind could feel so good! When that gust came up and blew our clothes and through our hair and in our faces—I felt like a kite! A kite. I've never flown a kite. If the wind's blowing tomorrow, can we fly a kite?

ETHER. I'm sure we can buy one in the village.

MAGGIE. Brilliant! Then we'll fly that kite and it'll lift above the library, above this dreary castle and it will fly higher and higher until we can't even see it, it's so high.

ETHER. We'll need a lot of string then.

MAGGIE. Once it gets so high, eventually we won't even need the string. After we've had our fun, we'll let it go and it will fly far, far away from here. Farther than I've ever been.

ETHER. Wonderful.

MAGGIE. Thank you. Thank you so much, Ether. I've never had such a beautiful day.

ETHER. Tell you the truth, neither have I.

MAGGIE. Have you traveled much, Ether?

ETHER. I went on a mission for my Church.

MAGGIE. Yes—your church. Where did you go?

ETHER. Ghana. That's in Africa.

MAGGIE. I know where Ghana is. That sounds beautiful. Did you see the savanna, the tall grass and the animals? Did that burning sun beat down on you and make you feel alive?

ETHER. Yeah, it did. I served in a lot of the villages, not much in the cities. I wouldn't have had it any other way. I got really sick a couple of times, but I wouldn't let them send me home, and I always got over it, just like I told them.

MAGGIE. I wonder what it's like to be sick. I suppose that's a different kind of adventure.

ETHER. It's not every pleasant. Wait, you've never been sick?

MAGGIE. And neither will you anymore.

ETHER. I suppose not. That's a weird thought.

MAGGIE. Morgana's spell kept away most diseases. My family would grow to a ripe, old age and then just pass away. Like the wind, just petering out . . .

ETHER. Growing old, with wrinkles and white hair—not something I'll experience, I guess.

MAGGIE. Don't think about that. *(Beat.)* Let's travel.

ETHER. Someday, perhaps.

MAGGIE. No, not some day. In a week. Maybe even tomorrow. I have plenty of money, I ran a lot of businesses on the internet. I've wanted to see Greece and Italy and America and Australia and China and Mexico—and then we can go back to where you were a missionary in Africa and then . . .

ETHER. I can't.

MAGGIE. Of course you can.

ETHER. And neither can you.

MAGGIE. Of course I can. No one can tell me that I can't.

ETHER. More must happen here first. There's still something that needs to happen.

MAGGIE. I don't care.

ETHER. I've dreamed it.

MAGGIE. I don't care! You don't decide my fate.

ETHER. I know I don't. But some choice you make, some path you take leads you to . . .

MAGGIE. Leads me to what?

ETHER. I don't know. A lot of stuff happens that I don't understand.

MAGGIE. What happens?

ETHER. I think you die.

MAGGIE. I—I die? And you didn't tell me?

ETHER. I don't think I understand it all. I could have misinterpreted it.

MAGGIE. I don't want to hear this.

ETHER. Then I won't say anything more about it.

MAGGIE. I—I think we're done for today, Ether.

ETHER. Maggie, I'm—I'm . . .

MAGGIE. The kite. We're going to fly that kite tomorrow.

ETHER. Okay.

MAGGIE. And we're going to ignore that dream.

ETHER. Maggie . . .

MAGGIE. No. It didn't happen, or if it did, you misinterpreted it, or it was just a dream. You do just have dreams sometimes, don't you?

ETHER. Yes.

MAGGIE. Then that's what it was.

ETHER. Okay.

MAGGIE. I'll see you tomorrow then.

ETHER. Wait.

MAGGIE. What now?

ETHER. You're a very special person to me, Maggie. I wish I could spend forever with you.

MAGGIE. Ether—I'm sorry for what Daniel did to you. Believe how sorry I am. But just because you're mourning your mortality doesn't mean that I'm anxious to meet mine. Do you understand?

ETHER. Of course.

MAGGIE. Good.

ETHER. God will get us through this.

MAGGIE. I—I didn't want to believe that once, you know. The whole God thing. There is Nature and She was the closest to God I ever had. But because of the curse I was denied any true relationship with even Her—until now. Well, I'm tired. Good night.

ETHER. Good night.

They kiss once more and ETHER *exits.* MAGGIE *smiles happily, but then grows serious and turns directly.*

MAGGIE. Come out, Frenzy. You can't hide from me.

FRENZY. How long did you know?

MAGGIE. You've been following me at a distance since we went outside.

FRENZY. I've only had to deal a veil ripper once before. He gave me a Dickens of a time. You're a rare breed.

MAGGIE. I think you'll find me a rare breed in all respects.

FRENZY. Indeed. No wonder the masters have had their eye on you.

MAGGIE. So tell me, Frenzy, how is this to go on? Is this some sort of cat and mouse game we're playing? Am I to always be guarded and are you to be ready to pounce whenever we're near each other?

FRENZY. Honestly, I don't know. My orders were always rather—vague.

MAGGIE. And how did those orders go? Or is that privileged information?

FRENZY. Oh, they were rather simple. Keep an eye on you and keep you alive.

MAGGIE. Yes, you mentioned keeping me alive before. Which concerns me—if the devils want me alive, what does that mean about my life?

FRENZY. Again, vague orders. I don't know what their plans are for you.

MAGGIE. Is that why—is that why Ether dreamed that I should be dead? Am I standing in God's way?

FRENZY. If there's one thing I've come to realize is that the Enemy is petty. He talks so much about love, but cross His will and you'll have a target on your head.

MAGGIE. So says the devil.

FRENZY. A devil.

MAGGIE. And a rather reluctant one at that.

FRENZY. What do you mean by that?

MAGGIE. Isn't it true?

FRENZY. No. I've proved my commitment. I'm a rising star in our kingdom.

MAGGIE. No, all devils are falling stars. And perhaps it extends farther than that. Perhaps we're all falling stars, humanity and devils alike. Certainly we can blaze with our momentary glory, our Camelots, but then we descend back into oblivion and darkness. But I don't want to be in the dark, Frenzy. For the first time in my life, I feel filled with light.

FRENZY. Well, I'm glad I've been given charge of someone with a little philosophy in her fiber, at least. It makes my time so much more bearable.

MAGGIE. So you're my protector then?

FRENZY. Ironic, isn't it?

MAGGIE. Am I bound to join your side? Am I evil then?

FRENZY. What is evil? We certainly don't feel like we're evil. We feel that we're justified, just like the Enemy does. We're fighting the good fight—even if we're bound to lose.

MAGGIE. You think you're going to lose?

FRENZY. Depends on who you ask. Some call the prophecies the Enemy's propaganda. But as far as I can see, they've been pretty accurate thus far.

MAGGIE. Well, I hope you're good at your job then. As reluctant as I am to have you around—I want to live.

FRENZY. I'll do my best. You have my word of honor.

MAGGIE. Hmpf. Honor. Frenzy . . .

FRENZY. Yes?

MAGGIE. Do you ever want to switch sides?

FRENZY. It's a little late for me.

MAGGIE. But if you could . . .

FRENZY. That's—that's traitorous talk, not worth entertaining.

MAGGIE. As much as I despise much of the traditional way women have been treated by the religious—there's—there's something that's drawing me to Ether and his kind. Even Arthur I'm warming up to.

FRENZY. My job is to keep you alive, not to influence your decisions.

MAGGIE. I guess I don't have much of a choice, do I?

FRENZY. I'm here whether you want me or not.

MAGGIE. Then I'm very tired. Time for bed.

FRENZY. And I'll watch over you and be here in the morning.

MAGGIE. Uh, that's kind of creepy, you know.

FRENZY. It's how we roll, I'm afraid.

Exit MAGGIE and FRENZY.

SCENE 4

Enter GUENEVERE *(previously referred to as the* VEILED WOMAN*) being pursued by* DANIEL. *She is trying to escape into her hidden door.*

DANIEL. Wait! Wait! Lánstad banríon cara dúinn adhaltranas! (*With the incantation,* DANIEL *freezes* GUENEVERE *in place.*) I said wait.

GUENEVERE. Let me go, Merlin!

DANIEL. I don't go by that name.

GUENEVERE. "Thou shouldst never hold a lady or gentle woman against her will."

DANIEL. Oh, please, don't quote those outdated oaths to me. If you didn't notice, I'm not one of your husband's archaic knights.

GUENEVERE. Yes, I remember. You always held yourself apart from the standards of society.

DANIEL. Exactly so. So, please, Guenevere, don't patronize me, don't test me, and don't expect me to grovel to your female whims and whiles! I'm not interested in protecting whatever shreds of supposed honor you managed to retain through your tempestuous existence!

GUENEVERE. How dare you . . .

DANIEL. I don't care about old relics of behavior. I don't care about codes of conduct. What I care about is smashing through all of these mysteries, allusions, and riddles!

GUENEVERE. You're one to talk, you hypocrite. You were the greatest mystery of Camelot.

DANIEL. Well, I don't know the man you, Morgana, and Arthur keep talking about. I would like to find out who Merlin is just as much as you do. But I'm going to address first things first. How are you still alive?

GUENEVERE. I could ask the same about you.

DANIEL. And I wouldn't be able to answer you. But you, I'm sure, haven't my complicated memory problems.

GUENEVERE. No. Unfortunately, my long life is branded upon my heart.

DANIEL. I wish I could say the same. But you still haven't answered my question.

GUENEVERE. I'll answer any question you put to me. Just let me go.

DANIEL. Saor banríon cara dúinn adhaltranas.

DANIEL casts off the spell, which frees GUENEVERE.

GUENEVERE. Thank you.

DANIEL. Legend says that you forsook Lancelot, even after Arthur's death. Supposedly you died serving God, praying in a nunnery for a remission of your sins.

GUENEVERE. Aye, all of that happened—minus the dying part. But Lancelot had to believe that I died, or else he would have kept coming back for me and kept tempting me. So I allowed him, and the rest of the world, believe that I had died of a broken heart. In one sense, it was true enough.

DANIEL. But how did you avoid death?

GUENEVERE. You—you really don't remember?

DANIEL. Remember? Why should I remember?

GUENEVERE. Merlin, *you* made me immortal.

DANIEL. With the grail?

GUENEVERE. Aye. It was said that the grail was brought to heaven after it was found by Galahad, but that wasn't the entire truth, was it? You had it. And you gave me the cup to give to Arthur. Arthur was dead. Mordred. Arthur and his son killed each other in that terrible last battle. But then you sent me and Morgana to bring him back to life . . .

DANIEL. Morgana? Morgana brought him back to life? Why would she do that?

GUENEVERE. She's more virtuous than you give currently her credit for. But you used to see her value. Don't you remember any of this? You sent Morgana and me to save him. We, with several other women of her order sailed a ship to Avalon—with his body—and the grail.

DANIEL. Avalon. Where's Avalon?

GUENEVERE. We're in Avalon.

DANIEL. We're in . . . ?

GUENEVERE. How did you get to this castle, Merlin?

DANIEL. I—I'm not sure, the battle with Morgana was so fast and so furious . . .

GUENEVERE. She said that not even you could find this place.

DANIEL. Ether. Ether led us.

GUENEVERE. The young man. The one who dreams.

DANIEL. Yes.

GUENEVERE. He has a special gift indeed to have worked past Morgana's defenses.

DANIEL. Wait, I'm confused . . .

GUENEVERE. This castle, this small piece of land—this is the last piece of Camelot. You and Morgana created it. You both set it apart, called it Avalon and then you instructed Morgana and I to protect it—you said to protect it even against yourself.

DANIEL. And what about Magdalena?

GUENEVERE. Her family has always been here, but never been here.

DANIEL. I'm sick of the double meanings! Talk straight with me!

GUENEVERE. They have remained here, to accomplish the task you set for them. Their family was part of our old world, but a part of the new world as well. To cross completely into one world or the other would have killed them—which is exactly what occurred with the Lady of Shallot.

DANIEL. That really happened? I thought it was just a poem.

GUENEVERE. Tennyson was a friend of the family of Shallot, you must understand, one of the few who actually was able to find them. Poets have a special power in finding the place.

DANIEL. Poets?

GUENEVERE. Poets, musicians, playwrights, novelist, artists. That whole sort. The entire Pre-Raphaelite movement found their way here. They generally have been the ones to help continue that family line, you see. Tennyson was an honorable family man, but others felt more than free, you understand. There were even those who remained here and married into the family, instead of going back to the fame that awaited them. But Byron, that man was a rascal. Poor Henrietta.

DANIEL. But the curse—If you were trying to hide Arthur, why did Morgana put the curse on the family of Shallott to find him?

GUENEVERE. Again, we were only following your instructions.

Enter MORGANA.

MORGANA. It nearly broke my heart to put that curse upon them, Daniel. They were innocents who should have never been dragged into this. But you said it was part of the spell, part of the contradicting tapestry. One force trying to protect, one force trying to liberate. One force trying to hide, one force trying to reveal. One force trying to retain Arthur's death, one force trying to resurrect Arthur's life. It was a deep magic, one that not even I completely understood.

DANIEL. Why did I tell you to do all of this?

MORGANA. I had hoped that you could answer that question for us.

DANIEL. But, I've told you, I don't remember any of you!

MORGANA starts to recite a spell and walks towards DANIEL.

MORGANA. Scaip Meabhair scamall . . .

GUENEVERE. Morgana, what are you doing?

MORGANA releases the spell upon DANIEL. DANIEL cries in pain and stumbles to the ground.

MORGAN. . . . in éineacht le beag dol meas!

GUENEVERE. Morgana!

MORGANA. I will not be left in the dark anymore, Guenevere. I am willing to be Merlin's queen. I am even willing to be even his bishop or his knight. But I will not be his pawn!

MORGANA releases another spell. DANIEL cries out in pain.

GUENEVERE. Morgana, stop it! You're killing him!

MORGANA. I am doing no such thing. Scaip draíocht gardáil in éineacht le beag dol meas!

MORGANA releases another spell. Again, DANIEL cries out in pain, more anguished than the last.

GUENEVERE. Then what are you doing?

MORGANA. Restoring his memory. Scaip Meabhair scamall in éineacht le beag dol meas!

MORGANA releases another spell. DANIEL gives one last cry before crumpling to the ground.

GUNEVERE. How is he?

MORGANA. Daniel? Can you hear me? Daniel?

DANIEL begins to rise.

DANIEL. My name is Merlin.

GUENEVERE. Morgana, you did it! He remembers.

MORGANA. Merlin? Do you remember me?

DANIEL. You are Morgan Le Fey. Half-sister of Arthur Pendragon . . .

MORGANA. Good. Now, Merlin, please, can you finally tell us why . . .

DANIEL. . . . and you are my most hated nemesis! Míshuaimhneas Pian!

DANIEL's sudden incantation strikes MORGANA fiercely to the ground.

GUENEVERE. Merlin, no! You don't understand, she's our friend now. You asked her to help . . .

DANIEL. Gearr Tinneas cuir míghnaoi ar!

DANIEL's incantation strikes GUENEVERE unconscious. MORGANA rises to her feet.

MORGAN. Merlin, stop, I'm not . . .

DANIEL. Lig glam agat istigh gortaigh!

DANIEL spell strikes MORGANA.

MORGAN. I am your ally!

DANIEL. Ally! You sent me back from my victory, Morgana! You are the one who took away my memory! You are anything, but my ally! You possess a different body, but I recognize the stench of your magic in any time, in any place! Olc mioscais tar isteach do anam!

DANIEL recites another incantation, which nearly knocks MORGANA off her feet.

MORGANA. Your magic is so strong. But before . . .

DANIEL. You made me weaker when you hid my memory from me, after our fiercest battle. But now, foolish witch, you have released my full grandeur once more.

MORGANA. I never took away your memory. My memory of the past is perfect, we never had any such battle!

DANIEL. It was not in your past. It is in your future.

MORGANA. Cúnaigh . . .

DANIEL. Pionós an bháis!

MORGANA tries to recite a counter spell, but before she can finish it, DANIEL finishes his spell, which crushes MORGAN. She falls dead. After a cold surveying of the scene before him,

DANIEL exits. GUENEVERE stirs into consciousness. She rushes to MORGAN's side and checks her vital signs.

GUENEVERE. No—no.

Tears well up in GUENEVERE's eyes and she exits in a panic.

SCENE 5

Enter MAGGIE, followed by FRENZY.

MAGGIE. Having you always around is getting kind of creepy. I've never had a ghost stalker before.

FRENZY. I'm not a ghost. I would have had to have had a body at some point to be a ghost.

MAGGIE. Now aren't we particular?

FRENZY. I hate when people call us ghosts. There are some very distinct differences, you know.

MAGGIE. Well then, Casper, let's get a move on.

FRENZY. I'm not a ghost!

MAGGIE. And must you really come out on my dates with me? I really don't need a chaperone every minute of the day.

FRENZY. I'm not your chaperone. You can do whatever you want, with whomever you want. My side of the fence is pretty free about that sort of thing.

MAGGIE. All while you're looking on. Perverts.

FRENZY. I'll look away, I promise. Not that you'll get much action with Mr. Mormon.

MAGGIE. I like it, actually. He's sweet and romantic with all of that. Keeps his hands where they should be. From what I hear from the outside world, I think I prefer his kind of . . . of . . .

FRENZY. Chivalry?

MAGGIE. That's not what I was going to say.

FRENZY. My oh my. Is he really getting to you?

MAGGIE. No—no!

FRENZY. You're blushing!

MAGGIE. I am not!

FRENZY. Well, I'm used to stoking the fires in your kind—but I'll let you in on a secret. I've always preferred watching over the gentlemen rather than the rakes.

MAGGIE. Gentleman. Yes, Ether's a gentleman.

FRENZY. You know, I applaud every feminist bone in your body, but a lot of the time it backfires and men like to interpret that feminism as a reason to mistreat women in the name of equality. Sometimes a woman, even a free and equal one, still yearns to be treated . . .

MAGGIE. . . . like a lady.

FRENZY. You're looking wistful.

MAGGIE. I never expected this to happen to me. I—I was beginning to think I was the end of the line for the Shallots. I had always heard the stories of the poets and the knights coming to us and soothing our loneliness—but I was losing hope.

FRENZY. Well, maybe the Enemy is having some mercy on you after all. I just wish he had a little left over for me.

MAGGIE. Are you supposed to confide with your assignments?

FRENZY. I don't know—normally they can't talk back. It's kind of nice.

MAGGIE. Maybe there's still hope for you—with Him, I mean.

FRENZY. You don't understand, Maggie. I made a decision. I knew the consequences, I knew who and what I was going against—I knew this would be permanent.

MAGGIE. Maybe He didn't tell you everything, maybe there's still . . .

FRENZY. No! Don't you get who I am, Maggie? Don't you get what I am? I enjoy this little budding friendship as much as you do, but one day my orders may change and I would not hesitate to bring you down. In the end, we're on different sides.

MAGGIE. But does it have to be that way? Even if there were no reward for it, no heaven or hell to pay, wouldn't it be nice to do the right thing just because it's right?

FRENZY. I am right! We are right! It's you pitiful weaklings who have never understood how the Universe should be ordered!

FRENZY turns to leave.

MAGGIE. I thought you weren't supposed to leave me!

FRENZY. I'm a devil! I don't always do what I'm told!

Exit FRENZY. Enter ETHER.

ETHER. Who were you talking to, Maggie?

MAGGIE. Just the shadows. *(Beat.)* Ether, how truly great is your God's mercy?

ETHER. I believe it's infinite. Why? What's wrong?

MAGGIE. Is it great enough to cover me?

ETHER. Of course it is.

MAGGIE. No, no, maybe it isn't. I've been plagued by devils all my life. The ability to see and hear them—well, maybe it's because I'm like them. It's like I'm a magnet for them. Their voices always hissing inside my head, their presence always just at the edge of my skirts— ravenous, hungry. Your gift is to see these beautiful visions of heaven. Why is mine to see to perpetually see evil? Is it even a gift? Or is it a fair curse, a just punishment, a part of my fallen nature?

ETHER. Maggie, really, you're being too hard on yourself.

MAGGIE. I'm being realistic. Ether, I want this life with you. I really want it. But, if you were to spend my life with me—what would you be marrying?

ETHER. An angel.

MAGGIE. An angel of what? Of where? Of whom?

ETHER. Maggie, why would a devil pay any attention to any one, unless they were meant to be an obstacle to their purposes? Don't you think they know your inherent worth? Don't you think that you've been targeted precisely because you have so much potential for good?

MAGGIE embraces ETHER tightly.

MAGGIE. Sometimes I don't know who I really am, Ether. Sometimes I don't know what it really means to be a woman. Sometimes I don't know what it really means to be a human. Sometimes I don't know what it really means to be me.

ETHER. As much as I would love to be your knight in shining armor with those questions, I'm afraid you're going to find out the answers for yourself. Especially the woman part, I really have no clue there.

MAGGIE kisses ETHER.

ETHER. What was that for?

MAGGIE. Do you ever doubt yourself?

ETHER. Every day.

MAGGIE. Then don't. When those doubts come, just know that I love you. That I believe in you.

MAGGIE turns to exit.

ETHER. Maggie—Maggie! Where are you going?

MAGGIE. Thank you for trying to see me, Ether. It helps.

ETHER. I love you, too.

MAGGIE. I know. You've already shown me.

Exit MAGGIE. ARTHUR wanders in, emotional, and stops surprised at seeing ETHER, not quite sure whether he's prepared to show this kind of vulnerability.

ETHER. Your Grace? Are you all right?

ARTHUR. *(Deciding to confide in ETHER.)* Sir Ether—come, come here. I stand in need of some company.

ETHER. What's wrong?

ARTHUR. Do you know what castle you are in?

ETHER. No. I had just assumed it was some generic . . .

ARTHUR. This was my home.

ETHER. Really? We're really in . . . ?

ARTHUR. It was more grand in its day. A vision. Time has taken its toll on it. Like many things.

ETHER. It's going to be quite the adjustment for you, isn't it? A whole new world.

ARTHUR. It is not the new world that troubles me at the moment, but the old one. This woman—Magdalena. I've seen you with her the past few weeks. How you look at her—how intense you get in your joy.

ETHER. Every knight must have his lady, I suppose.

ARTHUR. Guenevere—I loved her much like you love your lady. My heart fell fast.

ETHER. Guenevere . . .

ARTHUR. Do you trust this Maggie?

ETHER. I know I love her. But trust? I don't know yet.

ARTHUR. Then are all relationships between men and women doomed do such an uneasy truce?

ETHER. If the legends have survived intact, sire, then I believe there was another man involved in that scenario.

ARTHUR. Yes. Which made it even worse. Lancelot was my best knight—besides Merlin, I thought he was my truest friend.

ETHER. So, I guess the question truly is then, my lord, whether any of us can truly trust each other? Can we even trust ourselves?

ARTHUR. Indeed.

ETHER. I don't think I'm doing a very good job cheering you up.

ARTHUR. *(Laughs.)* No, you are not! But honesty is the best elixir to the soul, Sir Ether. Once you start simply telling me what I want to hear, that is when I should stop listening to you. That's why I could always trust Merlin. He would tell me the hard things.

Enter MERLIN.

ARTHUR. Speak of the devil and he will appear! Merlin, my friend!

DANIEL. My dear Arthur, you are in grave danger. Morgana and Guenevere have conspired against your life.

ARTHUR. We knew of Morgana—but Guenevere? How do you know this?

DANIEL. I caught them trying to poison our food supply. We had a bit of a wizard's duel and I am afraid that Morgana lost and is, well, dead.

ETHER. You killed her?

DANIEL. At least that incarnation of her. I've set a charm upon the castle that will prevent her from achieving another body for at least a couple of months, but I'm sure we will eventually have to deal with her again. That woman has more skins than a snake.

ETHER. But how could you kill her?

DANIEL. It was a necessary development. Remember that she did not spare you when we battled her before, Ether. You're going to have to develop more of a stomach if you're going into this knighting business. The sword you wear is not simply for show.

ETHER. *(Still wary.)* I—I suppose you're right.

ARTHUR. My friend, you must be very certain of what you know. By your honor, by our friendship, you are certain that Guenevere is involved in this plot?

DANIEL. She was the one holding the poison.

ARTHUR. She wasn't being coerced? She wasn't under a spell?

DANIEL. No! It was her, all right? Willingly, knowingly, gleefully she was planning all of our destruction!

ETHER. You don't need to get like that, Daniel.

DANIEL. Call me Merlin, I no longer go by Daniel.

ETHER. Well then, Merlin, you're being insensitive.

DANIEL. Insensitive! Well, here's a reality check. We are dealing with very volatile and powerful individuals here, so we don't have time to wince and mince around weeping choir boys!

ETHER. She was his wife.

DANIEL. She was the woman who brought down his kingdom.

ETHER. But that doesn't mean he can't still love her!

ARTHUR. It is all right, Sir Ether. As I said before, I need people who will be honest with me. Brutally honest.

Enter GUENEVERE in a rush.

GUENEVERE. Arthur! *(Upon seeing DANIEL, she stops.)* I am too late.

DANIEL. That's certainly true. Too late to cover your sins.

GUENEVERE. Too late to reveal yours.

ETHER. What do you mean by that?

DANIEL. As always, she's trying to keep her dress unspotted by casting the mud upon others. I hate to break it you, sweetheart, but you've cried wolf too many times.

GUENEVERE. Arthur, I know I broke your heart. I know I shattered your dreams. But I am asking you this, please, believe me in what I am going to tell you. Merlin is not to be trusted.

ARTHUR. I trust Merlin as much as I trust myself.

GUENEVERE. You said that once about me. Don't make the same mistake again. In a most blood thirsty fashion, he killed Morgana . . .

ARTHUR. He already told us that. It was a just punishment for her many crimes against my life.

GUENEVERE. Morgana unlocked his memories . . .

ARTHUR. Then even more reason to trust him, for the Merlin I knew remembers his promises in a more true fashion than you ever did.

GUENEVERE. My lord, my love . . .

ARTHUR. I was not your love. And one does not try to poison one's lord.

GUENEVERE. Poison? Is that what he told you?

ETHER. He told us that you and Morgana attempted to poison our food.

GUENEVERE. Then I am even more baffled, Arthur, for I once trusted this man as you do. He is the one who stationed us here to protect you. But why he has repaid our obedience with death and accusation, I do not know.

DANIEL. I never gave any such orders to you nor Morgana.

GUENEVERE. Now I know you lie!

DANIEL. Arthur, they trapped you here and then Morgana attacked us for trying to free you! You know this to be the truth!

GUENEVERE. Morgana was protecting you, Arthur! It was the charge given us. Merlin told us to even protect it against himself! Little did we know that we would have to do that very thing!

Enter MAGGIE and FRENZY.

MAGGIE. What's going on?

DANIEL. This doesn't concern you, little woman.

MAGGIE. Excuse me?

FRENZY. Do you see, Veil Ripper? The wizard . . .

MAGGIE. Oh. Oh, you're right . . .

DANIEL. And why is the Shade following you?

ETHER. The Shades are back?

ARTHUR. Show it to me, Magdalena! I'll run it through!

MAGGIE. No. She was sent here to protect me.

ARTHUR. You're in league with these devils now?

MAGGIE. No, of course not. But I'm not going to look a gift horse in the mouth.

ETHER. Get rid of the thing, Maggie! There's nothing good that can come from such dabblings!

MAGGIE. It's big, isn't it?

FRENZY. Very big. Legion. But there's something different about them . . .

MAGGIE. Different? How do you mean different?

ETHER. Are you really just talking with it?

FRENZY. It's—it's more feral. We're organized, but that thing—it's splitting apart at the seams. I've never seen one of us like that. There is definitely something wrong going on here . . .

ETHER. Make it go away, Maggie! Let Arthur kill it!

MAGGIE. Don't lecture me about what you don't understand, Ether!

ETHER. Maybe you were right, Arthur. Maybe our hearts are not to be trusted.

MAGGIE looks at ETHER sadly.

MAGGIE. This is important.

ETHER. I suppose we should re-consider flying our kite after all, Maggie.

MAGGIE. Just—just wait, Ether. I'll explain later . . .

ETHER. Maggie, please, evil spirits aren't just creatures you should be hanging out with . . .

MAGGIE. Ether, I'm still on your side. Trust me. Believe in me.

ETHER. I believe in God first.

FRENZY. Maggie, we really need to take care of this. Ask the warlock where it's from.

MAGGIE. Daniel, Frenzy wants to know . . .

DANIEL. I can hear and see the Shade just as well you can, Maggie.

ETHER. *(Growing suspicious.)* Since when?

DANIEL. Tell the little Dickens to mind its own business.

FRENZY. This isn't good, Maggie. That thing's not natural.

DANIEL. Mind your own damn business! Pionós an bháis!

With a quick and powerful incantation, DANIEL *casts a spell that knocks back both* FRENZY *and* MAGGIE. ETHER *runs to* MAGGIE's *side.*

ETHER. Maggie!

DANIEL. Let her go, Ether. She's devil-spawn.

ETHER. Look who's talking, dude. Maggie. Oh please, God, don't let me lose her. Maggie . . .

FRENZY. Ow—really, that—ow. That thing is—ow—tough. It's stronger than it should be, Maggie.

ETHER. Maggie!

MAGGIE. *(Becoming conscious and then whispering to ETHER.)* I'm fine. Not a scratch. But don't let him know that. That blast should have killed me.

ETHER. What?

MAGGIE. The scabbard. I have Excalibur's scabbard. Pretend I'm hurt.

ETHER. Oh. Oh! I mean, Oh, woe is me!

DANIEL. The whelp of a woman is still alive?

ETHER. Barely, no thanks to you, villain! I thought you were our friend!

GUENEVERE. Arthur, is this really the man you thought was your friend? A man who attacks people unprovoked?

ARTHUR. Merlin?

DANIEL. I was not unprovoked! Do you trust pagans and soothsayers over me?

ARTHUR. Merlin, you are a pagan and a soothsayer.

DANIEL. But a Christian one! Arthur, have I ever betrayed you? Have I ever given you reason to doubt me?

ARTHUR. No. But neither had Guenevere and Lancelot.

ETHER. There is one person you can trust right now, Arthur.

ARTHUR. And who is that?

ETHER. The Lord of the Grail.

FRENZY. Well, that's debatable.

ETHER. Arthur, trust in the Revelation.

> ARTHUR *pauses, doubtful, but then he then kneels, with Excalibur grasped in his hands.*

ARTHUR. Holy Lord, mine enemies have long plagued me with lying friendship. Please, guide my sword to the truth, and to the doom of error. In the name of thy holy child, Jesus, Amen.

> *There is a small moment of breathless silence.* ARTHUR *opens his eyes suddenly and stands to walk over to* GUENEVERE.

GUENEVERE. Arthur, don't fall for his . . .

ARTHUR. You are the one who most betrayed me when I most loved you. You are the one who turned my best knight against me and brought me to ruin.

GUENEVERE. Arthur, please . . .

ARTHUR. But where you hurt my heart, you never meant to hurt my body. I believe you love me still, as I love you.

> ARTHUR *turns and lunges towards* DANIEL, *Excalibur raised for a killing blow.* DANIEL *pulls out a sword he had hidden and deflects the blow.* ETHER *grabs his own sword and joins the battle. The two of them battle* DANIEL *for some time, but then Daniel delivers a quick incantation:*

DANIEL. Brú ri gan mheabhair!

The spell knocks back ARTHUR, *who falls to the ground uncon-scious.* GUENEVERE *rushes to* ARTHUR'*s side, while* ETHER *continues to battle* DANIEL.

GUENEVERE. Arthur!

ETHER. Traitor!

DANIEL. Sioc an fear ridire!

DANIEL recites another spell, which also knocks back ETHER. ETHER *lies on the ground, unable to move.*

ETHER. It—it's so cold. Maggie, I can't move . . .

DANIEL goes to GUENEVERE, *grabbing her by the hair.*

DANIEL. I don't know why you lot think I'm Merlin, but I certainly know who all of you are. And I tell you, Guenevere, we've been in this scenario before—or should I rather say, that we will be in it again. Your companions helpless, your hair in my hand—but, I'll let you in on a secret. In that future time, Morgan Le Fey saved you. She took my memory and sent me to the past with a rare and powerful spell. Unfortunately for you, however, Morgana is not here. There is no one to save you. So maybe it won't happen after all. Maybe I can kill you now. (*MAGGIE rises and tackles* DANIEL, *caught by surprise, he tumbles to the ground with her. They both rise to their feet and* DANIEL *recites another spell:*) Iompar speisialta bean sí! (*MAGGIE stands unaffected against it.*) What? What?!

MAGGIE. You're forgetting something, Merlin.

MAGGIE pats Excalibur's scabbard.

DANIEL. Clever.

DANIEL goes and grabs Excalibur, with which he, in turn, stabs MAGGIE. MAGGIE *smiles and then pulls out the sword, with which she stabs* DANIEL. DANIEL *gasps, and speaks with a completely different voice. He rips at his clothes, trying to tear at the burning in his skin. As he rips off his clothing, and at some points his skin, pieces of dark spirits emerge from*

DANIEL. *A limb here, a part of a face there, a glowing set of eyes, an agonized mouth.*

FRENZY. See, there it is, Maggie!

DANIEL. It stings, it hurts, get it out!

DANIEL pulls out the sword and guards it closely.

FRENZY. There are shades inside of him! But—I've never seen anything like this.

DANIEL. We are the Colony.

FRENZY. You're mutated. You're like a mass of limbs and eyes and mouths and spirit flesh all jumbled and jutting out of each other . . .

MAGGIE. We've got to get that sword, Frenzy. Send this thing to hell.

FRENZY. No, Maggie, I won't do that. Not one of my own.

MAGGIE. You said it yourself, that thing is not your own.

DANIEL. Oh, but we are, Frenzy. We have swallowed and consumed each other, drawing upon each other's powers and elements, and through that means we amplify this Warlock's powers. He is strong. With us He is Mighty. He is our city. We are His world.

FRENZY. But you're tearing at the seams, you're destroying yourselves.

DANIEL. Our essence will survive.

FRENZY. That was never the Deal. We were to keep what we had.

DANIEL. Times will change, Frenzy. Things will become desperate.

FRENZY. The Master authorized this?

DANIEL. In the future there is a schism.

FRENZY. A schism?

DANIEL. We no longer serve the Son of the Morning. He became old fashioned. There is a new master.

FRENZY. Then that is all that I needed to hear. Fervens Estus Vomica Exuro Incendia Veneficus!

FRENZY flares up and attacks DANIEL with her fiery elements. DANIEL screams.

DANIEL. Stop!

FRENZY. Traitors!

DANIEL. You can't kill us!

FRENZY. But it hurts like hell, doesn't it? Maggie, the sword!

MAGGIE rushes to DANIEL and struggles to wrest the sword from DANIEL.

DANIEL. Frenzy, stop her! You know what she will do to us!

FRENZY. My enemy is her enemy, which makes her my friend! This is why I was sent to protect her! So that she could help us destroy you. As bad as the Enemy and his servants are, an abomination like you is much worse. In you, Heaven and Hell have a common enemy!

DANIEL. No, we are not your enemy!

FRENZY. I am loyal to the Master!

DANIEL. You don't understand! You're in here with us!

FRENZY. You lie!

DANIEL. *(In FRENZY's voice.)* In your future, you become part of the Colony! You're a part of us! Your fire is burning your own spirit flesh!

FRENZY. No—no, it's a trick, I can imitate voices, too.

DANIEL. You must believe us!

FRENZY. Prove it!

DANIEL. There's not enough time!

MAGGIE tears the sword away from DANIEL, staggering back. Before she can thrust it into DANIEL, however, FRENZY breaks off her elements and rushes to MAGGIE and tears the scabbard off her body, leaving MAGGIE unprotected.

MAGGIE. Frenzy, no! You said you would protect me. I thought we—that we were friends.

FRENZY. You forgot something important, Maggie. First and foremost, I'm a devil.

DANIEL. Pionós an bháis!

> *DANIEL recites a powerful spell, which instantly kills MAGGIE. Unable to make any other movement, ETHER cries out in grief. In an instant, GUENEVERE rises from where she has been silently watching, scoops up Excalibur and, before anyone can react, she attacks DANIEL. They battle and DANIEL even stabs her a couple of times, but due to her immortality, his attacks have little effect. They continue to battle, but Guenevere eventually stabs DANIEL with Excalibur.*

GUENEVERE. You were right. There was no one to save me this time.

DANIEL. Get it out! Get it out!

GUENEVERE. So I'll just have to do it myself.

> *GUENEVERE twists the sword. A great cry is made from the spirits inside DANIEL, after which DANIEL falls to the ground, unconscious and liberated from the Colony's influence.*

FRENZY. What did you do? I was in there!

GUENEVERE. Morgana taught me to be a Veil Ripper, too, Frenzy. Don't come near me.

FRENZY. I'll burn the flesh off your bones!

GUENEVERE. Not before I thrust this into whatever you pass as a heart!

FRENZY. I have seen the future today, Guenevere. I will not forget what you did to me.

> *Exit FRENZY. GUENEVERE rushes to ARTHUR.*

GUENEVERE. My love—wake up. Please, wake up . . .

> *The spell worn off, ETHER is now able to move. He rises to his feet. He goes to MAGGIE.*

GUENEVERE. Is she . . . ?

ETHER. *(Devastated.)* Dead. Arthur?

GUENEVERE. Alive.

> DANIEL *stirs. He no longer has the spirits protruding from him. As he stands,* ETHER *grabs him and pins him to a wall.* GUENEVERE *rises and tries to restrain* ETHER.

ETHER. You're going to regret that you survived, Daniel!

DANIEL. Stop! Please, stop! I'm liberated now! I have my senses again! It wasn't me, I wasn't in control!

> ARTHUR *stirs awake.*

GUENEVERE. They—they were controlling you?

ETHER. Give me one reason that we should trust you.

DANIEL. Because I can undo what the Colony just did. I still have the Grail.

> DANIEL *pulls out the grail, which* ETHER *takes away from him.*

ETHER. No!

DANIEL. Ether, it is the only way we can save her!

ETHER. Like you saved me, to wander away from my God? To doom me as an exile until the end of the world? No, you will not save her. She is saved now.

GUENEVERE. Ether, think about what you're . . .

ETHER. If anyone tries to take the Grail away from me, I will kill them on the spot, I swear I will!

DANIEL. You saw her in the visions. She was with us in the end.

ETHER. I also saw parts of this battle. I saw her dead.

ARTHUR. *(Rising.)* And now you have the chance to merge the two visions, lad.

GUENEVERE. Arthur!

*GUENEVERE runs and embraces ARTHUR. ARTHUR hesitates,
but then embraces her warmly in return.*

ARTHUR. Guenevere. *(To ETHER.)* As you for you, Sir Ether, it is your
duty to protect Magdalena, not to condemn her to death.

ETHER. I am protecting her. I am safeguarding her salvation!

GUENEVERE. Is this about her, or is this about you?

ETHER. It isn't right. I didn't want it . . .

ARTHUR. God foretold it.

ETHER. I will not accept that God didn't want me in His arms as anxiously as I did!

GUENEVERE. Sir, this is not about God's love for you.

ETHER. Is it our place to say who lives?

DANIEL. Is it our place to say who dies?

ETHER. Shut up! You've already caused enough damage.

ARTHUR. Sir Ether, was it not our Lord himself who bestowed immortality on Saint John, until He should come again?

ETHER. And was it not Saint Peter who asked to return to the arms of
Jesus as soon as possible? They were both blessed according to their
desires. Both of them got what they asked for. I did not get what I
asked for!

GUENEVERE. And what would Magdalena ask for? What were her
desires?

DANIEL. She wanted to travel. She wanted to live.

ETHER. Shut up, Daniel!

DANIEL. Look, I won't be told where to get off! Perhaps I was wrong
to bring you back, Ether. If you never forgive me, I would understand. But that woman saved me from the grasp of evil—yes, an evil
I allowed, an evil I invited into me. They promised me the power
to conquer our enemies. Well, they kept that promise, but at a high
price, and I was lost. But Maggie and Guenevere saved me . . .

ETHER. I will protect her immortal soul!

DANIEL. And I will protect her mortal life, even if I have to knock you down and tie you up to do it!

ETHER. Come on then!

DANIEL. You know that you received a vision that showed Maggie in our future! If you have as much faith as you claim, then grow a backbone and do what needs to be done!

ETHER. What do you understand about faith, you warlock!

ARTHUR touches ETHER's arm, calming him.

ARTHUR. Ether, please. I, too, was once arrogant enough to think that I could decide a woman's fate and call myself just.

ETHER. It's not like that . . .

ARTHUR. Is it not? *(As much to GUENEVERE as to ETHER.)* I think these wondrous women have earned the right to have their own desires respected. If nothing else, trust in the Revelation.

ETHER pauses, considering, then:

ETHER. All right. You win. But I will take the responsibility for it. If she doesn't want it, then I'll be the one to pay for it. Can someone get something to drink?

ARTHUR fetches a bottle of something and hands it to ETHER. ETHER stoops to MAGGIE, takes her in his arms and allows her to drink. Soon MAGGIE stirs.

MAGGIE. Ether! You brought me back!

ETHER. I'm so sorry, Maggie. I . . .

MAGGIE embraces ETHER.

MAGGIE. Thank you! Oh, thank you.

Blackout.

SCENE 6

Enter ARTHUR and DANIEL.

ARTHUR. So, I was right. You have yet to meet the Arthur of my youth, the man I was.

DANIEL. The spell that Morgan used to send me back to this time—I think I remember it well enough to perform it. So, it seems to me, that I must go back even further. I go back to your father Uther Pendragon and help him first, and when he fails me, I assist in your birth, in your life and . . .

ARTHUR. . . . and you prepare for my re-birth. Including creating Avalon, warning Morgan and Guenevere about your younger self, and preparing for the final conflict which is yet to be.

DANIEL. Yes.

ARTHUR. I have been thinking about that. You—you knew all the time that Camelot was going to fail.

DANIEL. No, I don't know that, not technically. Oh, yes, now I know about Lancelot, Guenevere, Mordred and all of that shambolic mess. Yes, I know that Camelot fails in your time. But you have returned. Camelot can be reborn. We must try in your time surely—we must always try—but perhaps this time . . .

ARTHUR. But you will not be with me this time.

DANIEL. Won't I?

ARTHUR. You are travelling back.

DANIEL. So I am.

ARTHUR. I will be alone.

DANIEL. You won't be alone. Ether's visions have certainly confirmed that.

ARTHUR. Well, do not be gentle with me then.

DANIEL. Oh, I won't.

ARTHUR. It was your roughness that made me strong. I will miss you, my friend.

DANIEL. Miss me? I betrayed you . . .

ARTHUR. Merlin, I have learned through all of this that it may be true that I cannot fully trust anyone—even myself. We are all fallen from our true natures. Each of us has shown that.

DANIEL. True enough.

ARTHUR. But I will never let that painful truth dry up the depth of love that overflows in my heart. Even in the height of our darkest nights, I never stopped loving Guenevere. I never stopped loving Lancelot. I shall never stop loving you. And now, thanks to you, you will be God's instrument in helping us access the Grace that will change us—that will transform us from creatures of shadow, to beings of glory.

Enter MAGGIE, ETHER, and GUENEVERE. MAGGIE and GUENEVERE are now dressed in knight's clothing similar to ETHER's.

ARTHUR. Are we ready then?

MAGGIE. Aye, my grace.

ARTHUR. Kneel then. *(MAGGIE and GUENEVERE kneel ARTHUR pulls out his sword and raises it.)* "God make you a good woman and fail not of beauty. The Round Table was founded in patience, humility, and meekness. Thou art never to do outrageousity, nor murder, and always to flee treason, by no means to be cruel, and always to do ladies, damsels, and gentle women—as well as gentlemen—succor. . . . Thou shouldst be for all ladies—and gentlemen—and fight for their quarrels, and ever be courteous and never refuse mercy to him that asketh mercy, for a knight that is courteous and kind and gentle has favor in every place. Thou shouldst never hold a gentle woman—or gentleman—against her—or his—will. Thou must keep thy word to all and not be feeble of good believeth and faith. Right must be defended against might and distress must be protected. . . . Thou shouldst not fail in these things: charity, abstinence and truth. No knight shall win worship but if he be of worship himself and of good living and that loveth God and dreadeth God then else he getteth no worship here be ever so hardly. Do not anything that will in any way dishonour the fair name of Christian knighthood for only by stainless and honourable lives and not by prowess and courage shall the final goal be reached. Therefore be a good knight and so I pray to God so ye may be, and if ye be of prowess and of worthiness then ye shall be a Knight of the Round Table."

MAGGIE AND GUENEVERE. Amen.

ARTHUR. I dub thee Dame Magdalena, of Shallot. I dub thee Dame Guenevere, of Camelot. Knights of the Round Table. (*ARTHUR brings his sword down gently upon* MAGGIE's *shoulder and then crosses it over* MAGGIE's *head to the other, knighting her. He repeats the same action for* GUENEVERE. *They both rise.*) Now, my dear Guenevere, I shall never again leave you behind. You shall always be fighting at my side.

GUENEVERE. And, believe me, my love, I shall not disappoint. Immortal as we are, no one can now call us the weaker sex.

MAGGIE. Amen to that! And now, my lord, that I am thus immortal, I have no more need of Excalibur's scabbard. I restore it to you.

MAGGIE *hands the scabbard to* ARTHUR. ARTHUR *replaces it with the one he is currently using and places Excalibur within it.*

ARTHUR. Excalibur is now returned to its mate. All is well.

ETHER. So, Maggie, you finally consented to being a part of these horrible oaths and costumes.

MAGGIE. Even a kite needs to be attached to the earth before it can fly. I'm at peace, my love.

ETHER. (*To* ARTHUR *and* GUENEVERE.) Then, my lord and lady, we must leave you.

GUENEVERE. You finally get to see the world beyond your mirror, Maggie. Where to first?

MAGGIE. (*With a smile to* ETHER.) Africa. Then America, to Ether's home to meet his family and take care of some—business. Then

China and Greece and Jerusalem and—and who cares after that! We'll go everywhere!

ETHER. But, remember, when you need us . . .

ARTHUR pulls out a cell phone.

ARTHUR. Yes—the cellular phone. What a strange and wonderful new world.

MAGGIE. And don't forget to text me, Gwen. I want updates.

GUENEVERE. Certainly.

MAGGIE. We're off then. Goodbye.

They all give their final embraces and goodbyes. ETHER and MAGGIE exit.

ARTHUR. And I suppose you must be off as well, Merlin?

DANIEL. I suppose so.

GUENEVERE. You have been given a most rare gift. To revise our actions, to change our course. The opposing wheel that will change our ashes to splendor.

DANIEL. I am unworthy.

ARTHUR. Yes, you are. But we all play the shadows to a greater glory. God be with you, my friend.

DANIEL. Let's hope so. If not, then I'm in for one hell of a ride.

GUENEVERE. Goodbye, Daniel.

DANIEL. I am Daniel no more. Tá me an lag fear scáth cara dúinn an Críost. Tá me an faighteoir cara dúinn the análú tarrthála agus Slánaithe. Mé scrios am! An roth istigh an scáthán! Tá me Merlin!

MERLIN declares the incantation. There is a blinding flash and then blackout.

THE END

Stephanie Robertson as Guenevere, Chris Clark as Arthur, Jamie Denison as Morgana, Jason Kelly Fullmer as Daniel, Jyllian Petrie Unice as Magdalena, Jason Sullivan as Ether, Rebecca Minson as Frenzy, and Brian Randall as Tempest. Photo by Emily Bawden Drew.

Jyllian Petrie Unice as Magdalena Devonshire and Jason Sullivan as Ether Kimball. Photo by Emily Bawden Drew.

Jamie Denison as Morgana Le Fay.
Photo by Emily Bawden Drew.

Rebecca Minson as Frenzy, Jason Kelly Fullmer as Daniel, and Brian Randall as Tempest.

Jyllian Petrie Unice as Magdalena Devonshire
and Jason Sullivan as Ether Kimball.

Jyllian Petrie Unice as Magdalena Devonshire, Jason Sullivan as Ether
Kimball, and Jason Kelly Fullmer as Daniel.

Jason Sullivan as Ether Kimball, Jamie Denison as Morgana Le Fay, and Chris Clark as Arthur.

Jason Kelly Fullmer as Daniel and Rebecca Minson as Frenzy.

Jamie Denison as Morgana Le Fay, Stephanie Robertson as Guenevere, and Jason Kelly Fullmer as Daniel.

Jamie Denison as Morgana Le Fay and Jason Kelly Fullmer as Daniel.

Chris Clark as Arthur and Jason Sullivan as Ether Kimball.

Jyllian Petrie Unice as Magdalena, Stephanie Robertson as Guenevere, Chris Clark as Arthur, Jason Sullivan as Ether, and Jason Kelly Fullmer as Daniel.

The Emperor Wolf

A Post-Apocalyptic Fairy Tale

Production History

The current, full length version of *Emperor Wolf* premiered at Arizona State University on February 28, 2014, in Tempe, Arizona. It had the following cast and crew:

CAST

Madeline: Christine Conger
Shasta: Zach Turilli
Ebony: Chelsea Juaregi
Wandering Woman: Nikki Gallagher
Emperor Wolf: Salim Garami
Sphinx: Melissa Stone
Derrick: Isaac Kolding
Griffin: Phoenix Huber

CREW

Director: Brian Foley
Scenic Designer: Tyler Scivener
Costume Designer: Briana Gaydusek
Lighting Designer: Bret G. Reese
Sound Designer: Eric Lambert
Media Designer: Ryan Kirkpatrick
Stage Manager: Jeremy Leung

Emperor Wolf originally was a much shorter play that was less than an hour long. This succinct version premiered in a production by the DaVinci Academy for Arts and Sciences at the Edinburgh Fringe Festival's American High School Theatre Festival in Edinburgh, Scotland, on August 14, 2013. It had the following cast and crew:

CAST

Madeline: Natalie Hope Finamore
Shasta: Jacob Canyon Ward

Ebony: Sarah Howerton
Wandering Woman: Violet Taylor
Emperor Wolf: River Ward
Sphinx: Daniel Amsel
Derrick: Jayson Timothy Veillon
Griffin: David Sanders

CREW
Director: Adam Slee
Props/Technical Effects: Adam K.K. Figueira
Mask/Creature Design: Russ Adams, Escape Designs

Playwright's Note

People are not threatened by myths in the same way they are threatened by religion. Essentially, they both have the same purpose—to explore the contours of meaning. However, there is something more fluid and transformable about myth. More adaptable. Where established religion strives for orthodoxy, hard doctrine, and dogma—which, certainly, has value to the strictly objective mind that wants to nail down all truth to be measured, categorized, and labeled. Finalized. Meaning, as we call it, sometimes shies away from such treatment, though.

Meaning becomes more elusive when it's taken off the leash of creed and culture, darting in and out of the shadows, giving us no more than glimmers and winks, forcing us to probe, as it lures us playfully, but mysteriously, further and further into the woods. As we penetrate into the unknown, we are forced to discard our comforting technical instruments. We become explorers rather than scientists. Spirituality becomes about the journey rather than the conclusion—progression becomes eternal, not finite.

I am a religious man. The theology, ritual, and meaning making of my people is very important to me. So if you want to read with that lens in mind, you'll find much to mine in this play about who I am religiously. But I am also a mythical man. I believe there is a rich spirituality in myths to be discovered even for the irreligious. Even when a myth is non-literal, it does not make it any less true. This is the world I find myself continually drawn into and where my spirituality continues to flourish and change in unexpected ways as I've opened myself up to stories from many cultures that are not my own—but have become a part of me, nonetheless.

We teach our children through very direct means and have taught them the ways of each of our people's religion or irreligion. However, I find the language of myth, fairy tale, and story to be the place where that meaning comes vividly alive. They are different approaches to the same end—both we and our children are expanded by the act of meaning making.

This fairy tale is dedicated to my children Hyrum Irving and Charlotte Sophia. My wife Anne Marie and I are in the habit of reading to our son (and now our younger daughter) on a nightly basis. Between the two of us, we have covered most of *The Chronicles of Narnia, The Wizard of Oz, Ozma of Oz, The Hobbit, Matilda, Peter Pan, The Castle in the Attic, My Father's Dragon, The Princess and the Goblin, The Voyage of Basset,* the *Harry Potter* series, *Peter Pan, A Wrinkle in Time,* and are now moving onto Lloyd Alexander's *Prydain* series. That's just the tip of the proverbial iceberg when it comes to the magical worlds we plan on visiting in between the covers of books. So if the play seems thick with allusions to children's books and magical literature, then that is why. Books have meant a lot to me through the years, and now have become a vital part of the way I communicate, explore, and teach my children. This play is an extension of that, a theatrical representation of the sacred act of storytelling that I pass onto my children. It is one of the ways I pass on the True Myth.

The Emperor Wolf

Prologue

Enter the WANDERING WOMAN. *She is a goddess, dressed in an ancient style, perhaps Hebrew, or Egyptian, or Norse, or Greek, or Babylonian, or some sort of mixture thereof. Her hair is in an exceptionally long braid. The* WANDERING WOMAN *speaks to the audience in a storyteller's fashion. Depending on the style of the production, images of her "story" can appear projected, illustrated, portrayed through movement from the company, etc. behind/around her. The portrayal of the prologue, however, should be active and engaging, not stagnant.*

WANDERING WOMAN. Come and listen to the story. What kind of story really depends on which side of the veil you've been placed on. The destruction of one world can mean the creation of another. So whether you want to consider this an apocalypse tale or a creation myth is a matter of perspective. Whatever the case, the world had changed.

Even in my hidden places, I could feel it in the earth, the water, the sky. The vibrations were off. I went out from my hiding places, and began my wandering again. The cries of my children were too much to ignore, even if they still refused to see me. It would have been simpler if there had been someone to blame in the beginning, as easy as it was to have someone to blame in the end. But the fault was widespread, like an infection, like a pandemic.

There were really two wars happening at that time. There was the war between countries, but there was also the war between peoples. My children started again caring more about their differences than their similarities. There were no more presidents, or queens, or parliaments, or that sort of person anymore. They were all just broken up into smaller and smaller governments, until there were just governments of ten or five or two or one.

Until the Dread Awakening, that is.

A new ruling class, a whole new society of creatures arose. The things my children had only heard about in myths and fairy tales, but who I knew only too intimately. Sphinxes. Griffins. Elves and fairies and spirits and goddesses that had long been forgotten, or rejected, or relegated to books, were now warring with each other for possession of this newly created world. Many people didn't believe in these returning memories, the stories were just another reminder of how much they had lost and how far they had fallen. Whether they believed or not, however, the stories spread and became more convincing and more prevalent.

What was becoming obvious was that my children were disappearing. They were becoming rare, endangered. Instead of becoming hunters and gatherers, it appeared that they were the ones becoming hunted and gathered. For what reason, none of them knew. Out of all these stories, there was one that struck the most fear in the hearts of my children—the story of the Emperor Wolf.

SCENE 1

A MINOTAUR, or some other sort of mythical creature, is on stage. Enter MADELINE, who sees the MINOTAUR, but not clearly. MADELINE arms her bow, and lets off an arrow, hitting the MINOTAUR. She approaches the beast, expecting her arrow to have killed it. To her surprise, the MINOTAUR looks up at her, largely unaffected by the arrow. Startled, MADELINE's eyes widen in surprise, having never seen a creature like this before. Their scene freezes.

The SPHINX enters, killing unseen humans. SHASTA enters running, then stops upon seeing the SPHINX. The SPHINX turns on SHASTA *and is about to kill him as well, when the* WANDERING WOMAN *(unseen by* SHASTA, *but seen by the* SPHINX*) re-enters and motions to the* SPHINX *to stop. Their scene freezes.*

The MINOTAUR *attacks* MADELINE. MADELINE *releases another arrow, which still has no effect, so she takes out her dagger and stabs the creature. The* MINOTAUR *falls dead.* MADELINE *kneels down and touches where she stabbed the* MINOTAUR. *The* EMPEROR WOLF *enters, hovering above* MADELINE, *unable to be seen by her. Their scene freezes.*

The SPHINX *recognizes the* WANDERING WOMAN'*s authority and withdraws her attack on* SHASTA. *She kneels down in front of* SHASTA *and looks him in the eyes. She then rises and, to* SHASTA'*s bafflement, exits, following the* WANDERING WOMAN.

SHASTA. *(To the Sphinx:)* Why did you spare me?!

MADELINE. What are you?

MADELINE *recoils from the dead* MINOTAUR. *Both she and* SHASTA *start backing up until they are nearly back to back, full of fear in their separate moments of time. The* EMPEROR WOLF *touches Madeline, which she reacts to, although still unable to see him. Both Shasta and Madeline exit. The* EMPEROR WOLF *smiles, looking after* MADELINE, *and exits.*

EBONY *enters and sits beside a fire, with a wild, mystical looking staff.* EBONY *is a middle aged, blind woman with a sheath of cloth wrapped around her eyes, or sunglasses, and the staff laid across her lap. Enter* SHASTA, *a teenage boy who is slinking towards* EBONY. *He approaches her, entranced by the staff, attempting to take it.*

EBONY. I wouldn't try that, young man.

SHASTA. What?

EBONY. I said I wouldn't try that!

In a swift movement, EBONY *knocks down* SHASTA *and brings the staff down swiftly, stopping it just before it would crack his skull.*

SHASTA. You're blind!

EBONY. I am. In a matter of speaking.

SHASTA. It's the staff, I knew it! There's something special about it.

EBONY. And so you thought you would take it from me?

SHASTA. I—I don't know what I thought. I wasn't thinking. I think that was sort of the point. That staff—it called me. I think—I think it wanted me to take it.

EBONY. Is that how you excuse your thievery? The thing wanted to be stolen?

SHASTA. I—I really am sorry. I'm not usually a thief, I promise. I was raised differently than that.

EBONY. How we were raised may not matter anymore. I was raised differently, too, but this new world has made that irrelevant.

SHASTA. How did you get it?

EBONY. *(Good humouredly.)* I stole it.

SHASTA. *(Laughs.)* So you're a hypocrite.

EBONY. Yes, of course. This world has made us all thieves and hypocrites. *(Beat.)* The staff called out to me as well. I don't know how, but I could see it—certainly not how you see, not with my eyes. But with some sort of—third eye. It comes and goes, but it alerts me when I'm in danger—and allows me to "see" many beautiful things. *(Beat.)* But that still does not excuse stealing from a blind woman!

SHASTA. I'd feel more sorry for you if you hadn't given me so many bruises.

EBONY. I'd be happy to give you more.

SHASTA. Why does it seem like everyone here just want to hurt each other?

EBONY relaxes and feels around to help the boy up.

EBONY. You say "here" as if you're not from "here."

SHASTA. I'm not.

EBONY. From across the toxic desert? That's not possible, is it?

SHASTA. No. They're still as deadly as they were. We went around through the mountains.

EBONY. Those are just as deadly.

SHASTA. As my group found out.

EBONY. Where were you trying to get to?

SHASTA. Missouri.

EBONY. They don't let strangers in there.

SHASTA. We weren't strangers. You could say our people are from there. But we were driven away before we could get there.

EBONY. We? Are there others with you?

SHASTA. Not anymore.

EBONY. My daughter's coming, so you'd better make yourself scarce. She's not as merciful as I am.

SHASTA darts off, but rather than exiting he hides and lingers to watch once he sees MADELINE. Enter MADELINE.

MADELINE. I'm back, Mama. Found some—rabbit.

EBONY. *(À la Elmer Fudd.)* Be vewy, vewy quiet. I'm hunting wabbits. Heuh-heuh-heuh-heuh.

MADELINE. Mama, I still don't get that joke.

EBONY. *(Sighs.)* We have lost our culture.

MADELINE. Your culture was never my culture.

EBONY. Very true. It was an old classic that my parents showed me. Not that I could actually "watch" it anymore, even if there were still televisions.

MADELINE starts preparing the soup.

MADELINE. I already skinned it and cut it up, so it should be ready soon.

EBONY. Stumble across any other game which you can follow up on later?

MADELINE. No! Get off my case about it. *(Abruptly:)* Any trouble while I was gone?

EBONY. Not a bit.

MADELINE. I still wish you would let me take you with me.

EBONY. I'm sure a blind woman would be very helpful in hunting. I actually prefer when you're allowed to catch the food.

MADELINE. Don't know, I've seen you do some—weird things. Things you shouldn't be able to do. Ever since you found that staff a few months ago. I still don't know how you stumbled across it.

EBONY. I assure you, there was no stumbling involved. And, yes, it is why you don't need to worry about leaving me. I can take care of myself.

MADELINE. What aren't you telling me about that thing?

EBONY. The less you know about it, the safer you'll be.

MADELINE. *(Noting the fire.)* I keep telling you not to light those fires when I'm not here. It attracts thieves.

EBONY. Thieves are the least of our worries. *(In the direction of SHASTA.)* I can take care of thieves. What I'm concerned about is wolves.

MADELINE. There are no such things as wolves. Haven't been since before your day, if ever.

EBONY. I would hear them as a child. My father brought back a skin once, when they started encroaching on our property. That was before we moved to the city—before the city was abandoned to the gang lords, of course. But my father hung it right above the fireplace.

MADELINE. Mama, there are no wolves. Maybe you're remembering something you saw on your television thingy. You said it showed moving pictures . . .

EBONY. This is not the dream of a child! In my day we had wolves.

MADELINE. You're the one who told me they were just stories.

EBONY. So I did. *(Tense beat.)* About the Emperor Wolf. But not about the common wolves. Those have always been real.

MADELINE. The next thing you'll tell me is that Emperor Wolf himself is . . .

EBONY. I don't want to talk about the Emperor Wolf.

MADELINE. What has gotten into you?

EBONY. I—I have been re-thinking things since we found the staff.

MADELINE. You've let your imagination get away with you since you found that . . .

EBONY. I am not delusional.

MADELINE. I didn't say that.

EBONY. I've tried to protect you—help us to not live in fear—but maybe I have just made you as blind as I am.

MADELINE. You were right not to believe their stories, Mama. There are none of those things. There are no wolves, and there is especially no Emperor Wolf!

SHASTA reveals himself.

SHASTA. That's not true.

MADELINE swiftly takes out an arrow, drawing it into her bow and pointing it directly at SHASTA.

MADELINE. Get away from here!

SHASTA. I'm not afraid of your arrows.

EBONY. You should be.

SHASTA. Well, I'm not.

EBONY. No, really, she's quite good.

SHASTA. I'm not afraid of her arrows because I have seen much scarier things and had things—dark things, surreal things—attack me which are much more deadly than her. You don't believe your mother? You should. After seeing what I have—especially the Emperor Wolf—I can no longer be scared of anything else.

EBONY. You have seen the Emperor Wolf?

MADELINE. He's just another storyteller!

SHASTA. The Emperor Wolf stands on his hind legs like a man. He has great big hands with fierce claws. He has a snout of razor sharp teeth. He has eyes that remind you of your own blood. There is nothing that has made me more scared in my whole life than the Emperor Wolf.

MADELINE. You're a liar.

SHASTA. You can think I'm a liar . . . (SHASTA starts to approach Madeline, until he is eventually staring directly in front at the arrow which she is pointing at his forehead.) You can think I'm a thief. You can think I'm any number of things. But I am not scared of your arrow, for I have seen the Emperor Wolf, I know that I know it, and I know I have seen the other creatures you think are myths. I have seen griffins, and the Sphinx, and monsters. They scare me. You don't scare me.

> MADELINE lowers her arrow, reluctantly impressed by the SHASTA's boldness.

MADELINE. I still think you're a liar . . .

EBONY. Come, share our meal with us.

MADELINE. Mama, no . . .

SHASTA. Thank you. I'm very hungry. But I didn't say that for the food. (MADELINE goes back to preparing the soup with a pot. She pulls out a few bags of spices that are in her pack.) Are those spices?

MADELINE. What if they are?

SHASTA. You know how rare those are? And you have big bags full! You could trade so much for those.

MADELINE. We don't need to trade. We like the spices.

EBONY. Oh, yes, we do. Mmmm-hmmmm. I may be blind, but Madeline likes to indulge my other senses.

SHASTA. And you're sharing that soup with me? Spices and all?

MADELINE. Of course we are, you idiot. We can't exactly take the spices out of your part.

SHASTA. Well then, I have something to share as well then . . .

SHASTA digs in his bag, from which he pulls out a potato.

EBONY. What does he have?

MADELINE. He has a potato, Mama.

EBONY. A potato! I haven't had a potato for ages.

SHASTA. I actually have three potatoes, but I'm going to plant the other two soon and make more of them.

MADELINE. But you're sharing that one with us.

SHASTA. If you're feeding me soup with spices, I think that's only fair.

MADELINE nods, taking the potato and starts cutting it up.

MADELINE. Yes. Only fair.

EBONY. Thank you, young man.

SHASTA. No, thank you. (*Directed to* MADELINE:) Both of you.

MADELINE looks back, connecting with SHASTA momentarily, but then gruffly goes back to making the soup.

EBONY. I am Ebony. This is my daughter Madeline.

SHASTA. My name's Shasta.

EBONY. Shasta. That's a unique name.

SHASTA. It was the name of a character in a book that my father loved. He used read it to me when I was a child.

EBONY. Your father sounds like a good man.

SHASTA. He was. But he's gone now.

EBONY. I'm sorry. And your mother?

SHASTA. She's dead, too.

> MADELINE *looks up from her cooking at* SHASTA. *Her hardened expressions are softening a little.*

MADELINE. So you're alone.

SHASTA. Not completely alone.

> SHASTA *pulls out some books from his pack.*

MADELINE. What are those?

SHASTA. Well, they're books.

MADELINE. *(Feigning disinterest.)* So that is what books look like.

EBONY. Books? You really have books? And can you read them?

SHASTA. Yes, my mother taught me.

EBONY. You must value these very much.

SHASTA. Oh, yes. I've had people try to barter for them, but I won't give them up. Much like your spices.

EBONY. What books are they?

SHASTA. I have more in my pack, but these ones are *The Horse and His Boy*—the favorite I was telling you about. *The Wizard of Oz*— as a little boy, I used to think that the tornado it talks about was the thing that changed our world. And this one is the Doctrine and Covenants. It is part of my parent's religion.

EBONY. Not yours?

SHASTA. I suppose it's mine too. *(Beat.)* There aren't really many Churches to go to anymore, are there? Just us wanderers.

EBONY. Pilgrims. Pioneers. Prophets in the wilderness.

SHASTA. Are you religious?

EBONY. No. My family never was. But I always loved any kind of story. A man coming back from the dead? Yeah, I liked that. There are a few people I would like to bring back, too.

SHASTA. We used to have a lot more books, but those ones got destroyed in one of the great floods. It was soon after that when we saw the Emperor Wolf.

MADELINE. There is no Emperor Wolf! I'm sick of the lies.

SHASTA. I wish they were lies!

EBONY. Madeline, you need to apologize.

MADELINE. He's lying to us . . .

EBONY. We do not lightly call people liars.

MADELINE. But . . .

EBONY. Apologize!

MADELINE. *(Reluctantly:)* I'm sorry.

SHASTA. That's okay. But there is an Emperor Wolf.

MADELINE. Whatever.

Another tense pause.

EBONY. You said you have other books? Which ones?

SHASTA. There's one with a little man who finds a ring that made him invisible—and there is this part with a little monster who told riddles. And a dragon.

MADELINE. What, have you seen dragons, too?

SHASTA. Of course not. Dragons live in Europe.

EBONY. What else? What other books?

SHASTA. There's one about a boy sent to meet an old woman who was angry about a man who didn't marry her, so she kept wearing the wedding dress until it was all old and yellow and she never took down the wedding cake, so it was eaten by rats. In the house there was a little girl the old woman took care of that the boy liked, but I could never tell whether she liked him back. She was mean to him, but it seemed like she might actually like him. There is one called a—a play. You're supposed to perform it in front of other people.

MADELINE. Well, that's silly.

SHASTA. I always thought it sounded kind of nice. The play was about a wizard who lived alone on an island with his daughter and there was a monster and a fairy and a shipwreck . . .

MADELINE. These sound like stupid stories. Totally pretend, nothing real.

SHASTA. They were real to me.

MADELINE. Well, you also think wolves are real.

EBONY. Madeline!

MADELINE. Sorry.

SHASTA. Before the flood we even had more books! But they got destroyed by the Purgers. There were lots of stories in those, but I only remember some of them. Bits and pieces, that was a long time ago now—things were bad, but we at least had each other then.

SHASTA has a hard time containing his emotions.

MADELINE. Are you—are you crying?!

EBONY. I would hope you shed some tears for me when I am gone, Madeline.

MADELINE. I will not let you be gone, Mama.

EBONY. I'm afraid, darling, that may not be a choice you can make.

MADELINE. We've got many years ahead of us.

EBONY. Tell me, Shasta, did you ever read the story about a young girl at a horrible school who could move things with her mind?

SHASTA. No, I haven't read that one.

EBONY. I loved that one as a little girl, when I could still see and read. I had almost forgotten it until just now. How could have I forgotten it?

MADELINE. Maybe it didn't matter.

EBONY. It did matter. The girl in that story loved books, too. And you ought to know, Madeline, that you also were named after a little girl in a book.

MADELINE. You—you never told me that.

EBONY. It was a lovely book. With pictures.

MADELINE, *now curious, takes one of the books and starts inspecting it.*

SHASTA. Hey! Be careful with that . . .

MADELINE. I don't see anything so special about them. Just a bunch of black markings on white stuff . . .

SHASTA. Those markings are words.

MADELINE. I know that.

SHASTA. You can't read?

EBONY. I couldn't exactly teach her.

SHASTA. Did your dad die, too?

MADELINE. No, he's alive as far as we know. Wish he wasn't.

SHASTA. Don't say that.

MADELINE. He left us a long time ago.

SHASTA. Maybe he's out there. Maybe he's sorry. Maybe he thinks about both of you.

MADELINE. Well, I don't think about him. I won't waste my time.

SHASTA. But what if . . . ?

MADELINE. Look, I'm sorry your father died, but he was very different than mine. Okay?

SHASTA. Okay.

MADELINE. Dinner's ready.

MADELINE pulls out a few bowls and utensils from her pack, and pours the food in them. They all eat hungrily.

SHASTA. Oh, thank you. It reminds me of something my mother used to make. She was a good cook, too. This is so—so savory.

MADELINE. You think so?

SHASTA. Oh, yes.

MADELINE nods curtly, the best thing she can come up with for "You're welcome."

MADELINE. Are you a good hunter?

SHASTA. Uh, sure, kinda. Well—not really.

EBONY. Never mind, Madeline will take care of that. But I'm sure that Madeline will be more at ease having you with me when she's out and about.

MADELINE. What do you mean? Mother, he's not coming with us.

SHASTA. She's right. I travel by myself now.

EBONY. Not anymore you don't.

SHASTA. No, really . . .

MADELINE. Mama, you can't . . .

EBONY. I'm a stubborn old woman. Once I've decided something, Shasta, I won't take no for an answer.

SHASTA. Oh, but . . .

EBONY. Just say yes.

SHASTA. Uh—okay, I suppose. But I don't know for how long.

EBONY. As long as you're useful, I imagine. Can you read from those books to us?

MADELINE. Mother, you said useful.

EBONY. To a blind woman, a story is useful.

SHASTA. I would love to read to you—and it looks like we'll still have enough light for at least a little while. (*SHASTA opens one of his books and reads from it.*) "This is the story of an adventure . . ."

Blackout.

SCENE 2

Their fire has gone out and EBONY, MADELINE, *and* SHASTA *are asleep. The* EMPEROR WOLF, *within a dream-like setting suggesting that this is happening in their minds, appears.*

EMPEROR WOLF. I swallow suns. I eat souls. I take the light out of everything. Look in the mirror children, and you will see my face . . .

MADELINE. (*Still asleep.*) I'm nothing like you . . .

EMPEROR WOLF. I am the devourer in every reflection . . .

SHASTA. (*Also still asleep.*) You—you took my father . . .

EMPEROR WOLF. I feed on your black thoughts. I feed on your dark hearts. I feed on you!

EBONY. (*Awaking and lifting her staff, which suddenly flashes.*) Leave the children alone! (*The* EMPEROR WOLF *disappears in the flash. SHASTA and MADELINE still stir fitfully in their sleep.*) Madeline— Shasta—wake up!

MADELINE and SHASTA wake up.

SHASTA. That was so real . . .

EBONY. It was real.

MADELINE. What are you both talking about?

EBONY. You know what we are talking about, Madeline.

MADELINE. We were all talking about the Emperor Wolf. The conversation could have easily influenced all of us . . .

SHASTA. See, you did experience it! You know!

MADELINE. I—I don't know what I know, but that couldn't have
been . . .

SHASTA. People don't simply have mutual dreams . . .

MADELINE. I don't pretend to understand it—but what you're both
implying doesn't make sense—it just doesn't make sense!

SHASTA. The Emperor Wolf has our scent now.

MADELINE. Scent? It was a dream!

SHASTA. He smells our souls.

MADELINE. Ridiculous.

SHASTA. Madeline, this has happened to me before. This is how I lost
my father.

MADELINE. The Emperor Wolf isn't real, you lunatic!

SHASTA. No, no, you hear me now, you are ignorant!

MADELINE. What did you call me?

SHASTA. I'm no genius, but I know what I have seen, I know what I
have experienced!

MADELINE. Don't you dare talk to me like that—don't you dare! You
stand there with imaginary stories that pretend the world is something it isn't and then you try to make me believe fairy tales because
of dreams we had—dreams! If I'm ignorant, well, then you're stark
crazy! A kid who makes things up to make sense out of the horrible
things in his life. The rest of us deal with what is real.

EBONY. Stop it. Both of you.

MADELINE. But, Mother . . .

EBONY. Look, Maddy, I'm the one who taught you to be the skeptic—
for good reason. I'm proud of you. I'm proud of your mind.

MADELINE. Thank you, Mama . . .

EBONY. But he's right. Not because of any lack in you or your intelligence, but because of me. I just thought—thought it would better

that way. I wanted to protect my little girl from the monsters in the night.

MADELINE. Mama?

EBONY. There are things—there are things that I have never had the courage to explain.

MADELINE. Mama, why are you . . . ?

EBONY. I have never felt safe. There was always another tragedy willing to prey on me and I just took to escaping, hiding—hoping that the demons would pass me over. But they have found us.

MADELINE. Mama, you don't have to . . .

EBONY. Once the whole world collapsed and we were all left to fend for ourselves, the stories started coming—to life.

SHASTA. Let's get out of here. My parents were taking me to a colony in Missouri. My people are traveling there. It's supposed to be safe there. Maybe we can . . .

EBONY. Nowhere is safe. Maddy, your father followed that thing. He is a servant of the Wolf. That is why he left us.

MADELINE. What? No, you said that he was a horrible person who abandoned us . . .

EBONY. Your father was a good man once. Why else would he marry a woman with crippled sight and who totally depended on him?

MADELINE. You are not crippled! Did he make you feel that way? Did he call you crippled?

EBONY. No, he never would have . . .

MADELINE. That man was a fool for not really seeing you.

EBONY. You mustn't be too hard on him.

MADELINE. I certainly can be and will be!

EBONY. Derrick—he taught me to rely on myself and not on him. When he left, I thought he was preparing me for that moment.

MADELINE. There is no excuse for what he did.

EBONY. You don't understand. When I met him, he didn't see . . . *(motioning to her eyes)*

. . . this. He wasn't like that. He tried to make me feel good about myself, like you do. It's one of the reasons I loved him and why I find so much of him in you.

MADELINE. I am nothing like him.

EBONY. There was a lot of good in him. He used to be hopeful. Romantic. Optimistic. But when we met, I was the one who was—haunted. You don't know how I used to talk. What I would try to—do to myself.

MADELINE. You are strong, Mama. Stronger than you know.

EBONY. Sometimes I wonder if I was the Emperor Wolf's first target.

MADELINE. What do you mean?

EBONY. I have wondered if he took on the burden. Whether he offered himself in exchange . . .

MADELINE. Mama, you're not making sense.

EBONY. I was so bitter when he left us—I refused to see—I didn't know . . .

MADELINE. Didn't know what?

EBONY. The day he left, the Emperor Wolf was there.

MADELINE. Father lied to us!

EBONY. That is what I used to tell you. But I heard things. I felt things when he left. I've never told you, but I was awake when he left. He and I spoke—he did not sound like himself. Then I heard the Wolf. The sounds were—unearthly. The growls and the sounds—they weren't human.

MADELINE. Mama, you've been deceived.

EBONY. There were two voices. Who can make two voices at the same time?

MADELINE. He had help then—somebody helped him.

EBONY. All to trick a blind woman? For what? I—I felt its breath. Its hot, nasty breath. He rasped out with a voice that I still hear sometimes . . .

MADELINE. Mama, stop! Please, stop!

EBONY. You think I'm crazy, darling? Maybe so. But my senses told me that I experienced something that I have never been able to voice to you. Your father—he didn't want to leave us.

MADELINE. That's not true.

EBONY. That soulless wolf took him from us!

MADELINE. No, no, no, no, no. No!

EBONY. Maddy . . .

MADELINE. Mama, this is cruel. This isn't hope you're giving me, this isn't kindness wrapped in a lie—this is cruelty.

EBONY. The other story was the lie, to protect you. Now I'm telling you the truth.

MADELINE. We're packed. If we're gonna go, let's go. I just don't want to hear another word about . . .

EBONY. Shasta, have you been to the Forests of Whispers?

SHASTA. Yes, that's direction I just came from. But . . .

EBONY. Can you lead us there?

SHASTA. No! Why on earth would you want to go there? It's very dangerous.

EBONY. You said that you've seen the Sphinx.

SHASTA. Yes.

EBONY. We need to see her.

SHASTA. No! Please—she kills people. Eats them.

EBONY. Only if they can't answer her riddles.

SHASTA. Well, from what I've heard, they're kind of hard riddles.

MADELINE. Mama, he's lying. If he had seen the Sphinx, why is he still alive? Are you going to tell us that you answered this fairy tale's riddles?

SHASTA. No, of course not. I ran.

MADELINE. And skinny you, scrawny you were so fast that you escaped?

SHASTA. I don't know why—why I survived. Why she spared me.

EBONY. Spared you?

SHASTA. But the rest of my people—well, that's how my parents died. How my family and friends all died.

EBONY. Nevertheless, that is where we are going.

SHASTA. But why?

EBONY. If you answer her riddle, the Sphinx can give you knowledge.

SHASTA. Yes, I've heard that.

EBONY. What if . . . ?

SHASTA. Yes?

EBONY. If she can tell us, I want to know how to kill that monster wolf before he can hurt anyone else ever again.

MADELINE. Mama, we are not going to . . .

EBONY. Am I or am I not still your mother?

MADELINE. Am I or am I not the one that keeps us alive?

EBONY. I'm done hiding. Shasta, bring us back to where you ran from.

SHASTA. There was a reason I ran.

EBONY. I know. But maybe these monsters are as scared as we are. Maybe we just have to show a little courage.

MADELINE. Mama, please, we've been safe.

A light appears from the staff and points in a certain direction.

EBONY. Is that the direction you came from, Shasta?

SHASTA. Uhm, yes, actually.

EBONY. That's the direction we're going then.

SHASTA. Mama, it's pointless to . . .

EBONY. What are you scared of more, my child? That Shasta is wrong— or that he is right? Now hold my hand. Lead the way, Shasta.

Exit SHASTA, EBONY, *and* MADELINE.

SCENE 3

The SPHINX, *a beautiful but intimidating creature who is half woman, half lion, with great wings, flies down, or leaps onto to her perch.* DERRICK, *a graying, grizzled man enters, a sword in his hand. The* SPHINX *looks down on him casually.*

SPHINX. You have come again, have you?

DERRICK. I come as many times as my master bids me.

SPHINX. It is only because of your master that you are still alive.

DERRICK. I don't care who dies. You or me. It's all the same now.

SPHINX. I became an Eternal One long ago. You cannot kill me. *(DER-RICK lifts up his sword and lunges for the* SPHINX. *The* SPHINX *easily dodges him.* DERRICK *attacks again, and after the* SPHINX *dodges him this time, she claws his back. He withdraws injured and in pain.)* Tell the Wolf that next time I will really kill you.

DERRICK. I am just a shell to him. He would just send another.

SPHINX. And I can kill another. I do need the nourishment, after all. But this war between him and me needs to cease. Our kind should not be engaged in such things. You humans have proven where that leads.

DERRICK. My Master is very pleased with what has happened to the humans.

SPHINX. I'm sure he is, since he is at the root of it. His howl that created this world disturbed us from our sleep and brought us to feast
on the carnage he served. But not all of us were pleased with his
table. Are you pleased with this new world, mortal?

DERRICK. I had my opinions driven from me long ago.

SPHINX. Your vacant eyes may tell that tale. But is your heart so vacant?

DERRICK. My heart no longer exists.

SPHINX. Then I pity you all the more. Farewell, mortal, and good journeys. Come to me again and I will eat you.

> *The* SPHINX *is about to re-gain her perch when she sniffs in the
> air, catching a scent. She takes a prepped, combative position.*
> DERRICK *goes to exit, but upon hearing people walking near,
> hides. Enter* EBONY, MADELINE, *and* SHASTA. MADELINE
> *draws an arrow.*

MADELINE. Mother, Shasta, get behind me!

SPHINX. Your weapons can't hurt me, little girl. You may as well save
your arrows.

SHASTA. She's right, Madeline. I saw those who died use all sorts of
weapons against her. Nothing worked.

SPHINX. I spared you once, Shasta. You almost tempt me too far to
come when I am even more hungry.

SHASTA. How do you know my name?

SPHINX. I know all of your names. Have you come to pass into another
sphere, Ebony? Have you come to die, Madeline? It's almost your
time. But you, Shasta, you can still escape that fate, if you . . .

MADELINE. I—I don't know what you are, but . . .

SPHINX. What I am! You are right, you don't know what I am. I am
beyond you, I am above you. I see into your soul clearly, but my soul
is opaque to you. I repeat, have you come to die?

SHASTA. We have come to answer a riddle! That is what I say, right?

SPHINX. You are right. Nothing fancy, just the challenge. Who is your representative?

EBONY. I am.

MADELINE. Mama, no!

EBONY. If I die, then you two are to go on, to run from the Emperor Wolf the best you can. I don't know what to do after this . . .

MADELINE. Let me do it, let me . . .

EBONY. I am the representative! Do you heed me, Sphinx?

SPHINX. I heed you and I respect your challenge. But if you answer incorrectly you all die.

EBONY. No, the children must be spared, you can have me.

SPHINX. That is not how this works. And they are no longer children. They have come on a journey that is older than time.

EBONY. Children, if I answer wrong, you need to run. You need to . . .

SPHINX. Are you ready for the riddle, mortal? If you need a moment . . .

EBONY. Just ask me it.

SPHINX. Very well. In a box lies an important gift. It can be shared or it can be locked away. But either way it is how the world will know you. What is it?

SHASTA. Can we help her?

SPHINX. She is your representative—the burden belongs to her, but if she wants your help, that is her choice. It is her answer that matters. But, be careful, you may lead her astray more than you help her. Once she gives her answer, she can't ungive it.

MADELINE. She said it will be how the world knows us—clothing perhaps? The world judges on the outside appearance . . .

EBONY. I never have.

SHASTA. Anyway, she said it could be locked away or shared . . .

MADELINE. You can lock away or share clothes . . .

SHASTA. But then it's not how you're known, if you give them away, it's how someone else is known.

MADELINE. I don't see you coming up with any answers!

SHASTA. I'm thinking!

EBONY. Shhh—let me concentrate. (*There is a long silence as* EBONY *listens to her thoughts and tries to calmly work this out in her mind.*) You said it was in a box . . .

SPHINX. Be careful how you proceed with this. You can't ungive your . . .

EBONY. A voice. A voice is in a voice box. It can be shared or locked away. And that is how at least I know people. Am I right?

SPHINX. (*Beat.*)You have shown wisdom, Ebony, and seen where others could not see. A voice is the right answer. Forevermore, I will not eat you.

MADELINE. Mama—Mama, you did it!

SHASTA. Yes, yes, yes!

SPHINX. You have now all inherited her prize. What knowledge do you seek?

EBONY. We want to know how to kill the Emperor Wolf.

SPHINX. I cannot tell you how to kill the Emperor Wolf.

MADELINE. Wait, no, we had a deal . . .

SHASTA. Yeah, you're supposed to be fountain of all knowledge.

SPHINX. It is like asking me how to make the sun set in the east. I cannot tell you something that is not possible. The Emperor Wolf is immortal.

MADELINE. Then we have risked our lives for nothing!

SHASTA. Wait, wait, we have to—we have to think of another option.

MADELINE. Didn't you hear her? There is no other option!

EBONY. I'm sorry. I truly thought she could help us . . .

SHASTA. Wait, wait! There is always another option, there's always another way of thinking of something. We need to imagine another way!

MADELINE. Not all stories have the happy endings of your blasted books!

SHASTA. Not all books have happy endings! But some of them have smart characters. If we give up that easily, then you're right. There won't be any endings worth having. Let me think. Give me time.

SPHINX. You may ask something else of me, but I cannot . . .

SHASTA. If we can't kill the Emperor Wolf, can we—can we bind him somehow? Imprison him or banish him?

SPHINX. Yes. Yes, that is possible.

EBONY. Good work, Shasta! Please, majestic Sphinx, tell us how to bind the Emperor Wolf.

SPHINX. First you must capture a griffin . . .

MADELINE. A griffin!

SHASTA. Let me guess, you don't believe in griffins?

MADELINE. No, I'm starting to believe in everything now. It's just that a griffin sounds hard to catch.

SPHINX. Once you have captured a griffin, it will take you to the Wandering Woman. Obtain from her the braid of her hair. It is with that braid that you can bind the wolf. But first you must learn the value of the braid and how to use it. Seek Wisdom, may She bless you. Farewell.

> SHASTA *and* MADELINE *go to leave, but* MADELINE *lingers by the* SPHINX *for a moment. They speak privately.*

EBONY. Thank you. Thank you so much for helping us.

SPHINX. You were the one who helped your children.

EBONY. Oh, she's my daughter, but they're not both my . . .

SPHINX. Aren't they?

EBONY. Why do you care? You were about to devour us a moment ago.

SPHINX. The survivors become my children, under my protection.

EBONY. I hope you are a good mother.

SPHINX. Not a good one, no. But a fierce one. I see my children. I hope you can see yours.

EBONY. *(Listening to both SHASTA and MADELINE, who are chatting together happily. MADELINE laughs.)* I believe I can now. It's been a long time since I have heard her laugh. She pretends to not like the boy, but . . .

SPHINX. Be off on your journey now.

EBONY. But the Griffin, how do we find . . . ?

SPHINX. Shasta knows the way.

EBONY. *(Turning back to SHASTA and MADELINE.)* Shasta, she says you know the way to the Griffins.

SHASTA. I tried very hard to get away from those places, you know. *(Sighs.)* We'll follow the Northern Path nearly to its end. They live in that region of country. But they're big and strong and they can fly. I don't know how we're going to capture one.

MADELINE. Leave that to me.

> *Exit MADELINE, EBONY, and SHASTA. Exit the SPHINX. DERRICK re-emerges, following MADELINE, EBONY, and SHASTA.*

SCENE 4

Enter SHASTA, MADELINE, and EBONY.

SHASTA. It's not far now. We've made really good time. If we hurry we can . . .

EBONY. Wait, wait. I'm very tired, can we . . . ?

MADELINE. Mama, are you all right?

EBONY. Just the normal aches and pains. I'm not young anymore, Maddy.

MADELINE. Of course not. We need to stop, Shasta.

SHASTA. Okay. Sure. It is going to get dark soon, though . . .

MADELINE. Then we'll set up camp.

SHASTA. But we're almost . . .

MADELINE. We'll set up camp.

SHASTA. Okay. (*SHASTA and MADELINE start setting up camp, while EBONY rests. There is a long pause. MADELINE is definitely bothered by something.*) That was the most you've spoken since the Sphinx. Is everything all right?

MADELINE. Yeah, I'm fine.

SHASTA. I mean I would understand if you're a bit rattled. The Sphinx is kind of scary . . .

MADELINE. I said I'm fine! (*Another pause.*) It's that what we're doing is very dangerous.

SHASTA. It's okay to be scared.

MADELINE. I'm not scared—not scared for me, at least. (*They both look to EBONY, who has already fallen asleep.*) I don't ever care what happens to me.

SHASTA. You love her a lot.

MADELINE. She's the only one I love.

SHASTA. I can understand that.

MADELINE. I'm not sure if you can. You don't know what it's like to take care of someone.

SHASTA. What are you implying?

MADELINE. (*Pause.*) Nothing.

SHASTA. I know you don't like me. But you don't have to be cruel.

MADELINE. If you don't like it, just leave then.

SHASTA. *(Looking again at EBONY.)* I care about her, too, you know.

MADELINE. You don't even know her.

SHASTA. Not like you, sure. But she was willing to die for us. I think that makes the quality of her soul pretty evident.

MADELINE. Keep that kind of talk to yourself. I'm not pulled in by your stories.

SHASTA. Why are you so intent on not liking me?

MADELINE. What's there to like? You're all hot air and useless dreams.

SHASTA. You think I'm an intruder. Right? Horned in on your life and you would like nothing better than to drive me out of here.

MADELINE. Yeah, that's right! So why don't you just go?

SHASTA. Because we need each other.

MADELINE. Maybe you need us. But we don't need you. *(SHASTA doesn't move.)* I said get out of here!

SHASTA. Why are you afraid of what I have to offer?

MADELINE. I said that I'm not afraid! Get out! *(SHASTA is determined to stay.)* Selfish brat.

SHASTA. *I'm* selfish? You can't think of anyone besides you and Ebony. It's like the rest of the world doesn't exist to you! Like we don't matter!

MADELINE. Didn't you hear me? You don't matter. You're all just a set of distant stories, nothing to do with us. We don't need you!

SHASTA. You don't? Because, you know, I was right about the Sphinx, wasn't I? And I'm the one who is leading you to the Griffins, aren't I?

MADELINE. I didn't even want to go to the Sphinx or the Griffins! What's the point of trying to defeat the Wolf if we're going to be killed in trying to get it done? What would that accomplish? This is pointless!

SHASTA. But I was right, wasn't I? And you were wrong. And that's what irks you most. You didn't even know things like this existed, and you're too damn proud to face how ignorant you are! *(MADE-LINE punches SHASTA.)* Oh, is that how you argue your point? How eloquent! *(MADELINE punches SHASTA again.)* Are you tough now? Are you right now? *(MADELINE punches SHASTA again.)* Punch me all you want, Madeline! Beat me till I'm bloody and broken! Do everything this world has taught you! You learned your lessons well. It still won't change a thing.

MADELINE goes to punch SHASTA again, but then stops short and just pounds on his chest and he grapples with her.

MADELINE. Please, go—please, please, don't do this to us . . .

SHASTA. I'm not doing anything to you.

MADELINE. We were fine by ourselves—we were doing just fine . . .

SHASTA. You weren't doing just fine and I wasn't doing just fine.

MADELINE. You don't care about us—not really . . .

SHASTA. That's not true. But you don't care about me.

MADELINE. (Pause.) That's not true, either.

SHASTA. Isn't it?

MADELINE. You're just with us to help yourself.

SHASTA. I won't leave you like he did.

They are still locked in each other's grip, but now it loosens. It is now more like they are holding onto each other for dear life. It appears as if they might kiss. EBONY's voice pipes up from her "sleeping" place.

EBONY. Go to bed, kids.

MADELINE. Mama! How long have you been . . . ?

EBONY. Go to bed.

They both bolt to their sleeping areas and get under their blankets. Pause. MADELINE's head rises up, looking over at SHASTA. SHASTA's head then rises, too, matching her gaze. They just look at each other for a while and then smile. Lights dim.

SCENE 5

Lighting indicates a passage of time. EBONY, MADELINE, *and* SHASTA *are all still asleep.* DERRICK *enters. Quietly, stealthily* DERRICK *moves to* EBONY *and then just lingers above her for a moment.* DERRICK *then swiftly covers her mouth and drags* EBONY *a ways off as* EBONY *struggles.*

DERRICK, SHUT UP. I'm not here to hurt you.

EBONY calms down. DERRICK *uncovers her mouth.*

EBONY. Derrick?

DERRICK. I can't stay long. But my Master wants you.

EBONY. *(Backing away.)* Then he'll have to fight for me.

DERRICK. I'm not going to take you to him.

EBONY. You don't know what you'll do.

The EMPEROR *appears, dream-like.*

DERRICK. I—I'm trying to change.

EBONY. Then change. But you can't change with us. Too much has happened. Find a new life.

DERRICK. I still ache for you. I miss you and Madeline so much.

EBONY. And there's not a day that I don't miss you. But we can't help you anymore—we all have to keep moving.

DERRICK. Let me back in. Please.

EBONY. No.

DERRICK suddenly yells out in grief, which wakes up MADELINE *and* SHASTA.

MADELINE. What's happening?

EMPEROR WOLF. You can't hide from me, Derrick. You can't fight me. I found their scent again.

EBONY. Stay there, Maddy.

DERRICK. Filthy beast, stay away from them!

MADELINE. Get away from her!

SHASTA. Madeline!

In a swift moment MADELINE *picks up her bow and an arrow out of her quiver and draws it, pointing it directly at* DERRICK.

EBONY. No, Madeline, don't!

EMPEROR WOLF. You can't go back. They won't let you.

DERRICK. Maddy, it's me. I'm your dad.

MADELINE. I know who you are.

DERRICK. I am—you are . . .

EMPEROR WOLF AND DERRICK. You are forever mine.

A sudden blast of dark lights, sound and smoke emerge from DERRICK *and the light is overcome, causing a blackout. There is the sound of the bow firing its arrow and a surprising howl. The lights come on to reveal that* DERRICK *is gone, with the* EMPEROR WOLF *(no longer dream-like) in his place. There is an arrow protruding from his shoulder.*

EBONY. Maddy, Shasta—run!

MADELINE. Shasta, help me save her!

SHASTA. Right with you, Maddy!

SHASTA *takes* EBONY's *staff which is near him and* MADELINE *takes out her dagger. In an act of foolhardy bravery they attack the* EMPEROR WOLF *head on.*

EBONY. No—no!

EBONY *tries to grope forward as the battle between the* EMPEROR WOLF *and the two teenagers rages. Neither* MADELINE *nor* SHASTA *are pushovers, especially Madeline, and they both fight with desperate ferocity.* SHASTA, *however, is taken down first, knocked unconscious.* EBONY *has made her way to* SHASTA *and picks up her staff.*

MADELINE. Shasta!

EMPEROR WOLF. I have wanted your mind for a long time, Madeline.

EBONY. You won't have it!

> EBONY *has found her staff. She lunges forward to where she heard the* EMPEROR WOLF *and strikes him with the staff. There is a tremendous amount of light and sound, as something supernatural is happening:*

EMPEROR WOLF. Where did you get that? Stop it—stop it!

EBONY. You think you're the only one with power? You think you're the only one with abilities?

MADELINE. Mama, no, stop it, get away . . .

EBONY. Don't be scared, Maddy.

MADELINE. What are you doing?

EBONY. I can keep him down. I can keep fighting him. I can keep him at bay.

MADELINE. Don't you dare . . .

EBONY. Don't forget Shasta—he has no one else. We're all family now.

MADELINE. Mama, Mama, please . . .

EBONY. I love you.

> *There is a brilliant flash of light and immense sound. Then there is complete darkness and silence.*

SCENE 6

> *After a long pause, we hear* MADELINE *weeping. The lights slowly come up as we see her, distraught.* EBONY *and the* EMPEROR WOLF *are gone, but* EBONY's *staff has been left behind.* SHASTA *regains consciousness. He picks up the staff and goes to* MADELINE. *He kneels down next to her.*

SHASTA. Your mom?

MADELINE. Where did she go? Shasta, where did she go!

SHASTA. Madeline, we have to be calm . . .

MADELINE. Calm!

SHASTA. We have to figure out what happened.

MADELINE. I'll tell you what happened—we met you!

SHASTA. This isn't my fault—I told you both that we shouldn't have done this!

MADELINE. If we hadn't met you, we wouldn't have been pulled into this . . .

SHASTA. It was your father, Maddy, not mine! It was your father that brought this onto us, it's your father that came after her and you. I had nothing to do with this! My father was a good man!

MADELINE. I . . . I . . .

SHASTA. Oh, I didn't mean . . .

MADELINE. That monster.

SHASTA. We'll find her . . .

MADELINE. My father is a monster.

SHASTA. A griffin, the Wandering Woman . . .

MADELINE. I wish I was never born!

SHASTA. Don't say that. Please, don't say that . . .

MADELINE. What is this place, Shasta? What kind of world is this? I thought things were bad before, but this . . . I don't want to believe this kind of world can exist!

SHASTA. Maddy, you listen to me. I am glad I found you. I am glad that I found Ebony. Even if we've lost her . . .

MADELINE. We haven't lost her!

SHASTA. Please, please, just listen. Even if we've lost her, like I lost my parents—oh, Maddy, I know what you're feeling!

MADELINE. I—I know you do.

SHASTA. Even—even if we've lost her, we can't forget what she gave us. My parents—they're gone. I have no hope of seeing them anymore in this life.

MADELINE. Shasta . . .

SHASTA. But they're with me. I feel them sometimes. I know it sounds crazy, but . . .

MADELINE. It doesn't sound crazy. Not anymore.

SHASTA. You have to want to live.

MADELINE. Why?

SHASTA. Because if you stop then you become—really lost. I was there for a long time. Like I was in a land of shadows—like I was a shadow myself.

MADELINE. How did you . . . ?

SHASTA. I remembered. I remembered the stories they would tell me. I remembered falling asleep to their voices.

MADELINE. But doesn't that make it hurt even more?

SHASTA. A good hurt. Don't lose that ache, never forget them, but then it mingles with—such an exquisite joy. Don't stop feeling, because then you will really forget her. You will forget how she made you feel.

MADELINE. We'll get her back. We'll get a griffin, we'll find the Wandering Woman and get her braid—then we'll get her back.

SHASTA. Right. There is no reason to give up hope.

MADELINE. I'm really scared, Shasta.

SHASTA. Me too. *(They both reach for the staff.)* Oh.

MADELINE. It was my mother's, Shasta.

SHASTA. I know, but . . .

MADELINE. It doesn't belong to you.

SHASTA. It—it called to me.

MADELINE. It's not yours! (*MADELINE grabs the staff and backs away from SHASTA.*) Maybe it *is* best that I did this alone.

SHASTA. No. You can't.

MADELINE. Yes, I can.

SHASTA. Be reasonable . . .

MADELINE. You'll be safer if you don't come with me.

SHASTA. Nowhere is safe anymore! Please . . .

MADELINE. This isn't your fight. Ebony is not your mother. We are not your family.

SHASTA. That's not what she believed . . .

MADELINE. You're not my family!

SHASTA. But you're all the family that I have! Please, I don't want to be alone. Your mother said that we were all . . .

MADELINE. I don't care what she said! She's not here, is she? I can't depend on her anymore!

MADELINE breaks down crying. Shasta just stands there for a moment, not sure what to do.

SHASTA. Maddie . . .

MADELINE. Go away! I don't want to ever see you again!

SHASTA kneels in front of her, looking at her compassionately. MADELINE looks up.

SHASTA. I—I can leave, if you really want me to, but . . .

MADELINE. No!

MADELINE goes to SHASTA, clinging to him.

SHASTA. But you said . . .

MADELINE. Don't be an idiot. I'm just—I'm just—please, don't go.

SHASTA. Never.

MADELINE. I don't know if I can believe it anymore.

SHASTA. I—Honestly, I'm not sure how much I can believe myself. I mean—I could die, I could—could get lost, I could . . .

MADELINE. This is supposed to be comforting?

SHASTA. What I'm saying is—I can't see the future. But what I can see now is . . . is . . .

MADELINE. Is what?

SHASTA. Is worth staying for.

MADELINE. And you mean that?

SHASTA. What do I have in the world, Madeline, except you? *(MAD-ELINE touches SHASTA's face softly. She then hands him the staff.)* Are you sure?

MADELINE. Yes. *(Beat.)* I don't want to be alone either.

Blackout.

SCENE 7

A small light darts around the theater, playfully moving from place to place. Enter MADELINE and SHASTA. The little light "hides."

MADELINE. Are we there yet?

SHASTA. If you don't stop complaining I'll turn this thing right around and go right home.

MADELINE. What?

SHASTA. Uhm, another funny thing my Dad used to say. We would laugh so hard . . .

MADELINE. I don't get it.

SHASTA. Neither did I.

Beat.

MADELINE. Shasta—thanks for sticking around.

SHASTA. Well, you're kind of nice being—stuck to.

MADELINE. *(Laughs.)* That's really the best you've got?

SHASTA. Hey, beggars can't be choosers. You see any other potential boyfriends around here?

MADELINE. Is that what you think you are? My boyfriend?

SHASTA. Well, I don't think you're going to get any better offers.

MADELINE. Who said I wanted a boyfriend?

SHASTA. Oh, come on, you can't tell me it doesn't sound—nice.

They look at each other.

MADELINE. What's so—nice about it?

SHASTA. I don't know, the . . . the . . .

They draw closer, as if they are about to kiss.

MADELINE. Don't worry. You can be brave. *(The kiss is about to happen, when the light flies in between them, interrupting the moment.)* Agh! What is it?!

SHASTA. I can't believe it. I've heard stories, but—it's a fairy.

MADELINE draws her bow and arrow.

MADELINE. Be very quiet.

SHASTA. Stop! What are you doing?

MADELINE. I'm going to kill it, of course.

SHASTA. What? No!

MADELINE. It's one of them, Shasta. Who knows what horrible things it can do to us.

SHASTA. It's—it's beautiful.

MADELINE. Beautiful things can be deadly, too.

SHASTA. It's—it's alive! Doesn't that mean anything to you?

MADELINE. What means more to me is keeping us alive.

SHASTA. It hasn't done anything to us. Have some compassion.

MADELINE. I—I'm trying to protect us.

SHASTA. Maybe not all the creatures that came to our world—maybe they're not all bad. Maybe they need our protection, too.

MADELINE. We can't be naive . . .

SHASTA. My mother used to teach me that as broken as our world was, we were still stewards over it.

MADELINE. Stewards?

SHASTA. Protectors.

MADELINE thinks about this and then lowers her bow.

MADELINE. All right.

The fairy flies away.

SHASTA. *(Wistfully.)* "I believe in fairies."

MADELINE. Well, yeah.

SHASTA. It's a line from another book I have.

MADELINE. You and your books.

SHASTA. The fairies could make the children in the book fly.

MADELINE. Really?

SHASTA. With fairy dust.

MADELINE. I've always wanted to fly. I have dreams about it.

Suddenly the whole stage lights up with fairies (or fairy magic), accompanied by beautiful music.

SHASTA. Oh.

MADELINE. Shasta, it's—they're beautiful.

SHASTA. Do you hear them?

MADELINE. The words of their song—how can I understand them?

SHASTA. I don't know. They're—they're inviting us to stay. They say they can keep us safe.

MADELINE. We—we can't stay.

SHASTA. Wait, Maddy, let's think about this—are you sure this isn't what your mother would have wanted? She wanted us safe, that's why she sacrificed herself.

MADELINE. We can't abandon her to that monster.

SHASTA. I—I don't think we can beat him.

MADELINE. Neither do I. But that doesn't mean we don't try.

SHASTA looks longingly at the fairies.

SHASTA. But this—this could make us happy.

MADELINE. At what cost?

SHASTA. You're not listening . . .

MADELINE. At what cost!

SHASTA. I have survived, Maddy! After I saw my parents die—after I saw my whole community die—I was still standing! There must have been a reason for that.

MADELINE. When you stood against my arrow, told me you weren't afraid, I admired you then . . .

SHASTA. Maddy . . .

MADELINE. . . . but now I see you for who you really are. A coward. You want to know the reason why you survived and your community died when the Sphinx was after you? Because you ran. You gave up on them.

SHASTA. I did not give up on them!

MADELINE. You want to stay in your fairy world? Live by yourself in your books? Protect your hide? Go ahead! But I know where my responsibilities are.

SHASTA. Maybe the obligation has already been fulfilled for us . . .

MADELINE. Stop making excuses! You're just like him!

SHASTA. Like who?

MADELINE. You know who!

SHASTA. Your father, he . . .

MADELINE. He protected himself and left us to eat the scraps!

MADELINE turns to leave.

SHASTA. Madeline, wait.

MADELINE. What?

SHASTA. *(To the fairies.)* Thank you, friends, for your kind offer. I cannot accept it. *(Back to* MADELINE.*)* You're right. About all of it—except for one thing.

MADELINE. And what is that?

SHASTA. My books did not teach me to run.

Blackout.

SCENE 8

A GRIFFIN *is sleeping. The* GRIFFIN *can either be a dancer/actor in costume, or a large, beautiful puppet, or any other invention that occurs to the director/designers.* MADELINE *and* SHASTA *enter quietly.*

MADELINE. So—how do we catch it?

SHASTA. I have no idea.

MADELINE. I thought you were an expert on these things.

SHASTA. I said I knew where they were. I didn't say I was an expert.

MADELINE. Beautiful.

SHASTA. You are, you know.

MADELINE. What?

SHASTA. Beautiful.

MADELINE. *(A little embarrassed.)* You are so corny.

SHASTA. So I'm not Cassanova . . .

MADELINE. Who's Cassanova?

SHASTA. You know, I'm not sure. Just something my Dad used to say.

MADELINE. Well, I bet he was corny, too.

SHASTA. Probably.

MADELINE. But—I think you look good, too.

SHASTA. Thanks.

MADELINE. So—I'm going to go catch that Griffin now.

SHASTA. Have fun, sweetie.

MADELINE. I said stop being corny.

SHASTA. Sorry.

MADELINE kisses SHASTA on the cheek.

MADELINE. We can save that sort of thing for later.

SHASTA. Do you want my help?

MADELINE. Actually, no. No offense, Shasta, but you'd kind of get in the way. We may have only one shot at this.

SHASTA. Oh, I see how it is.

MADELINE. Just sit there and look cute and be supportive.

SHASTA. Now who's being corny?

They smile at each other before MADELINE takes some rope from her pack and makes a kind of lasso. She then approaches the GRIFFIN. As she nears it, the GRIFFIN wakes up. There is a tense moment between MADELINE and the GRIFFIN. They stare at each other momentarily and the GRIFFIN slowly rises. It spreads its wings.

MADELINE (CONT). Oh, no you don't! You're not flying off on me!

MADELINE grabs hold of the GRIFFIN. The GRIFFIN knocks her off. The GRIFFIN spreads its wings again. MADELINE grabs hold of the GRIFFIN again. The GRIFFIN knocks her off again. The process is repeated once more, after which the GRIFFIN *doesn't spread its wings again, but rather confronts* MADELINE.

MADELINE (CONT). There. That's what I was hoping for.

The GRIFFIN *hisses (or some sort of Griffinesque equivalent).* MADELINE *hisses back. The* GRIFFIN *and* MADELINE *circle each other, both of them wary.* MADELINE *tries to get the rope around the* GRIFFIN'S *neck. The* GRIFFIN *dodges. The* GRIFFIN *takes a swipe at* MADELINE. MADELINE *dodges.*

The two circle each other again. The GRIFFIN *rears up, trying to intimidate.* MADELINE *makes a swift movement and throws a rope over the* GRIFFIN'S *claw and tightens it. The* GRIFFIN *knocks* MADELINE *back.*

MADELINE *pulls on the rope, budging the* GRIFFIN *a bit. The* GRIFFIN *pulls back, toppling* MADELINE *onto her face.* MADELINE *rises. They both assess each other.*

The GRIFFIN *charges, knocking down* MADELINE. *The* GRIFFIN *rears up again, bringing its claw down.* MADELINE *moves her head to avoid the claw in the face, and then dodges the claw again. She rolls away just in time to avoid a claw in the chest.* MADELINE *rises again. The* GRIFFIN *hisses again.*

The GRIFFIN *then gets to higher ground.* MADELINE *tries to pull it down with the rope, but the* GRIFFIN *resists. The* GRIFFIN *then leaps from the higher ground, tackling* MADELINE. *They tumble and wrestle a bit, but* MADELINE *is able to extricate herself from the* GRIFFIN.

MADELINE *and the* GRIFFIN *then launch into a flurry of attempted strikes and swipes, with the possibility of the rope being used in some unique and inventive ways.*

They are both tired after this series of attempts. They recognize that they are pretty evenly matched. MADELINE *then smiles. She pulls on the rope again and, as before, it budges the*

GRIFFIN *a bit. The* GRIFFIN *pulls back, but this time* MADE-LINE *is ready for it and allows the force to launch her towards the* GRIFFIN.

The GRIFFIN *is too surprised to react and* MADELINE *uses the opportunity to twist onto the* GRIFFIN'S *back (if possible), or is at least clinging to the* GRIFFIN'S *shoulders from behind.*

The GRIFFIN *tries to twist, throw, and buck* MADELINE *off, to no avail.* MADELINE *just clings on tighter.* MADELINE *then grabs the* GRIFFIN'S *other front claw and twists the rope around it as well. With a pull, she causes the two claws to come together, toppling the* GRIFFIN *down to the ground.*

MADELINE *ties the* GRIFFIN'S *front claws together as she struggles with the* GRIFFIN. *The* GRIFFEN, *however, kicks* MADELINE *backwards with its back claws, sending her hurtling back.* MADELINE *drops the rope. The* GRIFFIN *stands on its hind legs and is about to take off and fly right before* MADELINE *scrambles and grabs the rope, just as the* GRIFFIN *leaps into the air.*

If it's possible, the illusion of flight would be appreciated here. MADELINE *is being dragged and yanked around from below, as she attempts to get a better grip on the rope.*

MADELINE *eventually finds a place where she can anchor herself. With some difficulty she ties the rope to some sort of stump, large rock, etc., which will prevent the* GRIFFIN *from flying away. She then, with a great deal of strain, not to mention an impressive feat of grit and strength, pulls down the* GRIFFIN, *hand over hand on the rope.*

The GRIFFIN, *once near* MADELINE, *tries to bite her with its beak.* MADELINE *avoids this and pushes the* GRIFFIN *onto its back, holding it down with her knee on its chest. With her hands now free she takes out her dagger, cuts the part of the rope that is tying it to the ground, and uses the rope to tie all the* GRIFFIN's *legs together, rodeo style. Once tied, the* GRIF-FIN *screams in fear and lashes about in what ways it can.*

MADELINE *stands, with a great deal of satisfaction.* SHASTA *comes to her with their things.*

SHASTA. Okay, I'm impressed.

MADELINE. So am I, actually.

SHASTA. But how are we going to get it to take us to the Wandering Woman?

The GRIFFIN *lashes and screams some more.*

MADELINE. Uhm—good point.

SHASTA. Wait. I have an idea.

SHASTA *goes to* MADELINE's *pack and pulls out one of the bags of spices. He then approaches the* GRIFFIN *with it.*

MADELINE. Wait, not the spices!

The GRIFFIN *quiets down and perks up, smelling the spices.*

SHASTA. Do you want to save your Mother or not?

MADELINE. But—but—but that's the oregano!

SHASTA. Yes. And the Griffin seems to want it.

MADELINE. Oh, all right. But I can't watch.

MADELINE *turns away.* SHASTA *approaches the* GRIFFIN *gently. The* GRIFFIN *is wary, but is also intrigued by what it's smelling in the bag.* SHASTA *puts some of the oregano in his hand and reaches it out to the* GRIFFIN. *The* GRIFFIN *tentatively eats a little and then immediately brightens, eating the entire morsel from* SHASTA's *hand.*

SHASTA. I thought you might like that.

SHASTA *takes more and puts it in his hand, which the* GRIF-FIN *continues to eat from.*

MADELINE. It's not a pet.

SHASTA. Give me your dagger.

MADELINE. Why?

SHASTA. I'm going to cut it loose.

MADELINE. You are not! Not after what I went through to . . .

SHASTA. It needs to trust us.

MADELINE. Where do you pull this stuff out of?

SHASTA. Good cop, bad cop.

MADELINE. What's a cop?

SHASTA. I don't know, but my parents used to do it to me. Now give me your dagger.

MADELINE. I'm not sure if I can catch another one.

SHASTA. I understand. But it needs to trust us—and you need to trust me.

MADELINE assesses SHASTA for a moment and then, with some resignation, gives him the dagger.

MADELINE. I must be as crazy as you are.

SHASTA then brings the dagger towards the GRIFFIN. The GRIFFIN then begins to panic, but SHASTA gently puts his hand on the GRIFFIN's neck, stroking it:

SHASTA. Shh—I'm a friend.

The GRIFFIN calms down and looks at SHASTA quizzically. SHASTA cuts the rope and sets the GRIFFIN free. The GRIFFIN looks as if it may fly away for a moment, but then it looks back at SHASTA, his hand extended again with more spice. The GRIFFIN goes to SHASTA and eats the spice. The GRIFFIN then nuzzles into SHASTA and coos.

MADELINE. Oh, I see, I do all the work, and then it likes you!

SHASTA. The privileges of being good cop. I can snuggle with you later, if you're feeling left out.

MADELINE. Har-har.

SHASTA. You think I'm joking.

SHASTA holds MADELINE's hand and the two look softly at each other. The GRIFFIN becomes jealous and separates the two, keeping SHASTA to itself.

MADELINE. Oh, great. Well, how do we tell it to take us to the Wandering Woman?

The GRIFFIN starts to nestle into a sleeping position.

SHASTA. It looks like we'll have to figure that out in the morning.

SHASTA goes to sleep by the GRIFFIN. The GRIFFIN puts its wing over SHASTA, protectively.

MADELINE. Come on, beasty. Can we be friends now? *(MADELINE tries to sit next to SHASTA, but the GRIFFIN pushes her away.)* Just great!

MADELINE stalks over a ways and sits, angry.

SHASTA. *(Quietly, to the GRIFFIN.)* Please—I love her.

The GRIFFIN looks at Shasta, then over at MADELINE. Then the GRIFFIN opens its wing, inviting. MADELINE hesitates, figuring out whether she still wants to be bitter or not. But then MADELINE dashes over to them and cuddles with SHASTA. The GRIFFIN then places its wing over both of them. SHASTA and MADELINE both glance at each other.

MADELINE. That was effective—what you did.

SHASTA. *(Looking at the stars.)* Why do you think they are there?

MADELINE. The stars?

SHASTA. Yeah.

All three of them, including the GRIFFIN, who curiously mimics them, look up at the stars.

MADELINE. Well, my mother says they are balls of fire in space.

SHASTA. *(Beat.)* I had a friend who had a book that said there were billions of stars out there that had no planets with life on them. They weren't giving light to anyone. He said that those stars were pointless, which proved that we were pointless.

MADELINE. I thought everyone you traveled with was part of your—tribe? Caravan? What were you exactly?

SHASTA. *(Dodging the question.)* My friend—Peter—we picked him up along the way. We sort of adopted him, like you and your Mom adopted me.

MADELINE. Even though he didn't believe what you believed?

SHASTA. What does that matter in the end? I mean, really, don't we all believe different things, even those who say they belong to the same groups? Even the same families . . .

MADELINE. And that's okay? For you?

SHASTA. *(Beat.)* Is it okay for you?

MADELINE. *(Pointing up in the sky.)* Look at that one! A falling star!

SHASTA *grabs her pointing hand, moving it with the star. They don't let go at first, but the* GRIFFIN *separates their hands with its beak.*

SHASTA. See how it doesn't go away? It's not a shooting star.

MADELINE. What is it then?

SHASTA. A satellite.

MADELINE. What's a saddle-light?

SHASTA. Some people on earth made it and shot it into the sky to send them information.

MADELINE. But no one can hear that message anymore?

SHASTA. Yeah. I suppose. It's just floating out there sending messages nobody is listening to.

Pause.

MADELINE. Something's bothering you.

SHASTA. *(Beat.)* Peter. Not everyone in my group treated him well. Because he didn't believe what we believed. But some of the things he said made sense.

MADELINE. I—you know, sometimes the things you've told me—they do make some sort of sense, too. *(Beat.)* Not that I'm saying you're right!

SHASTA. My father would say that the satellites weren't as important because they were made by humans.

MADELINE. From here they look the same to me as the stars.

SHASTA. That's sort of what I said. I said God made us, we made the satellite. If it's beautiful, then it's beautiful, it doesn't really matter where it came from.

MADELINE. Hm.

SHASTA. What?

MADELINE. I never saw you as one to argue with your parents.

SHASTA. I have my questions, too. I was kind of seen by some people as a—heretic.

MADELINE. A what?

SHASTA. Somebody who asks too many questions.

MADELINE. But you're always talking about . . .

SHASTA. Yeah, I know. After I lost my family, my group—well, I'm all that's left of them. I guess I believed it even more once they were gone.

MADELINE. I—I judged you.

SHASTA. I judged you, too.

MADELINE. I really didn't know you. But I really want to know you. But it's—scary.

SHASTA. I thought you weren't scared of anything.

MADELINE. I'm scared of a lot of things. That's why I make sure that I'm prepared. That's why I bare my teeth and shoot my arrows at them. That's why I show the whole scary world that I'm strong!

SHASTA. Except when you're not.

MADELINE. No, especially when I'm not. That's the time to look the strongest.

SHASTA. Doesn't that get exhausting?

MADELINE. Yes.

SHASTA. Then don't be strong. Not with me. With me you can be— yourself. However strong or weak you are in that moment.

MADELINE starts to cry.

MADELINE. Please, don't tell my Mom.

SHASTA smiles and takes MADELINE away from the GRIF-FIN's wings and both of them lay down next to each other, still stargazing. The GRIFFIN, curious, also lays on its back to get this new view of the stars.

SHASTA. It's a better view from down here.

MADELINE. Look another one. (*SHASTA grabs her hand once again to guide it with the satellite. This time, after the satellite is gone, they don't let go.*) Satellites and stars. They really are beautiful.

SHASTA. Then maybe that's why they are there.

MADELINE. And maybe that's why we're here.

Lights fade to black.

SCENE 9

Lights raise to reveal SHASTA, MADELINE, and the GRIFFIN sleeping. It is now morning and sitting beside them now, however, is the WANDERING WOMAN. The GRIFFIN stirs from its

sleep and sees the WANDERING. *The* GRIFFIN *coos and the*
WANDERING WOMAN *pets it face and neck affectionately.*

WANDERING WOMAN. Hello again, my darling. (*The* GRIFFIN *nuzzles into the* WANDERING WOMAN.) Thank you for calling me here.
(*The* WANDERING WOMAN *takes out one of Shasta's books from his pack and begins reading:*) "O God, where art thou? And where is the pavilion that covereth thy hiding place? How long shall thy hand be stayed, and thine eye, yea thy pure eye, behold from the eternal heavens the wrongs of thy people and of thy servants, and thine ear be penetrated with their cries?"

SHASTA *awakes to her reading.*

SHASTA. Who are you?

WANDERING WOMAN. You sought me, didn't you?

SHASTA. The Wandering Woman.

WANDERING WOMAN. That is one of my names.

SHASTA. I—I thought we would have to look longer for you.

WANDERING WOMAN. The Griffin called me. You first sought me with respect for my Wisdom in the Sphinx, and you came near me then; after that you sought me with actions when you caught the Griffin; and then you loved me when you freed the Griffin. When you both, together, implored me with wisdom, action, freedom, and love, how could I not answer you? You sought, you have found.

SHASTA. How—how am I supposed to approach you? How am I supposed to speak to you?

WANDERING WOMAN. As someone real.

SHASTA. Why do they call you the Wandering Woman?

WANDERING WOMAN. Because I have been denied my home. I have been thrust out of my dwelling place. So I wander the world, having left those that left me.

SHASTA. If I had a home, I would give it to you, Great Lady.

WANDERING WOMAN. And that is why I manifest myself to you, my dear boy.

SHASTA. You've come to me before . . .

WANDERING WOMAN. Yes, in your dreams. You floated like a corpse on the waters, the waters that so long ago I brooded over. But you were not a corpse. You still had life. The Emperor Wolf desired to have you, but I protected you, watched over you. And when you went out of my waters, you were born a new man.

SHASTA. When I heard your voice know me, name me, I felt such love from you. You knew I could be more than I even knew myself.

WANDERING WOMAN. And I still know that.

SHASTA kisses the WANDERING WOMAN on the cheek. She smiles at him and touches his face tenderly.

SHASTA. *(Looking to MADELINE.)* You need to talk to her, don't you? *(The WANDERING WOMAN nods.)* I will let you two alone then. Maybe it's about time I did some of the hunting, too.

WANDERING WOMAN. Yes. Equally yoked, equally weighted, you both will learn to be. Neither the master of the other, learning together, not apart.

SHASTA. Her and I . . . ? Are we to . . . ?

WANDERING WOMAN. Is that what you want? Is it what she wants?

MADELINE awakes.

MADELINE. What is going on?

WANDERING WOMAN. Hello, dear girl.

MADELINE. Who are you?

WANDERING WOMAN. I am the one you sought, but you did not know you were seeking until recently.

MADELINE. The Wandering Woman?

WANDERING WOMAN. Shasta has volunteered to go hunting while you and I talk.

MADELINE. Oh, but I'm the hunter . . .

WANDERING WOMAN. You both can be many things, often the same things. You can both be skilled in a whole myriad of proficiencies, without being afraid the other's skill diminishes yours. Don't be threatened.

MADELINE nods. SHASTA takes the bow and arrow and the knife.

SHASTA. I'll be back.

The WANDERING WOMAN takes out one of Shasta's books and sits next to MADELINE.

WANDERING WOMAN. Read with me.

MADELINE. I—I don't know how to read.

WANDERING WOMAN. A true answer. *(The WANDERING WOMAN kisses MADELINE's eyes.)* I have cured your blindness. Now read.

MADELINE. *(She takes the book hesitantly, attempting to read.)* "Dorothy lived in the midst of the great Kansas praries . . ." *(Pauses, shocked.)* I—I can read!

WANDERING WOMAN. You can do many things. Do not let shame divert your potential—it is a stone that diverts the stream.

MADELINE. Failure is a step, not a destination.

WANDERING WOMAN. You have gained Wisdom.

The WANDERING WOMAN magically reveals another book.

MADELINE. Another one?

WANDERING WOMAN. One that not even Shasta has read. You will be the first to read it to him.

MADELINE reads the title.

MADELINE. *Alice in Wonderland.*

WANDERING WOMAN. She had to figure out a new world. One that frightened her, too.

MADELINE. I'm not fright . . .

MADELINE can't finish saying it, realizing who she is talking to.

WANDERING WOMAN. You don't have to hide from me, my darling. Now that is not the end of my gifts for you.

The WANDERING WOMAN *takes out a sword. She uses it to cut off her own braid. She hands both the braid and the sword to* MADELINE.

MADELINE. What am I supposed to do with these?

WANDERING WOMAN. You will need both your strength and your tenderness. *(The* WANDERING WOMAN *kisses* MADELINE'S *forehead.)* The Griffin will take you to Ebony, just as the Griffin brought you to me. *(Beat.)* Fire is on the horizon. Take this moment of peace.

The WANDERING WOMAN *exits, with* MADELINE *looking after her breathlessly. She then nestles into the* GRIFFIN *and begins to read her new book.* SHASTA *enters with a dead animal, successful in his hunting excursion.* MADELINE *shows him her book.* SHASTA *shows her his animal. They both beam.*

SHASTA. We can do hard things.

MADELINE. But can we do this?

SHASTA. If we can't bind the Emperor Wolf, then there is nothing else to be done. He won't allow for co-existence. He is hunting all of us down. Either he swallows us whole . . .

MADELINE. . . . or we swallow him.

Blackout.

SCENE 10

DERRICK *sits across from* EBONY. EBONY *is in an incoherent state, as the dream-like* EMPEROR WOLF *hovers near her, working his incantations, etc.* DERRICK *tries to break into the "force field" that surrounds the* EMPEROR WOLF *and* EBONY *(which could be as simple as a pool of light).*

DERRICK. Ebony? Ebony, can you hear me? *(To the* EMPEROR WOLF.*)* What are you doing to her? Stay away from her! You promised me that if you took me, you would leave them alone! *(The* EMPEROR WOLF *does not respond.)* This is not how it happened with me. It did not take this long. What are you doing to her? Why would you want a blind woman?

EMPEROR WOLF. She will not be blind with me. And it is not her I want. She is the bait.

There is the sound of wings and the SPHINX *appears.*

DERRICK. Wh-what are you doing here?

SPHINX. I told you. I told you I would devour you, if you hurt any of them.

DERRICK. Master—Master, help me!

The Dream-like EMPEROR WOLF *does not acknowledge* DERRICK.

SPHINX. The Monster is having its own battle. It can't help you. It never could. It never would.

DERRICK *pulls out a dagger.*

DERRICK. Get away from me.

The SPHINX *attacks* DERRICK. *They scuffle and spar a bit, but then the* SPHINX *amps up her attacks and ends up tearing at his side, making him bleed.* DERRICK *swipes at the* SPHINX, *which she dodges.*

SPHINX. She was your wife. She was your daughter's mother.

DERRICK *swipes again, the* SPHINX *dodges again.*

DERRICK. You don't know the influence it had over me.

SPHINX. More influence than your own family?

DERRICK *swipes again, the* SPHINX *dodges.*

DERRICK. I—I was trying to be better.

SPHINX. To what end?

DERRICK. I was trying!

SPHINX. To what end!

DERRICK lunges in rage and grief at the SPHINX. She tears at his stomach and he staggers to the ground.

DERRICK. Please—please, don't kill me. I have to fix this.

SPHINX. You have doomed your wife to live with a demon inside her. You have doomed your daughter to a life without either parent. You have doomed yourself by allowing yourself to be an instrument of the dark one.

DERRICK. I didn't want this! I gave up because I was trying to protect them!

SPHINX. They would have been better served by a virtuous man who fought evil instead of conceding to it, instead of giving it room to breathe!

The SPHINX is about to deliver a killing blow to DERRICK, when a sudden blast of dark lights, sound and/or smoke emerge from EBONY and the light is overcome, causing a blackout. When the lights raise again, Ebony is gone and the EMPEROR WOLF (no longer dream-like) is now in her place.

DERRICK. No. Ebony, I thought you of all people might be able to . . .

SPHINX. This is what you've done, mortal. Look at your handiwork.

EMPEROR WOLF. You are not welcome here!

SPHINX. I never ask for anyone's welcome.

The SPHINX attacks the EMPEROR WOLF and the two of them battle. The GRIFFIN enters, bringing MADELINE and SHASTA with it. Seeing them, DERRICK rushes to them. Spooked by seeing her father again, MADELINE pulls out an arrow and pulls it into the bow, pointing it at her father.

MADELINE. Get away from us.

DERRICK. You both must stop them.

MADELINE. I said get away!

DERRICK. Madeline, the Emperor Wolf has taken over your mother.

MADELINE lowers her arrow.

SHASTA. Will you help us?

DERRICK. Yes, I'm free now . . .

MADELINE. No! We don't want your help.

DERRICK. Do you want that thing to own your mother?

MADELINE. No. But I can't trust you.

SHASTA. Maddy . . .

MADELINE. That man ruined my life, Shasta!

DERRICK. I know. I can't make up for that.

MADELINE. No. You can't.

DERRICK. But, please, I don't want another mistake on my head. You lost me. I don't want you to lose her, too.

MADELINE. I . . . No . . .

SHASTA. How can you help us?

MADELINE. We already have the help we need.

MADELINE pulls out the braid and the sword that the WAN-DERING WOMAN gave her. The EMPEROR WOLF is immediately aware of them. The EMPEROR WOLF ferociously thrusts the SPHINX aside, knocking her temporarily unconscious. The EMPEROR WOLF then lunges at MADELINE, knocking the items out of her hands and pushes her to the ground.

EMPEROR WOLF. You are mine, little one.

SHASTA. Get away!

SHASTA takes EBONY's old staff and attacks the EMPEROR WOLF with it. The staff begins to slowly glow brighter and brighter, which affects the EMPEROR WOLF. In the meantime MADELINE dashes to get the sword and the braid. DERRICK stops her before she can rush to the aid of SHASTA.

DERRICK. That staff—I don't know how you got it, but I have seen it used against him before. What the boy's doing is very dangerous. It's powerful, but it uses his life force.

MADELINE. What? Shasta, get away from him! That staff could kill you!

SHASTA. *(Looking at MADELINE sadly.)* I know. It told me.

The staff glows even brighter. MADELINE joins the fray, sword in hand, braid attached to her belt.

MADELINE. Shasta, I can handle this, please, don't . . .

SHASTA. We do this together.

The EMPEROR WOLF responds to the increasing light as if it is being burned. The SPHINX awakes and then attacks the EMPEROR WOLF, clawing at him, surprisingly actually hurting him. The SPHINX looks at the blood on her claws.

SPHINX. But how?

EMPEROR WOLF. That is not my blood. It is the Woman's.

SPHINX. But . . .

EMPEROR WOLF. Yes. I know. You fell for my snare. You made an oath not to hurt her or her children—you have broken your oath, broken your nature, broken your immortality. You are no longer Eternal. You are mine!

The EMPEROR WOLF extends his claw to the SPHINX, suddenly controlling her. The SPHINX stiffly (as if she were a puppet being controlled by string), but lethally attacks SHASTA, dividing the battle into two parts.

SHASTA. Madeline!

MADELINE. Shasta, get out of here!

DERRICK, overcoming an initial fear, pulls out his own dagger and lunges towards the EMPEROR WOLF, stabbing it. The EMPEROR WOLF howls in pain, but then pulls the dagger out, throws it aside, and then slashes DERRICK with a lethal attack.

DERRICK. Agh!

MADELINE. Father!

As the EMPEROR WOLF staggers back, tending to its wound, MADELINE dashes to her father.

DERRICK. It's getting weaker . . .

MADELINE. It's Mama we're hurting . . .

DERRICK. She does not want to be a slave to that thing anymore than I did, Madeline. The bond the Wolf and I share now—I could sense it—he's struggling. The staff did the trick. If we can find a way to . . .

The EMPEROR WOLF comes at them again and slashes DERRICK.

MADELINE. Father—Papa! (*MADELINE fights the EMPEROR WOLF back a bit. She draws and arrow and points it at the WOLF.*) Mama, I know you're still in there. I don't want to hurt you. So, please—back off! (*The EMPEROR WOLF steps back a bit.*) That's it, Mama, fight it.

EMPEROR WOLF. (*In EBONY's voice.*) Your Father . . .

MADELINE goes to DERRICK.

DERRICK. I know you were afraid to become like me . . .

MADELINE. This—this can be fixed. I can fix this.

DERRICK. You're nothing like me. You're like your mother.

DERRICK dies.

EMPEROR WOLF. (*Back in control.*) He lies. You're exactly like him.

MADELINE. Maybe I am. And tonight, maybe that's not a bad thing.

EMPEROR WOLF. I don't want your mother. I want you.

MADELINE. You want me for my mother? You want to make a deal?

SHASTA. *(Still occupied with the SPHINX.)* Madeline, don't!

MADELINE. Let's make a deal!

Suddenly the SPHINX kills SHASTA. The light in the staff goes out.

MADELINE. Shasta!

MADELINE shoots the SPHINX, killing her. MADELINE rushes to SHASTA, trying to rouse him.

EMPEROR WOLF. He's beyond your help.

MADELINE. *(Hardening.)* Then I have nothing left anyway.

EMPEROR WOLF. You would give yourself to me willingly?

MADELINE. Let go of my mother forever and you can do whatever you want with me. I don't care a thing about myself.

EMPEROR WOLF. Swear to me!

MADELINE. I am yours!

A sudden blast of dark lights, sound and smoke emerge from MADELINE and the light is overcome, causing a blackout. But instead of the lights returning to normal, as before, the lights change and refract and distort as we see the dream-like EMPEROR WOLF struggling to get into MADELINE, but MADELINE resists.

EMPEROR WOLF. You said you were mine . . .

MADELINE. I am—but I'm going to make sure I stick in your throat! *(MADELINE magically attaches the WANDERING WOMAN's braid to her own hair.)* Wandering Woman, your braid is connected to my head, and my head is connected to my mind, and my mind is connected to heart and my heart is connected to you—protect me! *(She then picks up the sword.)* I—I am understanding so many things. How am I . . . ? You—you caused this—our whole world was destroyed by you.

EMPEROR WOLF. Not by me. By all of you. Your little hatreds, your little divisions. You thought they were so harmless. Nursing a prejudice, holding a grudge, railing against your neighbor, bullying a child, persecuting someone who is different—they seemed such small things to you. But all the while you all were creating such fertile soil for me to go from person to person, sowing my rich harvest.

MADELINE. You were gone. They destroyed you.

EMPEROR WOLF. You think a few Vikings with axes and ships could truly destroy me?

MADELINE. They called you Fenris.

EMPEROR WOLF. It doesn't matter what they called me. They tried to name me, to bind me, to kill me. But my story did not die with my body. My astral form went from dream to dream, traversed a world which you all have forgotten about. There's a universal consciousness, a network as real as the roots of the trees here. I found my place into your minds, I found my place into your hearts, and you had all become so like me already that there was really no differentiation in the end. You didn't even recognize that I had taken possession of you.

MADELINE. The other creatures? You woke them up as well?

EMPEROR WOLF. No. The noise of the new world brought them forth.

MADELINE. You orchestrated our downfall.

EMPEROR WOLF. Look into the mirror and see your own face. See the face of every man, every woman, the potential of every child. I forced no one. They knelt before me as I devoured their wills. Just as you have given yourself to me. You have invited Ragnarök!

MADELINE. Then devour me and die!

EMPEROR WOLF. I cannot die!

MADELINE. Everything can die!

MADELINE raises her sword, rushing towards the EMPEROR WOLF. She stabs the EMPEROR WOLF and he simply looks down at her, continuing a steady, quiet, ominous breath.

EMPEROR WOLF. I nursed this world with the sword like a mother does its child. You think you can kill me with a blade?

MADELINE stares at him for a long while, then:

MADELINE. I have resisted you all my life—ignored you, tried to forget you, even tried to not believe in you. You were nothing but a story. Like Shasta's books, something made to scare children. But that is what you wanted, isn't it? That is where—that is where the fear came in. I wanted to obliterate your story. But a person only tries to destroy what she fears.

EMPEROR WOLF. There is so much to fear. Oblivion awaits you.

MADELINE. Death is not such an awful thing. *(MADELINE drops the sword.)* I will not struggle. I recognize you. Take me into your belly.

EMPEROR WOLF. You think I'm some mere puppy here to lick your face?

MADELINE. Lick my face, scratch it, tear it right off! But there is a part of me you may never have.

EMPEROR WOLF. I have every piece of you!

MADELINE. Not anymore. I don't need to destroy you. I just need to bind you, like the covers of a book.

EMPEROR WOLF. Nothing can bind me!

MADELINE. I am no longer afraid of the stories. I recognize your story, just like I recognize the higher stories.

EMPEROR WOLF. There are no stories higher than me!

Darkness rushes in as the EMPEROR WOLF goes in to devour MADELINE. However, before he can do so, she moves swiftly and brings the WANDERING WOMAN's braid around his neck.

MADELINE. There are many higher stories. Including the one of this braid. Be bound forever, you pitiful creature!

MADELINE tightens the braid around the EMPEROR WOLF's neck. There is a flash of bright light, the EMPEROR WOLF's pained howl, and then darkness again. The lights slowly raise to reveal EMPEROR WOLF gone and EBONY in its place. MADELINE has fallen on the floor, unmoving. EBONY touches the wounds she received from being the EMPEROR WOLF and then collapses.

Now all have fallen, except for the GRIFFIN, which stood aside the entire time, watching stoically and never interfering. Everyone else lays scattered on the stage, dead. The WANDERING WOMAN enters. The WANDERING WOMAN goes to the GRIFFIN and pets it gently. The GRIFFIN nuzzles into the WANDERING WOMAN, cooing in grief.

WANDERING WOMAN. I know that was hard for you to witness, dear one. *(The WANDERING WOMAN goes over to SHASTA, the GRIFFIN following her.)* You have suffered much, my boy. But many have gone before who have suffered likewise. Are you greater than them? *(The WANDERING WOMAN touches SHASTA's forehead and he revives.)* Welcome back, Shasta.

SHASTA. What happened?

The WANDERING WOMAN ignores the question. Instead she goes and revives the SPHINX.

WANDERING WOMAN. In your pursuit of justice, you harmed the innocent. But now even justice is overcome. Rise anew in love and learn what Eternal truly is. *(The WANDERING WOMAN then goes to EBONY and revives her.)* You continued on in blindness, Ebony, now continue on in sight.

To her overwhelming, emotional gratitude, EBONY can see now.

EBONY. I—I can see. Oh, thank you—thank you!

The WANDERING WOMAN *goes on to* DERRICK *and revives him.*

WANDERING WOMAN. Be reborn in body, Derrick, be reborn in spirit. Let the old world die. Let the old man die.

The WANDERING WOMAN *finally goes to* MADELINE. *Before she attempts to revive* MADELINE, *the* WANDERING WOMAN *sits on the ground next to her, bringing* MADELINE's *head into her lap. She strokes* MADELINE's *hair softly and gently. The* WANDERING WOMAN *then sings in an unknown language to* MADELINE. *The others gather around awestruck by the beauty and mystery of the song.*

DERRICK. What is she singing?

SPHINX. Some mothers sing their children to sleep. The Wandering Woman sings her children awake.

As the song nears its closure, slowly MADELINE *begins to awake. With the last beautiful strains of the song on her lips, the* WANDERING WOMAN *softly brings* MADELINE *to her feet.*

WANDERING WOMAN. You are stronger than you have ever been.

MADELINE. I had a dream that we were all dead.

WANDERING WOMAN. And so you are, so to speak. At least to that world. But see here—a new world. *(There is complete silence as the* WANDERING WOMAN *gives* MADELINE, SHASTA, EBONY, *and* DERRICK *kisses on the cheek or forehead.)* You all lived in a world of blood and fire and horror, but it is a new existence you have now, a new place you have inherited. Make it better than the one where you used to live. Although you were born on an earth of violence and death, and you perished on a world of violence and death, that can now be done away with. You have a chance to create peace and new life. To create anew, never to be disassembled.

All of that done, the WANDERING WOMAN *then gives them all one last wistful look and then exits, the* SPHINX *and the* GRIFFIN *following her out.* DERRICK, SHASTA, *and* MADELINE *all look at each other, still marveling, while* EBONY *takes her children's hands.*

DERRICK. I suppose I should leave you all alone now.

DERRICK goes to leave, but EBONY takes his hand.

EBONY. The Wolf is gone.

DERRICK. That doesn't change what I did.

EBONY. No—but you are changed back to the man I loved. We have a new world to re-build. Don't you want to be part of that?

DERRICK looks to MADELINE.

DERRICK. And you? You approve of this?

MADELINE. No. *(Pause.)* But I wouldn't mind being proven wrong. Just remember, if you don't take care of her—well, I can have softness, but as sure as the earth, I have strength.

DERRICK. I understand.

MADELINE goes to SHASTA. They look at each other softly for a moment. SHASTA touches the braid.

SHASTA. I kind of like this look.

MADELINE. I've never really been one for long hair. But it could grow on me, I guess. *(MADELINE touches SHASTA's face softly.)* I guess a lot of things have grown on me.

SHASTA. You make me sound like a fungus.

MADELINE punches SHASTA's shoulder.

MADELINE. I'm trying to be romantic.

SHASTA. Oh, is that why you're making that weird face?

MADELINE punches SHASTA's shoulder again.

MADELINE. If you don't do what I say then . . .

SHASTA. Then what, tough gal?

MADELINE punches SHASTA's shoulder again.

MADELINE. Then I'll do that! And then I'll . . . *(She inches closer to* SHASTA.*) . . .* do this.

MADELINE and SHASTA *kiss.*

THE END

Nikki Gallagher as the Wandering Woman. Photo by Tim Trumble.

Zach Turilli as Shasta, Nikki Gallagher as the Wandering Woman, and Christine Conger as Madeline. Photo by Tim Trumble.

Chelsea Juaregi as Ebony and Zach Turilli as Shasta. Photo by Tim Trumble.

Christine Conger as Madeline and Zach Turilli as Shasta. Photo by Tim Trumble.

Chelsea Juaregi as Ebony. Photo by Tim Trumble.

Chelsea Juaregi as Ebony, Salim Garami as the Emperor Wolf, Christine Conger as Madeline and Zach Turilli as Shasta. Photo by Tim Trumble.

Zach Turilli as Shasta, Christine Conger as Madeline, and Chelsea Juaregi as Ebony. Photo by Tim Trumble.

Melissa Stone as the Sphinx. Photo by Tim Trumble.

Melissa Stone as the Sphinx. Photo by Tim Trumble.

Isaac Kolding as Derrick. Photo by Tim Trumble.

Christine Conger as Madeline and the Company as the Fairies. Photo by Tim Trumble.

Phoenix Huber as the Griffin. Photo by Tim Trumble.

Christine Conger as Madeline and Phoenix Huber as the Griffin. Photo by Tim Trumble.

Christine Conger as Madeline. Photo by Tim Trumble.

Zach Turilli as Shasta and Phoenix Huber as the Griffin. Photo by Tim Trumble.

Nikki Gallagher as the Wandering Woman, Zach Turilli as Shasta, Phoenix Huber as the Griffin and Christine Conger as Madeline. Photo by Tim Trumble.

Nikki Gallagher as the Wandering Woman, Zach Turilli as Shasta, Phoenix Huber as the Griffin, and Christine Conger as Madeline. Photo by Tim Trumble.

Zach Turilli as Shasta and Nikki Gallagher as the Wandering Woman. Photo by Tim Trumble.

Christine Conger as Madeline and Nikki Gallagher as the Wandering Woman. Photo by Tim Trumble.

Melissa Stone as the Sphinx, Salim Garami as the Emperor Wolf, and Chelsea Juaregi as Ebony. Photo by Tim Trumble.

Zach Turilli as Shasta and Melissa Stone as the Sphinx. Photo by Tim Trumble.

Salim Garami as the Emperor Wolf. Photo by Tim Trumble.

Salim Garami as the Emperor Wolf, Christine Conger as Madeline, and Chelsea Juaregi as Ebony. Photo by Tim Trumble.

Salim Garami as the Emperor Wolf and Christine Conger as Madeline. Photo by Tim Trumble.

Zach Turilli as Shasta, Melissa Stone as the Sphinx, Nikki Gallagher as the Wandering Woman, Christine Conger as Madeline, and Isaac Kolding as Derrick. Photo by Tim Trumble.

Zach Turilli as Shasta, Christine Conger as Madeline, Isaac Kolding as Derrick, and Chelsea Juaregi as Ebony. Photo by Tim Trumble.

Acknowledgments

One of the reasons I love theatre is that it is a collaborative art. In the process of bringing these plays to the stage, and then to print, I have made many friends, and collected many debts.

As always, my first line of defense is my wife Anne, my best, most honest critic, while still building my confidence with her loyal support and encouragement. My children Hyrum and Charlotte also were great respondents, giving the necessary child's eye to plays like *Emperor Wolf*. It's been wonderful finally sharing some of my work with my little elves and pixies.

I had a splendid group of readers for these plays; many of them were part of the staff and my cohort at Arizona State University while I was earning my MFA there. A number of these plays were developed as part of the Dramatic Writing program. For their input on many of these particular plays I am deeply grateful to Guillermo Reyes, Philip Taylor, Gitta Honneger, Jeff McMahon, Pamela Sterling, William Partlan, Erika Hughes, Jacob Pinholster, Brian Foley, Alice Stanley, John Perovich, Kirt Shineman, Ryan Noble, Miranda Giles, Cody Goulder, José Zaraté, Shelly Sarver, Jess Cochrane, Kathleen Arcovio Pennyway, Chelsea Pace, and the many others I'm sure I'm forgetting that made ASU such a wonderful environment for my creative and artistic development.

For prepping this manuscript with their superb editing skills, I am deeply indebted to Tricia Harris Evanson and Hillary Sterling particularly, who have excellent eagle eyes for editing, but also are both deeply encouraging and supportive of these plays. It's nice when you feel like you have a fan club.

Donovan Glass, Georgia Brain, and Jess Cochrane were super helpful in giving me an Aussie perspective on *Evening Eucalyptus*. Although I lived there for two years, in the end I am still an outsider.

I can't name off all the directors, actors, designers, and crew that helped on each of these plays, but please take a look at the casts and crews listed before each of the plays to recognize how much work and effort is made by so many people to put on even the most humble of plays. I have always been surrounded with talent, unusually so, which always brings the productions of my plays to another level.

Finally, I can't say how grateful I am to Zarahemla Books for publishing these plays. I'm sure Drama isn't the most lucrative of genres, but my publisher Chris Bigelow has shown nothing but support. Marny Parkin has made a beautiful interior, as she did with my volume *A Roof Overhead and Other Plays*. Liz Pulido's artwork for the theatre poster of *Evening Eucalyptus* was so amazing that I insisted it be used, which Jason Robinson incorporated into his excellent cover design.

Drama, indeed, is a communal art form.